INTRODUCTION TO CATALOGING, VOL. II:
ENTRY HEADINGS

McGRAW-HILL SERIES IN LIBRARY EDUCATION
Jean Key Gates
University of South Florida

INTRODUCTION TO CATALOGING, VOL. II: ENTRY HEADINGS

with emphasis on the cataloging process
and on personal names

JOHN J. BOLL

Library School of the University of Wisconsin, Madison

with special contributions by
RICHARD D. WALKER
PEGGY O'NEILL BARRY
ETHEL FARRIS HEISE

McGRAW-HILL BOOK COMPANY

New York • St. Louis • San Francisco • Düsseldorf • Johannesburg • Kuala Lumpur • London
Mexico • Montreal • New Delhi • Panama • Paris • São Paulo • Singapore • Sydney
Tokyo • Toronto

INTRODUCTION TO CATALOGING, VOL. II: ENTRY HEADINGS

1 2 3 4 5 6 7 8 9 0 E B E B 7 9 8 7 6 5 4 3

Boll, John J   1973
    Introduction to cataloging.

    Includes bibliographical references.
    CONTENTS: v. 1. Descriptive cataloging—v. 2. Entry
headings, with emphasis on the cataloging process and on personal
name entry headings.
    1. Cataloging.   I. Title.
Z693.B64   025.3'07   73-87296
ISBN 0-07-006412-1

This book was set in Press Roman and Univers by John T. Westlake Publishing Services.
The editor was Janis Yates; the designer was John T. Westlake Publishing Services; and
the production supervisor was Judi Frey.
Edwards Brothers Incorporated was printer and binder.

ACKNOWLEDGMENTS

I gratefully acknowledge permission granted by publishers and/or authors of the following books to reprint
materials copyrighted by them. *The Agitator; a Collection of Diverse Opinions From America's Not-so-
popular Press.* Edited by Donald L. Rice. A Schism Anthology. American Library Association, 1972.
American Iron and Steel Institute, *Study of Industrial Health Practices For the Iron and Steel Industry.* April
1953. Anderson, Hans, *Three Tales of Hans Anderson.* With Twenty-two Illustrations by Linley Samborne.
London, Macmillan and Co., 1910. *Anglo-American Cataloging Rules. North American Text.* American
Library Association, 1967. Baker, Ray Stannard, *Woodrow Wilson, Life and Letters: Youth, 1856-1890.*
Doubleday, Page & Co., 1927. Bancroft, Elizabeth Davis, *Letters From England, 1846-1849.* With portraits
and views. Charles Scribner's Sons, 1904. Carlson, Ruth Kearney, ed., *Folklore and Folktales Around the
World.* Prepared by the IRA Library and Literature Committee. International Reading Association, 1972.
Casey, Robert S. and others, *Punched Cards, Their Application to Science and Industry.* 2d ed. Van Nostrand
Reinhold Co., 1958. Ceram, C. W., *Gods, Graves, and Scholars; The Story of Archaeology.* Translated from
the German by E. B. Garside and Sophie Wilkins, 2d rev. and substantially enlarged ed. Copyright 1951,
1967 by Alfred A. Knopf, Inc. Chapman, John L., *Atlas, the Story of a Missile.* Harper and Row. Copyright
© 1960 by John L. Chapman. Chiera, Edward, *They Wrote on Clay; the Babylonian Tables Speak Today.*
Edited by George G. Cameron. The University of Chicago Press, © 1938. Danielou, Jean and others, *Intro-
duction to the Great Religions.* Fides Publishers, 1964. Dickerson, Milton B., Essel R. Dillavou, Harry M.
Schuck, *Business Law by the Case Method.* Prentice-Hall, Inc., 1957. Dickinson, Emily, *Letters.* Edited by
Mabel Loomis Todd. New and enl. ed. Harper and Row, 1931. Doolin, Dennis J., ed., *Communist China; the
Politics of Student Opposition.* Hoover Institution for War, Revolution and Peace, 1964. Drabble, Margaret, *A
Summer Bird-cage.* Weidenfeld and Nicolson, 1963; William Morrow, 1964. © 1962 Margaret Swift. Dumond,
Dwight L., ed., *Southern Editorials on Secession.* Century Co., 1931. © by Dwight L. Dumond. Du Rietz, G.

ACKNOWLEDGMENTS (CONTINUED)

Einar, *Life-forms of Terrestrial Flowering Plants.* Uppsala, Almqvist & Wiksells Boktryckeri A. B., 1931.
Fassett, Norman C., *Grasses of Wisconsin.* With an Essay, *The Vegetation of Wisconsin,* by John T. Curtis.
University of Wisconsin Press. Copyright 1951 by The Regents of the University of Wisconsin. Ferris, Walter,
Death Takes A Holiday; a Comedy in Three Acts. Based on a Play of this same Title by Alberto Casella.
Copyright 1928, 1930, by Walter Ferris; Copyright 1955 (In Renewal), by Walter Ferris; Copyright 1957 (In
Renewal), by Walter Ferris. (Title page reprinted by permission of Samuel French, Inc.) Froman, Robert.
Title page from *Quacko and the Elps,* by Robert Froman, illustrated by Jean Macdonald Porter. Copyright ©
1964 by Robert Froman and reproduced by permission of David McKay Company, Inc. Frost, Robert,
Collected Poems. H. Holt, 1930. Reproduced by permission of Holt, Rinehard and Winston, Inc. Giorgione,
All the Paintings of Giorgione. Text by Luigi Coletti, Translated by Paul Colacicchi. Hawthorne Books, ©
1961. Gordon, Edgar S., ed., *A Symposium on Steroid Hormones.* The University of Wisconsin Press.
Copyright 1950 by The Regents of the University of Wisconsin. Grayson, David, *Adventures in Friendship.*
Illustrated by Thomas Fogarty. Doubleday, Page & Co., 1910. Copyright 1910 by Doubleday, Page & Co.;
copyright 1908, 1909, 1910 by The Phillips Pub. Co. Hale, Lucretia P., *The Complete Peterkin Papers.*
Houghton, Mifflin Co., 1959. Lamarck, Jean B., *Hydrogeology.* University of Illinois Press, 1964. Le Galley,
Donald P., ed., *Space Exploration,* by Robert M. L. Baker, Jr. and others. McGraw-Hill Book Co., 1964.
Lehndorff, Count Hans von, *Wast Prussian Diary; a Journal of Faith, 1945-1947.* Copyright 1963 for English
translation by Oswald Wolff (Publishers) Ltd., London. Lenski, Lois, Title page from the book *Strawberry
Girl* written and illustrated by Lois Lenski. Copyright 1945, by Lois Lenski. Reproduced by permission of J.
B. Lippincott Company. *The Manly Anniversary Studies in Language and Literature.* The University of
Chicago Press, 1923. Mellon, M. G., *Chemical Publications, Their Nature and Use.* 4th ed. McGraw-Hill Book
Co., 1965. *Merit Students Encyclopedia,* Selected pages reprinted with permission from Volume I of *Merit
Students Encyclopedia.* © 1967 Crowell Collier Educational Corporation. Read, Miss, *Village Diary.*
Houghton, Mifflin Co., ©1957 by Dora Jessie Saint. Reed, W. Maxwell and Wilfrid S. Bronson, *The Sea for
Sam.* Rev. ed., edited by Paul F. Brandwein. Copyright 1935, © 1960 by Harcourt, Brace & World, Inc.
Renoir, Pierre Auguste, *Pierre Auguste Renoir (1841-1919)* Text by Milton S. Fox. Published by Harry N.
Abrams, Inc., in association with Pocket Books, Inc. Copyright 1953 by Harry N. Abrams, Incorporated.
Scribe, Augustin E., *Le verre d'eau; ou, Les effets et les causes.* Edited with notes and vocabulary by Charles
A. Eggert. D. C. Heath, 1900. Smitt Ingebretsen, Herman, *En dikter og en herre; Vilhelm Krags liv og
diktning.* Annet opplag. Forlagt av H. Aschehoug & Co. (W. Nygaard), Oslo, 1943. Strauss, Lucille J., Strieby,
Irene M., and Brown, Alberta L., *Scientific and Technical Libraries: Their Organization and Administration.*
Interscience Publishers, 1964. Thompson, James W., *An Introduction to Medieval Europe,* by James Westfall
Thompson and Edgar Nathaniel Johnson. Copyright 1937 by W. W. Norton & Company, Inc. Copyright
renewed 1965 by Edgar Nathaniel Johnson. With permission from the Publisher. U.S. Library of Congress,
The National Union Catalog, 1966. (Selected entries) Van Dalen, Deobold B., *Understanding Educational
Research.* With two chapters by William J. Meyer. McGraw-Hill Book Co., 1962. Van Loon, Hendrik Willem,
The Story of the Bible. Written and drawn by Hendrik Willem Van Loon. Copyright, 1923, by Boni &
Liveright, Inc. Title page and verso reprinted from *The Year the Yankees Lost the Pennant, a Novel* by
Douglass Wallop. By permission of W. W. Norton & Company, Inc. Reprinted by permission of Curtis Brown,
Ltd. Copyright © 1954 by John Douglass Wallop. Welter, Rush, *Problems of Scholarly Publication in the
Humanities and Social Sciences.* A report prepared for the Committee on Scholarly Publication of the
American Council of Learned Societies. Copyright 1959 by the American Council of Learned Societies.
Wilson, Louis R., *The University Library,* by Louis Round Wilson and Maurice F. Tauber. 2d ed. Columbia
Unversity Press, 1956. Title page from *The Wisconsin Blue Book, 1973.* (Grateful acknowledgment is made to
the Wisconsin Legislative Reference Bureau.) Booz, Allen & Hamilton, Inc., *Problems in University Library Management.*
A study conducted for the Association of Research Libraries and the American Council on Education. Washington,
Copyright 1970 by the Association of Research Libraries.

CONTENTS

PREFACE

This study text is the second of several volumes which together form an introduction to cataloging. It is an amalgam of text, illustrations, and exercises-with-answers that is designed to involve the student actively in the learning process. The preliminary edition of this text has proved useful as a text for regular classroom study as well as a substitute for formal classroom instruction and laboratory sessions, in independent individual study, and in extension study. When used in lieu of lectures in a formal classroom situation, this text releases the instructor from much routine but permits him to insert himself at any point in the learning process for individual counseling, lecture treatment of related topics, or testing. When used for independent study, the text permits the student to study at his own pace and to check continuously his progress and comprehension.

This text and its companion volumes are based on the belief that any librarian needs to know the theory and basic practice of description, entry headings, and subject control; that in these areas theory and practice are inalienably entwined; and that once this foundation stone has been mastered, the student can use it as a point of meaningful departure to the broader realms of systematic bibliography and information retrieval theories and techniques. Of these areas this volume covers three parts: an overview of all types of entry headings; typical sequences of steps involved in entry heading cataloging; and a detailed introduction to the personal name entry heading rules of the *Anglo-American Cataloging Rules, North American Text.* An attempt was made throughout this volume to help the student to recognize clues—Chapter 7, for example, deals essentially with clues—to learn professional terminology, and to apply the AA with judgment. The last chapter treats differences and similarities between the 1949 and 1967 codes.

It is a pleasant task to give thanks to the many individuals and organizations that helped directly and indirectly with this text. The Library School of the University of Wisconsin—Madison has supported it in many ways through the persons of its directors, Margaret E. Monroe, Jack A. Clarke (Acting), and Charles E. Bunge. Ethel Heise had a major role in helping to draft the preliminary edition which was developed at the Library School under a grant from the Carnegie Corporation to the Articulated Instructional Media Program (AIM) of the University's Extension Division. The preliminary edition has been in continuous use at the Library School* and was tested both on and off campus. Many students contributed much valuable advice, most of all their instructor Valmai Clark, who was also kind enough to read critically the current edition. The

---

*We find it best to use this volume after students have been exposed to an overview of catalogs and cataloging and a brief introduction to descriptive cataloging (see Volume I, *Descriptive Cataloging,* "Introduction" through Chapter 4). Several patterns are workable. We *either* assign for each class meeting a relatively small portion of this volume and then devote the class periods to deepening or expanding the area covered, to theoretical concepts, quizzes, etc. *Or* we hold first an introductory class meeting during which we explain and assign a substantial portion of the volume, *in lieu* of a predetermined number of class and laboratory meetings. At the end of this predetermined period the class meets again for group discussion or lecture, and for testing. Then the process is repeated for the next substantial portion. During these weeks the instructor is available daily for individual consultation and may wish to arrange pertinent exhibits or to conduct extra laboratories.

manifold assistance and advice of Lorene Bryon, Peggy Davey, Kenneth Ferstl, E. Bernice Gibson, James Krikelas, Sister Luella Powers, Jill Bast Rosenshield, Harry Whitmore, Patricia Wickersham, Paul W. Winkler, and the reference staff of the University of Wisconsin—Madison Library are gratefully acknowledged. The humane and contageous teaching technique of Rachel K. Schenk, late director of the University of Wisconsin—Madison Library School, has remained a model to emulate. My wife Ruth, who helped in many ways, deserves most affectionate thanks.

Any shortcomings are, of course, solely the responsibility of the undersigned. Suggestions that may lead to improvements of future editions are very welcome.

John J. Boll

Madison, Wisconsin

HOW TO USE THIS TEXT

This text is designed for use with the *Anglo-American Cataloging Rules, North American Text.* Therefore, *before you start,* please buy

The *Anglo-American Cataloging Rules, North American Text* (Chicago: American Library Association, 1967). List price: cloth, $9.50; paper, $4.75. Available through your local book store, or directly from the American Library Association, 50 East Huron Street, Chicago, Illinois 60611. Please order the *Rules* at once; it takes a while to get them.

The Study Situation

Wherever you study, at home or in the library, it is important to have a place that is well-lighted, free from interruptions, relatively quiet, and with adequate table space for the two books you will be using together: this text and the *Anglo-American Cataloging Rules.* If you take notes you will also need space for your notebook.

The Study Schedule

For best results, plan a regular daily study schedule. Because this text requires concentrated study, we suggest that you study no more than an hour at a time, or two to three half-hour periods with short breaks in between. Study should be done when you are rested and alert, if it is to be effective.

Guidelines to Studying This Text

- To get the most out of this study text do not skim it. Rather, read it thoughtfully and in detail. It requires mastery of principles and careful understanding of the concrete examples.

- The illustrations, the exercises, and the *Anglo-American Cataloging Rules* are an integral part of this text. Their mastery is part of the learning objective. Handle them at the point they are presented, for the text builds on previously gained knowledge.

- Examine the illustrations carefully. Follow the arrows in a diagram; note the highlighted elements in an example; compare and contrast the title pages with the catalog cards that describe them. No other way of study will suffice.

- Study carefully those parts of the *Anglo-American Cataloging Rules* (AA) to which this text refers you, for all exercises are based on the AA.

- While doing an exercise, do not hesitate to refer to earlier parts of this text or to the AA. Once you have recorded your answer, compare it with the one in the Answer Book. If the two answers disagree, restudy the pertinent AA Rules and the pertinent portions of the text.

- Take time to reflect on new ideas. If an idea is not clear or seems to conflict with another concept, do not begrudge the time needed for rereading sentences, paragraphs, or even whole sections of the text and the AA.

- If even a careful restudying of the sections on which you are working does not clarify your question, then ask for help from your instructor or someone else with experience.

- Complete a section before you stop your study. Do not stop in the middle of an idea. If you are interrupted, go back far enough to be sure you are maintaining the sequence of ideas.

PART A: AN INTRODUCTION TO ENTRY HEADINGS

CHAPTER ONE ENTRY HEADINGS: AN OVERVIEW

HIGHLIGHTS

Cataloging consists of (1) Putting a collection of books and other library materials into some kind of logical order ("classification"), and (2) making up a record for it that will serve as its index (the "catalog"). Most books, films, phonograph records, etc. are "entered" in the catalog, that is, described individually in it.

The unit of description is called an entry. Entries consist typically (but not always) of the book's main author, title, edition statement, place of publication, publisher, date of publication, the number of its pages, and other elements (see illustrations in the text). Entries can be stored on individual catalog cards (in a "card catalog"), in a catalog that is in the form of a book, (a "book catalog"), in a computer storage device, or anywhere else suitable.

This volume deals with entry headings, that is, the names or words under which the entries are filed in a catalog. Most card catalogs contain several identical entries for each book (or filmstrip, microfilm, etc.). These identical units of description (also called in a card catalog "unit cards") contain typically at the head (the "main entry heading") the name of the book's main author and, at the bottom (the "tracings") the names of other people or organizations prominently associated with the book, the book's title, the title of the series of books to which it may belong, and the name(s) of the subject(s) it covers in depth. Each unit card thus contains a record of all names or words under which its various copies are filed, for each tracing is also typed above ("overtyped") the main entry heading on a different unit card (thereby becoming an "added entry heading") so that the first line of each catalog card in a set for a book differs. Each card is then filed by its first line, that is, one card under the main entry heading, every other card under an added entry heading. This makes it possible for the catalog user to learn, by looking in the catalog, whether or not a library has a book by a certain author, with a certain title, in a certain series, or on a certain subject.

Tracings are numbered partly in Arabic, and partly in Roman numerals, and in a definite sequence, to permit clerical assistants to distinguish easily between subject and other tracings, and also to guide the sophisticated catalog user.

Names can be transcribed in a unit card (in an entry) without having to become added entry headings. But no roman numeral added entry heading should be made for a name that has not been transcribed. They must be "justified."

Five types of headings exist: Names of people ("Personal name entry headings") are the most frequent. Other types are: the names of organizations ("corporate entry headings"); the book's real title; for certain ancient works a standard "uniform" title; and for laws, treaties, and similar items a made-up heading called a "form heading." Each of these five types can become a main or an added entry heading.

BEFORE GOING FURTHER
PLEASE READ "HOW TO USE THIS TEXT,"
Page xii

ENTRY HEADINGS: AN OVERVIEW

Cataloging consists of (1) putting a collection of books and other library materials into some kind of logical order, and (2) making up a record for it that will serve as its index. This record is the catalog. Most books, films, phonograph records, etc. are "entered" in the catalog, that is, described individually in it. This unit of description is called an entry. Entries may be stored on individual catalog cards, or in a catalog that is in the form of a book, or in a computer storage device, or anywhere else suitable. Mostly they are stored on catalog cards or in a catalog that is in the form of a book.

An entry on a
catalog card,
for use in a
card catalog.

Alter, Dinsmore, 1888–1968.
  Pictorial astronomy [by] Dinsmore Alter, Clarence H. Cleminshaw and John G. Phillips. 3d rev. ed. New York, T. Y. Crowell [1969]
    328 p. illus., charts. 28 cm. 10.00

    1. Astronomy.   ɪ. Cleminshaw, Clarence Higbee, 1902–   joint author. ɪɪ. Phillips, John Gardner, 1917–   joint author. ɪɪɪ. Title.
  QB44.A42 1969   520   69–15412
  Library of Congress   [3]   MARC

ALTBACH, Philip G
Turmoil and transition; higher education
and student politics in India. NY, Basic
Books, 1968. 277p. illus.

ALTER, Dinsmore.
Pictorial astronomy, by D. Alter, C. H.
Cleminshaw & J. G. Phillips. 3d rev. ed.
NY, Crowell, 1969. 328p. illus.

ALTMAN, Frances.
The something egg. Illus. by M. Kleitz.
Minn., Denison, 1969. 48p. illus.

The same entry
as it might be
stored in a
book, that is,
in a "book
catalog."

The same entry
as it might be
stored on a
punched card

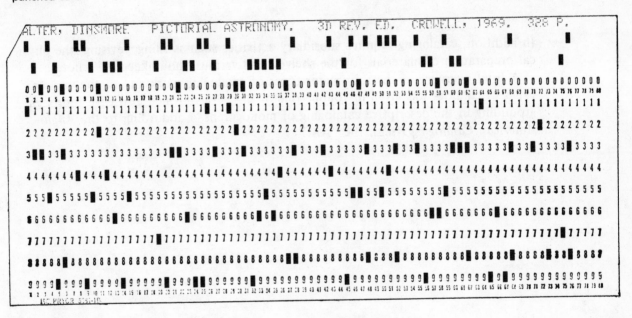

The same entry, as stored
in a computer disk storage,
is invisible to the naked eye.

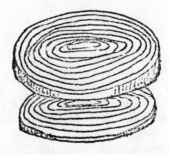

The arranging of the collection and the creation of an index are achieved by means of four major types of work:

CLASSIFICATION $\left\{\vphantom{\begin{array}{c}a\\a\end{array}}\right.$ The orderly arranging of the materials

DESCRIPTIVE CATALOGING
ENTRY HEADING WORK
SUBJECT HEADING WORK $\left\{\vphantom{\begin{array}{c}a\\a\\a\\a\end{array}}\right.$ The three activites which create the record that makes possible the use of most, though not all, materials in the library collection

In addition, cataloging requires subsidiary activities such as filing, revising, the physical preparation of materials for the shelves, and various "housekeeping" chores.

A brief overview of the four major types of cataloging work and of the various types of catalogs was given in volume one of this series* which also gave thorough grounding in the descriptive cataloging of monographs** addording to the *Anglo-American Cataloging Rules,* the "AA."***

---

* John J. Boll, *Descriptive Cataloging, and an Overview of Catalogs and Cataloging.* New York, McGraw-Hill Book Co. [c1970] (*His Introduction to Cataloging,* v. I).

** A monograph is a work that is complete in itself. It may consist of more than one physical volume but is, typically, only one volume. In other words, a monograph is what the layman calls a "book." Librarians and bibliographers distinguish monographs from periodicals and other serials which are issued continuously, in successive parts.

*** *Anglo-American Cataloging Rules. North American Text.* Prepared by the American Library Association, the Library of Congress, the Library Association, and the Canadian Library Association. (Chicago, American Library Association, 1967.)

This second volume deals with entry headings, that is, the names or phrases under which the entries are filed in a catalog. It will first give an overview of all types of entry headings, (Chapter 1); secondly a detailed introduction to related policies and techniques, (Chapters 2-7): thirdly a detailed introduction to the AA entry heading rules for personal names (Chapters 8-17); fourthly, a comparison between the AA and its predecessor (Chapter 18).

EXERCISE

Please complete the following statements. (You may want to re-read these four pages first.) Then check with the suggested answers in the "Answer Book," Answers numbers 5-1 and 5-2.

An entry is (1) _____

_____

An entry heading is (2) _____

_____

To get the most benefit from this volume, you should know something about the kinds of catalogs and the kinds of catalog arrangement that exist, should know the related terminology, and should be familiar with our principles and rules for descriptive cataloging. If you have just finished volume one in this series, or have learned these matters through other means, study the following illustration to refresh your memory, and then proceed with this text. But *if you have had no exposure to descriptive cataloging, or are rusty,* turn now to Appendix I (pages 409 to 410) which will not teach you descriptive cataloging, but will at least introduce you to terminology and to basic concepts. Study Appendix I carefully, and then return to this page.

An entry heading is really an avenue of approach to a work listed in a catalog or bibliography.* To make this approach as convenient as feasible, most catalogs list each book (or filmstrip, phonograph record, map, microfilm, etc.) under several entry headings. Typically, these entry headings permit us to approach a work** through

- the name of its author or authors
- its own name, that is, its title
- the name of the series of books to which it belongs, if any, and
- the name of each subject that it covers in depth, that is, its subject headings

---

* A bibliography is a list of items that exist and that could be located anywhere. Like the catalog, a list of entries. (The term has additional meanings which are outside the scope of this text.)

** The term "book" is used here and on the next few pages generically. Obviously, the same kind of multiple approach is useful for all types of library materials.

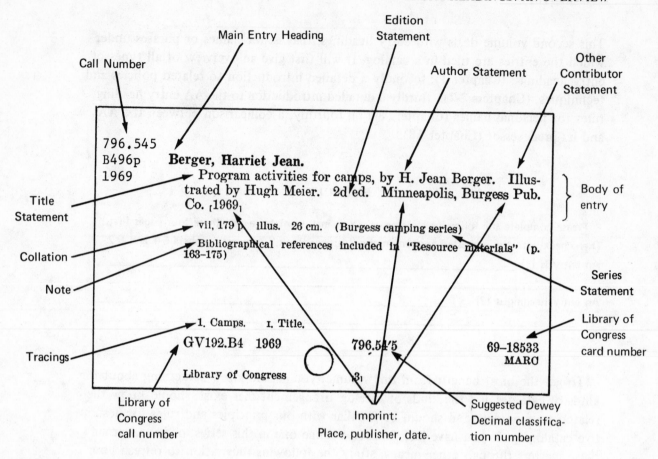

Call Number

Main Entry Heading

Edition Statement

Author Statement

Other Contributor Statement

Title Statement

Collation

Note

Tracings

Body of entry

Series Statement

Library of Congress card number

Library of Congress call number

Imprint: Place, publisher, date.

Suggested Dewey Decimal classification number

796.545
B496p
1969

Berger, Harriet Jean.
Program activities for camps, by H. Jean Berger. Illustrated by Hugh Meier. 2d ed. Minneapolis, Burgess Pub. Co. ₁1969₁

vii, 179 p. illus. 26 cm. (Burgess camping series)

Bibliographical references included in "Resource materials" (p. 163–175)

1. Camps.   I. Title.
GV192.B4   1969

Library of Congress

796.54′5

₃₁

69–18533
MARC

Form of Personal Name Entry Headings

As in telephone directories, entry headings for persons are typically given in inverted form to permit finding a work under the person's surname.

The book being cataloged may say:	The entry heading is typically given as:
. . .by James H. Miller	Miller, James H

CARD SETS

For each book that is to be cataloged, a library typically either buys or produces a set of cards: One card for each entry heading in the catalog, and other cards for supporting files.

A set of cards purchased from the Library of Congress arrives like this in the library. Note that all four "LC cards" are identical at this stage.

CARD SETS

Library of Congress Set of Unit Cards

Berger, Harriet Jean.
　　Program activities for camps, by H. Jean Berger.　Illustrated by Hugh Meier.　2d ed.　Minneapolis, Burgess Pub. Co. ₍1969₎

　　　vii, 179 p.　illus.　26 cm.　(Burgess camping series)

　　　Bibliographical references included in "Resource mate-
163–175)

　　　1. Camps

Berger, Harriet Jean.
　　Program activities for camps, by H. Jean Berger.　Illustrated by Hugh Meier.　2d ed.　Minneapolis, Burgess Pub. Co. ₍1969₎

　　　vii, 179 p.　illus.　26 cm.　(Burgess camping series)

　　　Bibliographical references included in "Resource materials" (p.
163–175)

　　　796.54′5　　　69–18533
　　　　　　　　　　　MARC

Berger, Harriet Jean.
　　Program activities for camps, by H. Jean Berger.　Illustrated by Hugh Meier.　2d ed.　Minneapolis, Burgess Pub. Co. ₍1969₎

　　　vii, 179 p.　illus.　26 cm.　(Burgess camping series)

　　　Bibliographical references included in "Resource materials" (p.
163–175)

　　　1. Camps.　　I. Titl
　　GV192 B

Berger, Harriet Jean.
　　Program activities for camps, by H. Jean Berger.　Illustrated by Hugh Meier.　2d ed.　Minneapolis, Burgess Pub. Co. ₍1969₎

　　　vii, 179 p.　illus.　26 cm.　(Burgess camping series)

　　　Bibliographical references included in "Resource materials" (p.
163–175)

　　　1. Camps.　　I. Title.　　　796.54′5　　　69–18533
　　　　　　　　　　　　　　　　　　　　　　　　　MARC
　　GV192.B4　1969

　　Library of Congress　　　　₍3₎

Library-Produced Set of Unit Cards

If the library produces its own set of cards, the sequence of steps may be as follows:*

1. The cataloger writes or types or edits a workslip.**

796.545 B496p 1969	00° BIP	Buckram Pambind
	OR✓ PTLA	
	PC° ABPR	
	NUC✓ CBI	
	1969 BM	

HEADING

Berger, H*arriet* Jean.

BODY

Program activities for camps, by H. Jean

Berger.∧ 2d ed. Minneapolis, Burgess

Pub~~lishing~~ Co. [1969]   *Illustrated by Hugh Meier.*

COLL

vii, 179 p. illus. 26 cm. *(Burgess camping series)*

NOTES

Bibliographical references included in "Resource materials" (p. 163–175)

TRCGS

1. Camps. I. Title.

---

* Other possibilities exist, but many libraries use this sequence. It can, thus, serve as an example. In computerized systems, the cataloger's job remains, essentially, the same but the clerical steps differ considerably. The professional sequences of steps which precede card-production are outlined in Chapter 6, page 130ff.

** Workslip: A temporary record of bibliographical information. Most frequently, a record on which the cataloger constructs an entry, along with supplemental information, from which the typist prepares a stencil master for duplication. It may range from an ordinary P-slip to a preprinted, highly organized, 5″ x 8″ sheet of paper. For a complete sample, and an explanation, see pages 411-412.

2. The typist transfers this information onto a stencil according to a standard formula.

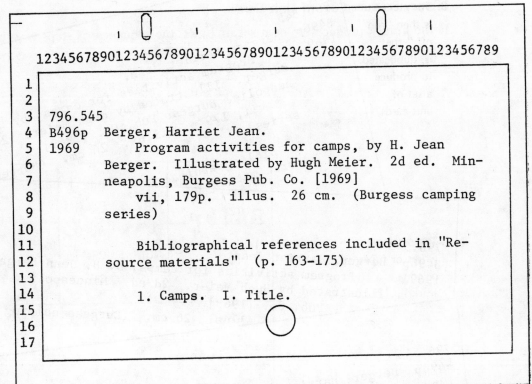

```
          1234567890123456789012345678901234567890123456789012345678901234567890123456789

 1
 2
 3    796.545
 4    B496p  Berger, Harriet Jean.
 5    1969       Program activities for camps, by H. Jean
 6           Berger.  Illustrated by Hugh Meier.  2d ed.  Min-
 7           neapolis, Burgess Pub. Co. [1969]
 8               vii, 179p.  illus.  26 cm.  (Burgess camping
 9           series)
10
11               Bibliographical references included in "Re-
12           source materials"  (p. 163-175)
13
14               1. Camps.  I. Title.
15
16
17
```

3. The stencil
is then "run
off," that
is, duplicated,
to produce
a set of
unit cards.

796.545
B496p Berger, Harriet Jean.
1969   Program activities for camps, by H. Jean
Berger. Illustrated by Hugh Meier. 2d ed. Minneapolis, Burgess Pub. Co. [1969]
        vii, 179 p. illus. 26 cm. (Burgess camping
series)

        Bibliographical references included in "Re-
source material...

796.545
B496p Berger, Harriet Jean.
1969   Program activities for camps, by H. Jean Berger
Illustrated by Hugh Meier. 2d ed. Minneapolis,
...ss Pub. Co. [1969]
                illus. 26 cm. (Burgess camping

796.545
B496p Berger, Harriet Jean.
1969   Program activities for camps, by H. Jean
Berger. Illustrated by Hugh Meier. 2d ed. Minneapolis, Burgess Pub. Co. [1969]
        vii, 179 p. illus. 26 cm. (Burgess camping
series)

        Bibliographical references included in "Re-
source materials" (p. 163-175)

        1. Camps. I. Titl...

796.545
B496p Berger, Harriet Jean.
1969   Program activities for camps, by H. Jean
Berger. Illustrated by Hugh Meier. 2d ed. Minneapolis, Burgess Pub. Co. [1969]
        vii, 179 p. illus. 26 cm. (Burgess camping
series)

        Bibliographical references included in "Re-
source materials" (p. 163-175)

        1. Camps. I. Title.

Many large libraries do not use a stencil (see page 9) but transfer the information from the workslip (see page 8) to a clean card which is then Xeroxed as many times as needed, to produce a set of unit cards. Note that at this point you have with any of these three methods identical entries on cards. Since each card in such a card set contains the same entry—the same unit of information—these cards are called **unit cards.*** Please note this term: Unit cards. In a card catalog entries are typically recorded on unit cards.

EXERCISE

Please explain briefly how an entry differs from a unit card. _____

_____

_____

_____

* Before duplicating machines became common in libraries each card had to be typed individually or, still earlier, written by hand. To save preparation time, libraries typed then only the main entry card completely and with tracings. All other cards, (the added entries) had no tracings and were far less complete, perhaps like this:

ADDED ENTRY

```
796.545     CAMPS
B496p  Berger, Harriet Jean.
1969        Program activities for camps.  2d ed.   [1969]
```

```
796.545
B496p  Berger, Harriet Jean.
1969        Program activities for camps, by H. Jean
       Berger.  Illustrated by Hugh Meier.  2d ed.  Min-
       neapolis, Burgess Pub. Co. [1969]
            vii, 179 p.  illus.  26 cm.  (Burgess camping
       series)

            Bibliographical references included in "Re-
       source materials"  (p. 163-175)

            1. Camps.  I. Title.
```

MAIN ENTRY

Since these cards do not contain the same unit of information in the main entry heading and the body of the entry, they are not unit cards.

ENTRY HEADINGS vs. TRACINGS

The basic rule for entry headings says that, if possible, a book should be entered in the catalog first under the name of the person primarily responsible for its intellectual content, the author. This name becomes typically the book's **main entry heading** —Berger, Harriet Jean in the previous example—and thus the heading on the unit card.

The names of every one else who had a "significant share" in creating the book's intellectual content are listed at the bottom of the unit card, as **tracings**. Other tracings made are typically, one for the book's title, sometimes one for the series* to which a book may belong, and one or more for the subjects which it treats in depth. On unit cards, then, tracings are librarians' shorthand to show under what headings additional entries for a book—the added entries— are to be filed in the catalog. (See page 6). In printed cards, tracings appear in the front. This is the preferred location with typed cards as well. However, when space limitations make this impossible, the tracings are put on the back or on a second, or extension, card.

Each unit card in a set thus has the same main entry heading and, typically, at the bottom, tracings. The first card of the set is filed in the catalog "as is," under the main entry heading, and is called the main entry card.

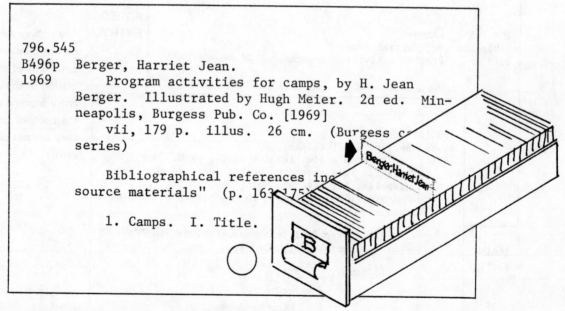

```
796.545
B496p   Berger, Harriet Jean.
1969        Program activities for camps, by H. Jean
        Berger.  Illustrated by Hugh Meier.  2d ed.  Min-
        neapolis, Burgess Pub. Co. [1969]
            vii, 179 p.  illus.  26 cm.  (Burgess c
        series)

            Bibliographical references in
        source materials"  (p. 163 175

            1. Camps.  I. Title.
```

---

* If you come across terms that require clarification, please turn to the *Glossary* at the end of this volume, and to the *Glossary* at the end of the *Anglo-American Cataloging Rules.* The *Glossary* in this volume is intended only as a supplement to the one in the AA.

The typist copies the first tracing above the main entry heading of the second unit card, like this.

MAIN
ENTRY
CARD

796.545
B496p   Berger, Harriet Jean.
1969   Program activities for camps, by H. Jean
        Berger. Illustrated by Hugh Meier. 2d ed. Min-
        neapolis, Burgess Pub. Co. [1969]
            vii, 179 p. illus. 26 cm. (Burgess camping
        series)

            Bibliographical references included in "Re-
        source materials" (p. 163–175)

            1. Camps. I. Title.

ADDED
ENTRY
CARD

796.545   CAMPS
B496p   Berger, Harriet Jean.
1969   Program activities for camps, by H. Jean
        Berger. Illustrated by Hugh Meier. 2d ed. Min-
        neapolis, Burgess Pub. Co. [1969]
            vii, 179 p. illus. 26 cm. (Burgess camping
        series)

            Bibliographical references included in "Re-
        source materials" (p. 163–175)

            1. Camps. I. Title.

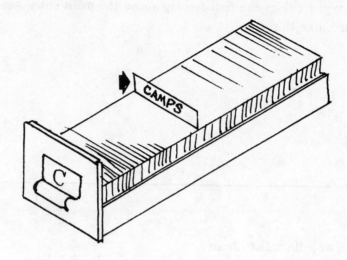

In this fashion, every tracing becomes an added entry heading when it is typed over the main entry heading of another unit card, which thereby becomes an added entry card. This process is called "overtyping."

EXERCISE

Which process causes a unit card to become an added entry card?

_____

_____

Every catalog card is filed in the catalog by its first line of text. The last card of the set, however, (see pages 7 and 10) is filed in a different file, the shelflist,* by its call number.**

---

* Shelflist: A file of cards, or a printed list, arranged in the order in which the books are shelved, that is, by call number.

** Call number: A number, or group of numbers, used to assign a book to its proper location on the shelves. In the United States, the call number consists typically of a subject number (class number) followed by an author number.

CATALOG vs SHELFLIST

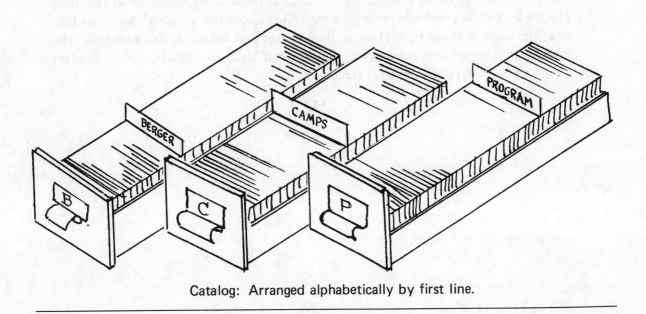

Catalog: Arranged alphabetically by first line.

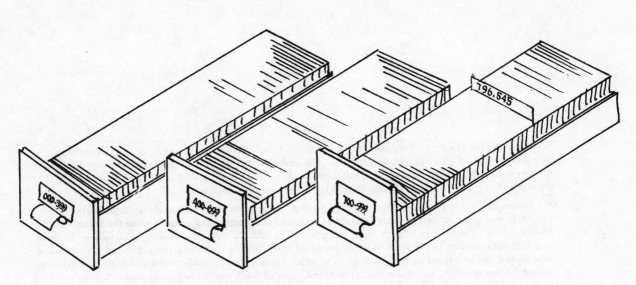

Shelflist: Arranged numerically by call number (in shelving order)

Tracings are numbered in definite sequences: (1) **A first sequence of Arabic numerals for subject tracings.** The major subject is usually listed first, but need not be. (2) **A second sequence of Roman numerals for non-subject tracings**, in this order: Personal names in the order listed in the entry; corporate names in the order listed in the entry; title of the book; (rarely also) a variant form of the title; the series tracing;* (rarely also) a tracing for a second series.

These sequences are maintained to permit easy distinction between tracings for subject on the one hand, and tracings for joint authors, titles, or series on the other: The reader who is checking, perhaps, a card filed under the author's name, can tell what the book is about by looking at the tracings that follow Arabic numerals. The typist who is overtyping (see page 14) knows that tracings following Arabic numerals are to be overtyped as subject tracings.**

---

* Until 1971, the Library of Congress used no number for the series tracing but enclosed it in parentheses. (See bottom card on pages 21 and 44). It needed this device at that time for its card sales program. Most other libraries copied the same style, without a real need. In 1972, L.C. began to omit parentheses around series tracings and to number them as the last item in the Roman numeral sequence.

** Libraries like to overtype subject added entry headings either in red with regular library capitalization or, preferably nowadays, entirely in black capitals. This permits easier separation of cards when the library uses a divided catalog, it sometimes helps in filing, and it is said to help the user when looking at a group of headings in a dictionary catalog. The typist who overtypes added entry headings onto unit cards does not need to waste time making the sometimes difficult decision as to which headings are for subjects and which are not: Whatever tracing follows an Arabic numeral is overtyped in red, or in all black capitals; whatever tracing follows a Roman numeral is overtyped in black with regular library capitalization. The numbers are, of course, not overtyped into the added entry headings since the headings are filing devices.

EXERCISE

Please examine the sequence of tracings on page 13 and in the following example. Note that
(1) Not every name transcribed in the description is listed as a tracing; (2) The form in which a
name is transcribed in the description does not always agree with its form as a main entry heading
or as tracing; (3) When a title or a series is to become an added entry heading, the tracing consists
merely of the word "Title," or "Series," unless the wording of the added entry heading must
differ from the title or series in the transcription.

We shall soon study the pertinent rules and the reasoning behind them.

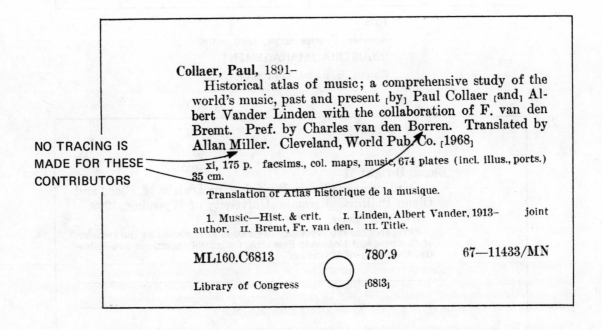

NO TRACING IS
MADE FOR THESE
CONTRIBUTORS

Collaer, Paul, 1891–
    Historical atlas of music; a comprehensive study of the
world's music, past and present ₍by₎ Paul Collaer ₍and₎ Albert Vander Linden with the collaboration of F. van den
Bremt. Pref. by Charles van den Borren. Translated by
Allan Miller. Cleveland, World Pub. Co. ₍1968₎
    xi, 175 p. facsims., col. maps, music, 674 plates (incl. illus., ports.)
35 cm.

Translation of Atlas historique de la musique.

    1. Music—Hist. & crit.   I. Linden, Albert Vander, 1913–   joint
author.   II. Bremt, Fr. van den.   III. Title.

ML160.C6813   780'.9   67—11433/MN

Library of Congress   ₍68i3₎

Now list the following tracings in correct order, and correctly numbered.

1.

Newman, William Herman, 1909–
The process of management: concepts, behavior, and practice [by] William H. Newman, Charles E. Summer [and] E. Kirby Warren. 2d ed. Englewood Cliffs, N. J., Prentice-Hall [1967]

xii, 787 p. illus. 24 cm.

Title.
Summer, Charles Edgar, joint author.
INDUSTRIAL MANAGEMENT.
Warren, E Kirby, joint author.

2.

Blood, Dwight M
Outdoor recreation in Wyoming, by Dwight M. Blood and Clynn Phillips. Laramie [University of Wyoming, 1969.
3 v. illus. 28 cm.
"Prepared for the Wyoming Recreation Commission by the Division of Business and Economic Research, College of Commerce and Industry, University of Wyoming."

Wyoming. Recreation Commission.
OUTDOOR RECREATION—WYOMING.
Phillips, Clynn, 1935-   joint author.
Title.
University of Wyoming. Division of Business
and Economic Research.

After checking the answer to the preceding question in the Answer Book, use the tracings from the first card, above, to "overtype" the following added entry cards for the same book. Please watch the capitalization and punctuation. (While it may seem picayune at this stage, this sometimes affects the filing of entries, especially subject added entries, and thus their accessibility.)

3.

Newman, William Herman, 1909–
    The process of management: concepts, behavior, and practice ₍by₎ William H. Newman, Charles E. Summer

Newman, William Herman, 1909–
    The process of management: concepts, behavior, and practice ₍by₎ William H. Newman, Charles E. Summer

Newman, William Herman, 1909–
    The process of management: concepts, behavior, and practice ₍by₎ William H. Newman, Charles E. Summer

THESE ARE ADDED ENTRY CARDS. FOR MAIN ENTRY CARD SEE PAGE 18.

Newman, William Herman, 1909–
    The process of management: concepts, behavior, and practice ₍by₎ William H. Newman, Charles E. Summer ₍and₎ E. Kirby Warren. 2d ed. Englewood Cliffs, N. J., Prentice-Hall ₍1967₎

    xii, 787 p. illus. 24 cm.

Nomenclature of Catalog Cards

Unfortunately, library terminology at this state is not precise, and the term "added entry card" or "added entry" for short, means different things to different people. To avoid confusion it is best to think of all entries by more specific names:

- Main entry, usually a personal author main entry

  Joint author added entry (The joint author is
  someone virtually as responsible for the book
  as the main author)

- Contributor added entry (A contributor is someone
  typically responsible for either a relatively minor
  contribution, or for a specific intellectual aspect
  of the book, such as the illustrator, translator,
  adaptor, or editor of someone else's work)

- Title added entry
- Series added entry
- Subject added entry

EXERCISE

Please indicate in the margin the types of entry shown. The top example is filled in for you.

Joint author added entry _____

> 328   Melinat, Carl Herman, 1912–
> H669s Hirshberg, Herbert Simon, 1879–
>   Subject guide to United States government
>   publications, by Herbert S. Hirshberg and Carl H.
>   Melinat. Chicago, American Library Assn., 1947.

(1) _____

> 021.3
> M522e Melinat, Carl Herman, 1912–
>   Educational media in libraries. Syracuse,

(2) _____

> 025.171   MANUSCRIPTS.
> H529a Hepworth, Philip.
>   Archives and manuscripts in libraries.

(3) _____

> 016.981   Library guide for Brazilian studies.
> J14*l*   Jackson, William Vernon.
>   Library guide for Brazilian studies. Pitts-

(4) _____

> 021.3   LIBRARIES AND SCHOOLS
> M522e Melinat, Carl Herman, 1912–
>   Educational media in libraries. Syracuse,

(5) _____

> 021.3   LIBRARIES AND READERS
> M522e Melinat, Carl Herman, 1912–
>   Educational media in libraries. Syracuse,

(6) _____

> 920
> I2i   Ireland, Norma Olin, 1907–
>   Index to scientists of the world, from

(7) _____

> 021.3   Frontiers of librarianship, no. 6
> M522e Melinat, Carl Herman, 1912–
>   Educational media in libraries. Syracuse,

(8) _____

> 022   Frontiers of librarianship, no. 1
> Y9c   Yenawine, Wayne Stewart, 1911–
>   Contemporary library design. Syracuse,

(9) _____

> 384
> E53i   Emery, Edwin.
>   Introduction to mass communications [by]

(10) _____

> 021.3   Educational media in libraries.
> M522e Melinat, Carl Herman, 1912–
>   Educational media in libraries. Syracuse,
>   N. Y., School of Library Science, Syracuse
>   University, 1963.
>   39 p. 23 cm. (Frontiers of librarianship,
>   no. 6)
>
>   Bibliography: p. 31.
>
>   1. Libraries and schools. 2. Libraries and
>   readers. I. Title. (Series)

---

* Under the 1972 policy referred to in the first footnote on page 16, the series tracing would be "II. Series."

Fill in below the proper term: Joint author;   Contributor.

Someone who is typically responsible for a specific intellectual aspect of a book:

(1) _____

Someone who is virtually as responsible for the book as the main author:

(2) _____

FINDING A BOOK

To find a book the reader can:

- Go to the card catalog:

    Look under a name or under
    a title that he happens to
    know, **or**

    Look under a subject that
    he thinks exists;

- Find the book listed in the
  card catalog;

- Note its call number in the
  upper left corner of the card;

- Use the call number to find
  the desired book on the shelves.

RICHARD GOLDHOWER'S BOOK ?

320
G568b   Goldhower, Richard Lyndon.
              The basic value system
          political process in a
          1971.
              xii, 357 p.

MAIN AND ADDED ENTRY HEADINGS

Among the various entry headings the main entry heading is generally considered the most important one. It helps us to assign primary responsibility for a work. This means, it helps us to use the same "handle" that is apt to be used in bibliographies, bibliographical footnotes, and whenever reference is made to the book. This makes it easier to **find** the book: not just in the catalog but in many of the lists that librarians and library patrons must consult. Indeed, many bibliographies, and virtually all union catalogs,* order lists for new books,** accession lists,*** and exchange lists† record a book **only** under its main entry heading. In such lists the main entry heading is typically the only approach that leads to a desired item. It is, therefore, important to assign the main entry heading correctly and according to a definitely established and known pattern.

EXERCISE

Please answer the following questions: What is a union catalog?

(1) _____

_____

_____

Does it, typically, list a work only under its main entry heading?

(2) _____

One can make a strong case for making a work's title the main entry heading. Logically it is the work's own name, and practically one is apt to remember a title fairly well. But our cataloging codes have been constructed on the assumption that the use, whenever possible, of the author's name as main entry heading helps the catalog user even more.

- The reader does not have to know or remember a book's exact title. (Titles change in translation and sometimes in revision.) The author's name, which is rather stable, leads him to the listed works.

---

* Union catalog: A catalog that lists the cataloged books and/or other materials of more than one library. Typically, it contains only main entries. It can be a card catalog or a book catalog or a computer catalog.

** Order list: A list of titles which the library wishes to order from a book dealer. These orders can also be sent out on individual slips.

*** Accession list: A list of all or selected titles newly received and cataloged. Many libraries issue such lists periodically to inform their patrons, or as a public relations gesture.

† Exchange list: A list of titles (usually of duplicate copies) which a library is willing to exchange with other libraries in return for titles it needs.

READ
UP

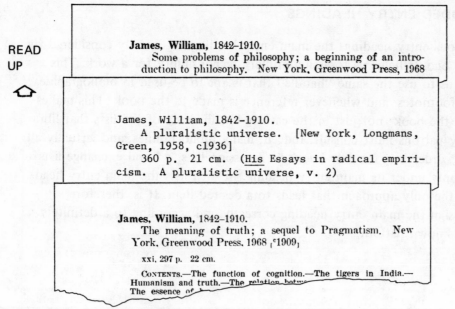

If the titles were the main entry headings for these works in a typical union catalog, these works would be listed far apart under "S," "P," and "M" (initial articles are commonly ignored in filing) and the reader would have to know their precise titles to find them.

- It permits finding next to each other all of one author's works that the library has cataloged. This gives the user an easier overview.

- Even in a bibliography or union catalog that lists a work only once (under its main entry heading) the reader can see at a glance the listed works for which an author is primarily responsible. In a typical catalog, which lists a work several times, the reader can find next to each other the cataloged works for which an author is either primarily, or secondarily, responsible. This is an added advantage to the user.

```
              Erickson, Ernst Walfred, 1911-      joint
027.7            author.
K955r  Kuhlman, Augustus Frederick, 1889-
              Report of a survey of the libraries of Murray
          State University for the University, by A. F.
          Kuhlman, E. W. Erickson [and] A. Robert Rogers.
          Murray, Ky., Murray State University, 1968.
```

Main and added
entry headings
for one person

```
020
Ac7   Erickson, Ernst Walfred, 1911-
no. 25     College and university library surveys, 1938-
       1952.  Chicago, American Library Association, 1961.
          viii, 115 p.  tables.  24 cm.  (ACRL monograph
       no. 25)

       "Based upon the author's doctoral dissertation,
       which was completed at the University of Illinois
       in 1958."
```

In most catalogs—dictionary, divided, or classed*—the main entry heading is only one of several approaches to a book. Patrons do not care what type of heading leads them to the book they want. They just want to find it quickly. To serve them it is as important to select helpful added entry headings as it is to select the proper main entry heading.

---

* The various types of catalog arrangement are described and illustrated in Chapter Two of the author's *Descriptive Cataloging, op. cit.* In summary, for **Dictionary Catalog**, see the *Glossary* in the AA; A **Divided Catalog** uses separate files for different types of entries, as follows: The **Vertically Divided Catalog** uses typically one alphabet for subject entries and one for all other entries. It may, instead, use one alphabet for subject entries, one for titles of works, and one for all other entries. The **Horizontally Divided Catalog** is divided by date, using one alphabet for all items published or received before a certain date, and another alphabet for items published or received after that date. The **Classed Catalog** is a catalog in which author, title and series entries are filed alphabetically in one file while subject entries are filed in another file numerically by class number rather than alphabetically by subject heading.

Therefore, when we think of establishing entry headings we must learn to think of **all** entry headings needed for a book, of **all** approaches.*

What is the purpose of these multiple approaches? To make it possible for a librarian or patron to find out, by looking in the catalog, whether or not a library has a book.

- by a certain AUTHOR
- with a certain TITLE
- in a certain SERIES
- on a certain SUBJECT,

depending upon which of these elements he happens to desire or to recall. Catalogs must furnish all of these approaches because readers come with different information and desires. A reader may want to find out whether the library has any books on Benjamin Franklin, or whether it has *For Whom the Bell Tolls,* or whether it has anything on HOCKEY. We must make it possible to find the answer regardless of which approach the reader uses.

EXERCISE

Explain briefly the difference between a main entry heading and an added entry heading.

_____

_____

_____

_____

* It has been said that the universal advent of the computer produced catalog will bring with it the demise of the concept of the main entry heading. Entries (the basic unit of description) would begin with the title and consist of the usual descriptive information. The author's name would be included only in the author statement and in the tracings. Thus, entries would be stored in the computer as titles entries but would be printed out also under the various tracings.

   This would avoid the necessity of deciding which is the main entry heading. But it would not avoid the necessity of knowing entry headings as such, and the principles according to which they are constructed, to permit their sophisticated use. Bibliographers and patrons would still have to know the various forms of headings, the likely filing order, and the depth of indexing practiced. They would undoubtedly still do most of their searching via the author's name, and they would still need multiple approaches to one work.

What's That to Me?

The catalog and the other bibliographical tools that librarians use are highly sophisticated organisms. Although most of them are arranged alphabetically their effective use requires far more than a knowledge of the alphabet. While anyone can use a catalog to some extent, its effective use requires solid grounding in bibliographical techniques and a knowledge of the standard and of all the elements that go into creating such a bibliographical tool.

This is the reason that even librarians who never catalog a book must be thoroughly familiar with our system of entry heading and filing rules. We must at least know the established patterns according to which books are listed in our tools; we must be able to recognize deviations from these patterns; and we must be able to create the various bibliographical tools that are the librarian's means of communication.

Personal Name Main Entry Headings

Apart from subject added entry headings which are outside the scope of this volume, the most frequent headings in a catalog or bibliography are the names of individuals. The personal name entry heading is the most frequent main entry heading, and it is the most frequent added entry heading. This is why this volume deals with personal name entry headings in depth.

EXERCISE

YANKEE SI!

The Story of Dr. J. Calvitt Clarke
and his 36,000 Children

By EDMUND W. JANSS

With a Foreword by
Dr. Daniel A. Poling

New York, 1961

WILLIAM MORROW & COMPANY

Judging from the title page, who is the author of this work?

(1) _____

Who is the contributor? (2) _____

Corporate Main Entry Heading

If the book's author is an organization rather than an individual, the main entry heading is the name of that organization. This type of entry heading is called a corporate main entry heading. Each of the following works is considered the work of a corporate body.

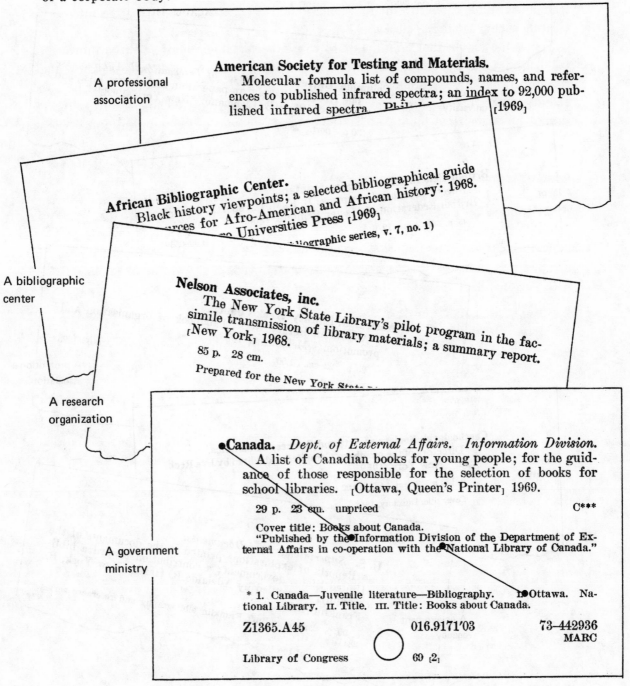

A professional association

American Society for Testing and Materials.
Molecular formula list of compounds, names, and references to published infrared spectra; an index to 92,000 published infrared spectra. Phil... ... [1969]

A bibliographic center

African Bibliographic Center.
Black history viewpoints; a selected bibliographical guide ...rces for Afro-American and African history: 1968. ...o Universities Press [1969]
...liographic series, v. 7, no. 1)

A research organization

Nelson Associates, inc.
The New York State Library's pilot program in the facsimile transmission of library materials; a summary report. [New York] 1968.
85 p. 28 cm.
Prepared for the New York Stat...

A government ministry

●**Canada.** *Dept. of External Affairs. Information Division.*
A list of Canadian books for young people; for the guidance of those responsible for the selection of books for school libraries. [Ottawa, Queen's Printer] 1969.

29 p. 23 cm. unpriced   C***

Cover title: Books about Canada.
"Published by the●Information Division of the Department of External Affairs in co-operation with the●National Library of Canada."

* 1. Canada—Juvenile literature—Bibliography.   ●Ottawa. National Library. ii. Title. iii. Title: Books about Canada.

Z1365.A45   016.9171'03   73–442936
                                                                  MARC
Library of Congress   69 [2]

* Under a policy initiated in 1972, the first Roman numeral tracing would have become "National Library of Canada." But the structured heading, above, is the one still used in most catalogs and bibliographies.

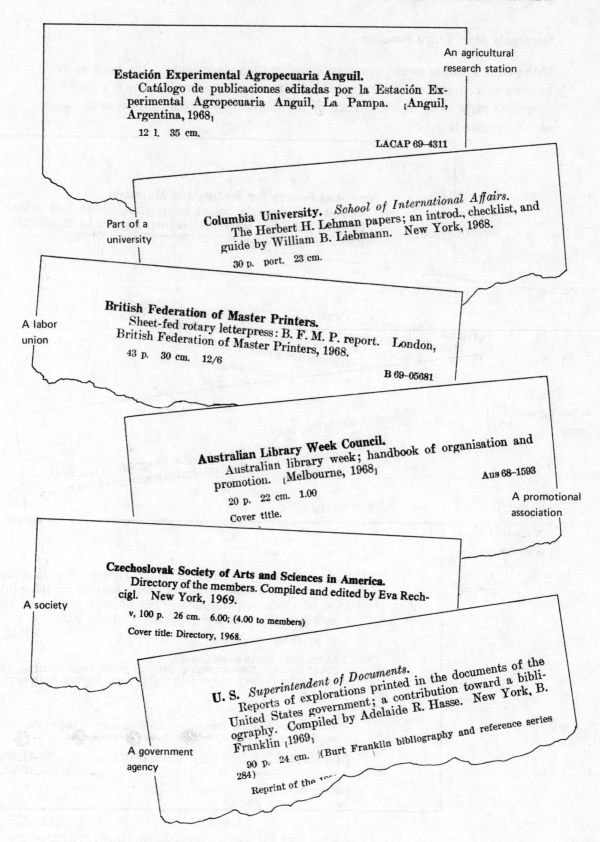

An agricultural
research station

Estación Experimental Agropecuaria Anguil.
   Catálogo de publicaciones editadas por la Estación Experimental Agropecuaria Anguil, La Pampa. ₍Anguil, Argentina, 1968₎

   12 l. 35 cm.

LACAP 69–4311

Part of a
university

Columbia University. *School of International Affairs.*
   The Herbert H. Lehman papers; an introd., checklist, and guide by William B. Liebmann. New York, 1968.

   30 p. port. 23 cm.

A labor
union

British Federation of Master Printers.
   Sheet-fed rotary letterpress: B. F. M. P. report. London, British Federation of Master Printers, 1968.

   43 p. 30 cm. 12/6

B 69–05681

Australian Library Week Council.
   Australian library week; handbook of organisation and promotion. ₍Melbourne, 1968₎

   20 p. 22 cm. 1.00

   Cover title.

Aus 68–1593

A promotional
association

A society

Czechoslovak Society of Arts and Sciences in America.
   Directory of the members. Compiled and edited by Eva Rechcigl. New York, 1969.

   v, 100 p. 26 cm. 6.00; (4.00 to members)

   Cover title: Directory, 1968.

A government
agency

U. S. *Superintendent of Documents.*
   Reports of explorations printed in the documents of the United States government; a contribution toward a bibliography. Compiled by Adelaide R. Hasse. New York, B. Franklin ₍1969₎

   90 p. 24 cm. ₎(Burt Franklin bibliography and reference series 284)

   Reprint of the 19__

While personal names as entry headings are typically listed under the surname* corporate names as entry headings are often re-arranged in structured order. Note, in the second example above, that

The Information Division of the Department of External Affairs of Canada	} becomes as entry heading {	Canada. Dept. of External Affairs. Information Division.
The National Library of Canada		Ottawa. National Library.**

The specific rule in this area are outside the scope of this text. But their effect is to group frequently the entries for sub-units of an organization next to the parent organization. This permits the user a better overview of what the library has.

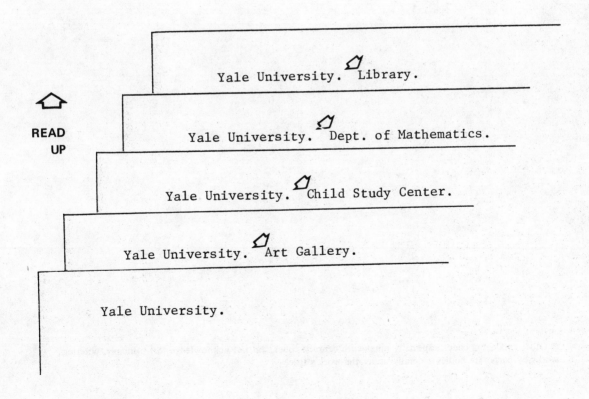

READ
UP

Yale University. Library.

Yale University. Dept. of Mathematics.

Yale University. Child Study Center.

Yale University. Art Gallery.

Yale University.

---

* Mentioned on page 6.

** Under a policy initiated in 1972, this particular heading would become "National Library of Canada." But the structured heading, above, is the one still used in most catalogs and bibliographies.

Intellectual Responsibility

The personal name main entry heading and the corporate main entry heading are assigned on the basis of intellectual responsibility. The cataloging codes of the English speaking countries have operated for over a century on the principle that a corporate body can be intellectually responsible for its corporate writings just as it can be held legally responsible for its corporate actions.*

But for material that does not have an author in the usual sense we cannot use the principle of intellectual responsibility. Yet, the reader must have a "bibliographical handle," some kind of heading that will come easily and naturally to his mind, to lead him to the material he seeks, and to bring all variations of the same material together. Therefore, we adopt for such materials a main entry heading which we think will provide the greatest convenience for the reader and act as a substitute for the personal or corporate main entry heading. Three such substitutes exist: Real title main entry heading, Uniform title main entry heading, and Form heading.

---

* Other cataloging codes, especially nineteenth century codes, did not acknowledge this principle, entering works by corporate bodies generally under the work's title.

Title Main Entry Heading (Real Title)

If the author is unknown and cannot be determined, or if there are so many authors that responsibility is difficult to assign, we enter a book under its real title. Following are examples of title main entry headings.

BOOKS
ENTERED
UNDER
THEIR
REAL
TITLE

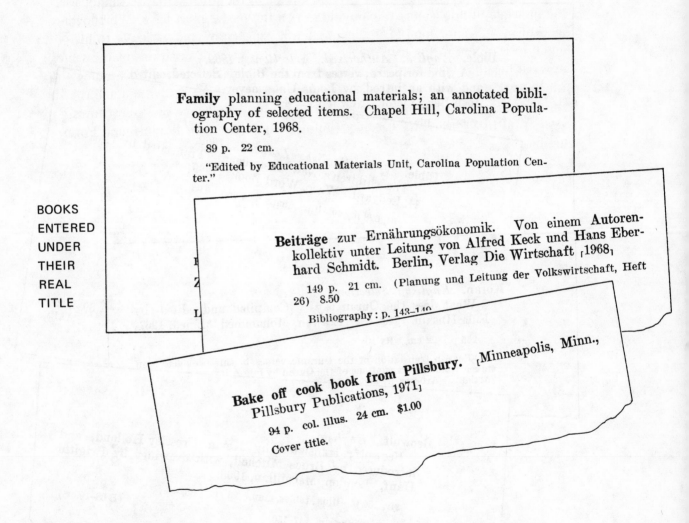

Family planning educational materials; an annotated bibliography of selected items. Chapel Hill, Carolina Population Center, 1968.

89 p. 22 cm.

"Edited by Educational Materials Unit, Carolina Population Center."

Beiträge zur Ernährungsökonomik. Von einem Autorenkollektiv unter Leitung von Alfred Keck und Hans Eberhard Schmidt. Berlin, Verlag Die Wirtschaft ₁1968₁

149 p. 21 cm. (Planung und Leitung der Volkswirtschaft, Heft 26) 8.50

Bibliography : p. 143–149

Bake off cook book from Pillsbury. ₁Minneapolis, Minn., Pillsbury Publications, 1971₁

94 p. col. illus. 24 cm. $1.00

Cover title.

The title is in the regular author position, but the entry continues without interruption. For spacing regulations for this "hanging indention" format, see page 410.

Uniform Title Main Entry Heading

For ancient works of unknown authorship, which are commonly referred to by one title although they have appeared under many titles in different languages, namely sacred books (such as the *Bible,* the *Koran,* or the *Bhagavad Gita*) and anonymous classics* (such as the *Arabian Nights* or the *Roman de Renart*) we use the best known of these titles as a substitute for the author, calling it a "Conventional title,"

Bible. *English. Authorized. Selections. 1969.*
　　A time for peace; verses from the Bible.　Selected, edited
and with an introd. by Louis Untermeyer.　I̶l̶
Joan Berg Victor.　New York, W̶
　　[64] p.　ill̶

Bible. *N. T. English. Ledyard. 1969.*
　The children's New Testament.　Translated by Gleason
H. Ledyard.　Waco, Word Books [1969]
　　viii, 628 p.　col. illus., maps.　24 cm.　6.95

Koran. *English. Selections.*
　　What does the Quran say?　[Compiled and edited] by
Fida Husain.　[1st ed.　Etawah, Mohammed Ahmed, 1967]
　　255 p.　22 cm.　Rs 10

　　"English translation of the Quranic verses in this book has been
taken from the translations of the Quran by late A̶l̶l̶
Arthur J. Arberry ... and o̶f̶ ̶M̶

69–20228
MARC

Beowulf. *English.*
　　Beowulf; translated by Kevin Crossley-Holland, and
introduced by Bruce Mitchell, with drawings by Brigitte
Hanf.　London, Macmillan, 1968.
　　xiv, 150 p.　illus., tables, map.　23 cm.　35/–　　(B 68–19995)
　　Bibliography: p. 147–150.

or a "Uniform title." Note that the uniform, or conventional, title is in the main entry heading position and contains additional prescribed terms indicating the language, whether the edition is less than complete, and sometimes other elements such

* This term is, unfortunately, not used any more although it describes well such non-religious works which are commonly designated by a commonly accepted (conventional) title. The current term is "Early anonymous work."

as the date of publication. The precise rules for this are somewhat intricate and outside the scope of this text. Their purpose, however, becomes clear when you remember that all entries are filed by their first line. Thus, headings like this permit us to list together, say, all of a library's French language editions of the *Koran*, or all the English language editions of the *New Testament*. Since hundreds of editions exist of each anonymous classic, and thousands of editions of sacred works (and especially of the Bible), and most with differing titles, some kind of orderly arrangement is essential. This makes it relatively easy for a user to find what he needs, such as a French language edition of the *Koran*, even if he does not know its exact title. Also, it permits him to see at a glance entries for **all** such works the library owns, and he can fairly easily select the one that seems to meet his need. If the following entries were filed by their real title, instead of by a uniform title, the entries would be scattered throughout the catalog and the reader could not possibly have an overview.

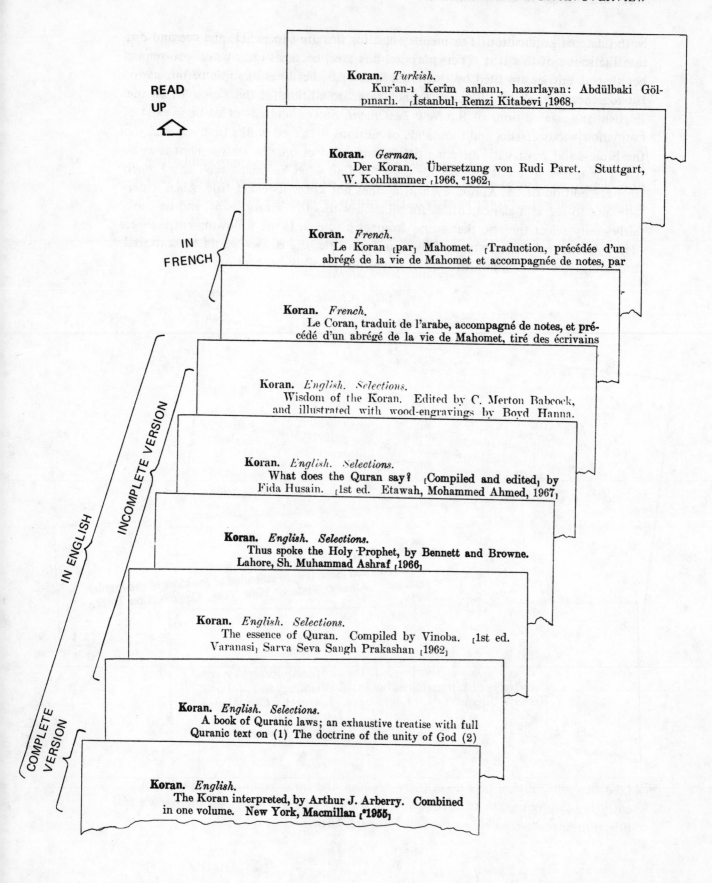

READ
UP

Koran. *Turkish.*
Kur'an-ı Kerîm anlamı, hazırlayan: Abdülbaki Göl-
pınarlı. ₁İstanbul₁ Remzi Kitabevi ₁1968₁

Koran. *German.*
Der Koran. Übersetzung von Rudi Paret. Stuttgart,
W. Kohlhammer ₁1966, ᶜ1962₁

IN
FRENCH

Koran. *French.*
Le Koran ₁par₁ Mahomet. ₁Traduction, précédée d'un
abrégé de la vie de Mahomet et accompagnée de notes, par

Koran. *French.*
Le Coran, traduit de l'arabe, accompagné de notes, et pré-
cédé d'un abrégé de la vie de Mahomet, tiré des écrivains

Koran. *English. Selections.*
Wisdom of the Koran. Edited by C. Merton Babcock,
and illustrated with wood-engravings by Boyd Hanna.

Koran. *English. Selections.*
What does the Quran say? ₁Compiled and edited₁ by
Fida Husain. ₁1st ed. Etawah, Mohammed Ahmed, 1967₁

Koran. *English. Selections.*
Thus spoke the Holy Prophet, by Bennett and Browne.
Lahore, Sh. Muhammad Ashraf ₁1966₁

Koran. *English. Selections.*
The essence of Quran. Compiled by Vinoba. ₁1st ed.
Varanasi₁ Sarva Seva Sangh Prakashan ₁1962₁

Koran. *English. Selections.*
A book of Quranic laws; an exhaustive treatise with full
Quranic text on (1) The doctrine of the unity of God (2)

Koran. *English.*
The Koran interpreted, by Arthur J. Arberry. Combined
in one volume. New York, Macmillan ₁ᶜ1955₁

INCOMPLETE VERSION

IN ENGLISH

COMPLETE VERSION

Note that, unlike in the title-main-entry-heading situation (page 33) the conventional title is placed in the main entry heading position in lieu of an author, and the book's real title begins the body of the entry, as in any ordinary author-title situation. For spacing regulations for this standard format, see page 409.

Form Headings

For other works, for example laws and treaties that usually have impossibly long titles which are hard to remember, we create a heading that fits anything in that category, calling it a "form heading." This results in headings such as

> France. *Laws, statutes, etc.*
>
> Maryland. *Laws, statutes, etc.*
>
> New York *(City) Charter.*
>
> U.S. *Constitution.*

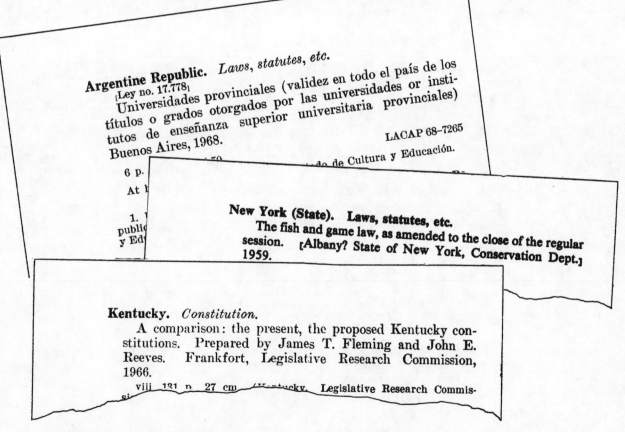

Like the conventional-title main entry heading, the form heading is in the main entry heading position and is followed, in the body of the entry, by the book's real title. For spacing regulations for this standard format, see page 409.

Advantages of Uniform Titles and Form Headings

Uniform titles, and form headings, bring together in the catalog, under one heading, all editions of an anonymous classic, or of the *Bible,* or of a city charter, that the library has, since they all have the same main entry heading. Thus, these headings achieve what personal and corporate main entry headings achieve for personal and corporate authors: The reader can find a specific item without knowing its exact title, provided he knows something about the entry heading formula. Also, the reader will find listed together all cataloged editions of one type of material (such as the Constitution of the State of New York) and can thus make his preliminary selection rather easily.

The illustration on page 24 shows how this works with a personal author, and the illustration on page 36 how conventional titles try to achieve it. Below are examples, taken from the *National Union Catalog,** showing files of entries for a corporate author and for form headings.

---

* The *National Union Catalog* is a union catalog of books and other items recently cataloged by the Library of Congress and about one thousand other United States and Canadian libraries. It is published monthly in book form and cumulates for periods of up to twenty years.

Nathan (Robert R.) Associates, Washington, D.C.
Economic development plan for the Trust
Territory of the Pacific Islands. Submitted to
the High Commissioner. Saipan, Mariana
Islands, 1966.
4 v. in 3.
1. Pacific Islands (Ter.)—Econ. condit.
2. Economic development—Pacific Islands (Ter.)
1. Pacific Islands (Ter.) High Commissioner.
1. Title.
CarS   NUC68–106642

Nathan (Robert R.) Associates, Washington, D.C.
An economic feasibility study of the Port
Harcourt Aba road and of related road facilities
in the Port Harcourt area. Washington, 1967.
1 v. (various pagings)
Prepared for the Agency for International
Development.
1. Roads—Nigeria. 2. Nigeria—Roads.
1. U.S. Agency for International Development.
II. Title. III. Title: Port Harcourt Aba road.
DS   NUC68–86849

Nathan (Robert R.) Associates, Washington, D.C.
Margins speculation and prices in grains
future markets. ₁Washington₎ Economic
Research Service, U.S. Dept. of Agriculture
₁1967₎
iv, 245 p. illus.
1. Grain futures. 2. Grain—Prices. I. U.S.
Dept. of Agriculture. Economic Research
Service. II. Title.
MH–BA IU   NUC68–56318

Nathan (Robert R.) Associates, Washington, D.C.
Recreation as an industry in Appalachia.
Prepared for the Appalachian Regional Commis-
sion by Robert R. Nathan Associates and
Resource Planning Associates. Washington,
D.C., 1966.
vi, 131 p. illus. 27 cm.
Bibliography: p. 77–89.
1. U.S. Appalachian Regional Commission
₁Founded 1965₎
IU NhD MH–BA N   NUC68–9849
NIC

Nathan (Robert R.) Associates, Washington, D.C.
Recreation as an industry in Appalachia;
field study summary reports. Prepared for the
Appalachian Regional Commission, by Robert
R. Nathan Associates and Resource Planning
Associates. Washington, 1966.
71 p. maps, 27 cm.
1. U.S. Appalachian Regional Commission
₁Founded 1965₎   NUC68–8767

Montana. *Laws, statutes, etc.*
Election laws of the State of Montana, 1968. Arranged
and compiled from the Revised codes of Montana of 1947,
as amended. Compiled by Frank Murray, secretary of state.
₁Helena₎ 1968.
409 p. 26 cm.
1. Election law—Montana.   1. Montana. Secretary of State.
II. Title.
KFM9420.A3 ·1968   340   68–64677

Montana. *Laws, statutes, etc.*
Liquor control laws, 1966. Compiled from the Revised
codes of Montana of 1947, as amended by the laws of 1949
to 1965, inclusive. ₁Helena₎ Montana Liquor Control Board
₁1966₎
114 p. 26 cm.
At head of title: State of Montana.
1. Liquor laws—Montana. 2. Liquor traffic—Montana.
1. Montana. Liquor Control Board.
KFM9375.A3 1966   66–64776

Montana. *Laws, statutes, etc.*
Livestock sanitary laws of Montana, and Attorney General's opinions. ₁Helena₎ Montana Livestock Sanitary
Board, 1967 ₁1968₎
iii, 107 p. 26 cm.
1. Animal industry—Law and legislation—Montana.
1. Montana. Attorney General's Office. II. Montana. Livestock Sanitary
Board. III. Title.
KFM9246.A3 1967   340   68–63963

Montana. *Laws, statutes, etc.*
1967 Montana retirement laws relating to: public employees retirement system, game wardens retirement system,
judges retirement system, social security. Compiled for
the Board of Administration, Public Employees' Retirement System. Indianapolis, A. Smith Co. ₁1967₎
58 p. 26 cm.
1. Montana—Officials and employees—Salaries, allowances, etc.
1. Montana. Public Employees' Retirement System. Board of Administration. II. Title. III. Title: Montana retirement laws.
KFM9435.5.A3 1967   340   68–64609

Montana. Laws, statutes, etc. The Occupational
disease act of Montana
see Montana. Laws, statutes, etc. Workmen's
compensation act. Workmen's compensation
act ... Helena, 1967.

Montana. *Laws, statutes, etc.*
₁Workmen's compensation act₎
Workmen's compensation act and occupational disease
act of the State of Montana. Compiled from the rev.
codes of 1947 as amended by 1949, 1951, 1953, 1955, 1957,
1959, 1961, 1963, 1965, and 1967 Legislative Assemblies.
Administered by the Industrial Accident Board. Helena,
1967.
130 p. 23 cm.
1. Workmen's compensation—Montana. 2. Occupational diseases.
Montana. Laws, statutes, etc. The Occupational disease act of
Montana. II. Montana. Industrial Accident Board. III. Title.
KFM9342.A3 1967   340   68–64276

New York (State) Constitution.
The constitution of the state of New York,
amendments effective January 1, 1959, effective
January 1, 1960. Albany, N.Y., C.K. Simon,
Secretary of State, 1960.
24 p.
Cover title.
I. New York (State) Secretary of State.
FTaSU   NUC68–6503

New York (*State*) *Constitution.*
The Constitution of the State of New York, as revised,
with amendments adopted by the Constitutional Convention of 1938 and approved by vote of the people on November 8, 1938. As amended and in force January 1, 1967.
₁Albany? 1967₎
267 p. 23 cm.
KFN5680 1938.A35   342′.747′01   67–65631
N

New York (*State*) *Constitution.*
New York State Constitution, as revised, with amendments adopted by the Constitutional Convention of 1938 and
approved by vote of the people November 8, 1938, and
amendments subsequently adopted by vote of the people
during the years 1939–1965, inclusive. Amended to January
1, 1966. ₁Albany₎ John P. Lomenzo, Secretary of State
₁1966?₎
12A, 346 p. illus., ports. 16 cm.
1. New York (State) Dept. of State.
KFN5680 1938.A34   342.747′01   67–65630
MH–L MiU–L

EXERCISE

Please indicate the types of entry headings shown at left. Each represents one of the five types we have encountered: Personal, corporate, real title, uniform title, and form heading.

Kentucky. *Constitution.*
A comparison: the present, the proposed Kentucky constitutions. Prepared by James T. Fleming and John E. Reeves. Frankfort, Legislative Research Commission,

EXAMPLE:
Form heading
_____

FILL IN:

Boykin, James H   1936–
Industrial real estate: an annotated bibliography, by James H. Boykin. Washington, Society of Industrial Realtors, 1969.

(1) _____

Utah. *State Board of Education.*
Minority groups; a bibliography. Salt Lake City, Office of the State Superintendent of Public Instruction, 1968.

(2) _____

Index to Federal aid publications in sport fish and wildlife restoration and selected cooperative research project reports, March 1968. Washington, U. S. Dept. of the Interior, Departmental Library, 1968.
    1 v. (unpaged) 26 cm.

(3) _____

Chanson de Roland.
The song of Roland. Translated by Patricia Terry. With an introd. and bibliography by Harold March. Indianapolis, Bobbs-Merrill [1965]

(4) _____

Kentucky.   Laws, statutes, etc.
Kentucky narcotic, barbiturate, and amphetamine drug laws and regulations. 1965 ed. Frankfort, Kentucky State Dept. of Health, Office of Investigation & Narcotic Control [1965]
    28 p.   22 cm.

(5) _____

American Antiquarian Society.
    A society's chief joys; an exhibition from the collections
of the American Antiquarian Society. Worcester ₁Mass.,
1969₁   *(6)*

Arabian nights.
    Arabian nights. ₁Selected and edited₁ by Andrew Lang.
Illustrated by William Dempster. Santa Rosa, Calif.,
Classic Press ₁1968₁   *(7)*

New York (State).   Laws, statues, etc.
    Law against discrimination (as amended through May 3,
1967) New York, State Commission for Human Rights ₁1967₁   *(8)*

Directory of Australian booksellers. Sydney, Joint Publishers
Committee of The Australian Book Publishers Association and
The Publishers Association of the United Kingdom, 1969.   *(9)*

    157 l.   22 cm.   Aus***

McKerrow, Ronald Brunlees, 1872–1940.
    A dictionary of printers and booksellers in England, Scot-
land and Ireland, and of foreign printers of English books
1557–1640, by H. G. Aldis ₁and others₁ General editor:
R. B. McKerrow. London, Bibliographical Society, 1968.   *(10)*

    xxiii, 346 p.   22 cm.   60/-   B 69–22868

    First published in 1910.
    Bibliography : p. ₁xxl₁–xxiii.

Five Types of Main and Added Entry Headings

Any one of these headings may be a main entry heading, any one of them may be an added entry heading, depending on the characteristics of the book being cataloged.

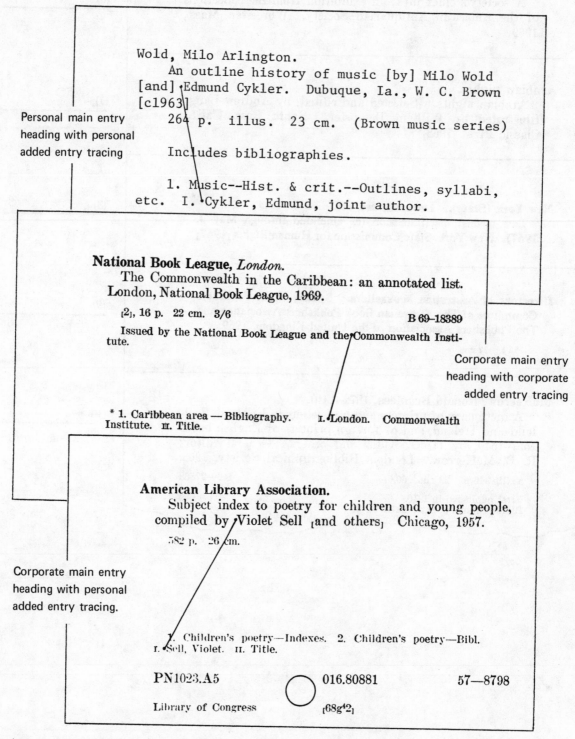

Personal main entry heading with personal added entry tracing

> Wold, Milo Arlington.
>   An outline history of music [by] Milo Wold [and] Edmund Cykler. Dubuque, Ia., W. C. Brown [c1963]
>   264 p. illus. 23 cm. (Brown music series)
>
>   Includes bibliographies.
>
>   1. Music--Hist. & crit.--Outlines, syllabi, etc. I. Cykler, Edmund, joint author.

> **National Book League,** *London.*
>   The Commonwealth in the Caribbean: an annotated list. London, National Book League, 1969.
>   [2], 16 p. 22 cm. 3/6   B 69–18389
>   Issued by the National Book League and the Commonwealth Institute.
>
>   * 1. Caribbean area — Bibliography.   I. London. Commonwealth Institute. II. Title.

Corporate main entry heading with corporate added entry tracing

Corporate main entry heading with personal added entry tracing.

> **American Library Association.**
>   Subject index to poetry for children and young people, compiled by Violet Sell [and others] Chicago, 1957.
>   582 p. 26 cm.
>
>   1. Children's poetry—Indexes. 2. Children's poetry—Bibl. I. Sell, Violet. II. Title.
>
>   PN1023.A5   016.80881   57—8798
>
>   Library of Congress   [68g⁴2]

* Under the policy mentioned on page 29, the first Roman numeral tracing would change to "Commonwealth Institute, London." But the structured form, above, is the one found in most catalogs.

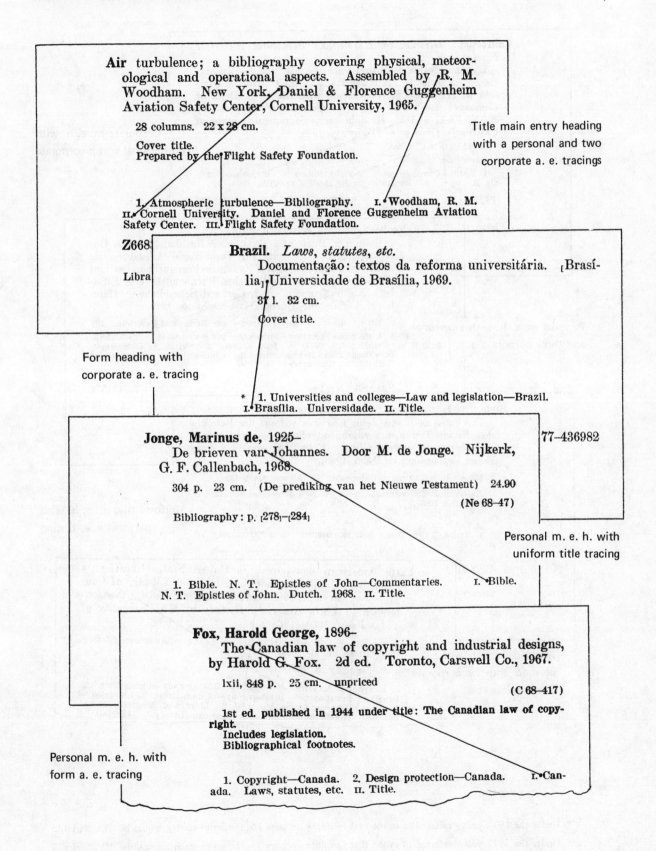

Air turbulence; a bibliography covering physical, meteorological and operational aspects. Assembled by R. M. Woodham. New York, Daniel & Florence Guggenheim Aviation Safety Center, Cornell University, 1965.

28 columns. 22 x 28 cm.

Cover title.
Prepared by the Flight Safety Foundation.

1. Atmospheric turbulence—Bibliography. I. Woodham, R. M. II. Cornell University. Daniel and Florence Guggenheim Aviation Safety Center. III. Flight Safety Foundation.

Title main entry heading with a personal and two corporate a. e. tracings

Z668

Libra

Brazil. *Laws, statutes, etc.*
Documentação: textos da reforma universitária. [Brasília] Universidade de Brasília, 1969.

37 l. 32 cm.

Cover title.

Form heading with corporate a. e. tracing

* 1. Universities and colleges—Law and legislation—Brazil.
I. Brasília. Universidade. II. Title.

Jonge, Marinus de, 1925–
De brieven van Johannes. Door M. de Jonge. Nijkerk, G. F. Callenbach, 1968.

304 p. 23 cm. (De prediking van het Nieuwe Testament) 24.90

(Ne 68–47)

Bibliography: p. [278]–[284]

77–436982

Personal m. e. h. with uniform title tracing

1. Bible. N. T. Epistles of John—Commentaries. I. Bible. N. T. Epistles of John. Dutch. 1968. II. Title.

Fox, Harold George, 1896–
The Canadian law of copyright and industrial designs, by Harold G. Fox. 2d ed. Toronto, Carswell Co., 1967.

lxii, 848 p. 25 cm. unpriced

(C 68–417)

1st ed. published in 1944 under title: The Canadian law of copyright.
Includes legislation.
Bibliographical footnotes.

Personal m. e. h. with form a. e. tracing

1. Copyright—Canada. 2. Design protection—Canada. I. Canada. Laws, statutes, etc. II. Title.

* The first Roman numeral tracing is in the form in which it will be found in most library catalogs. But under the new policy initiated in 1972, it would have been "Universidade de Brasilia."

California.   *Division of Highways.   Structural Materials Section.*

Dynamic full scale impact tests of cable type median barriers: test series IX. A study made by the California Division of Highways in cooperation with the U. S. Dept. of Commerce, Bureau of Public Roads. ₍Report prepared by R. N. Field and M. H. Johnson. Sacramento₎ State of California, Division of Highways, 1965.

39, 15 l. illus. 29 cm.

Cover title.

1. Roads—Guard fences.   I. Field, Robert N.   II. Johnson, Melvin H.   III. U. S. Bureau of Public Roads.   IV. Title.

TE228.C36   625.7'9   70–625460
                                                         MARC

Library

Corporate m. e. h. with two personal and a corporate a. e. tracing

Noelle-Neumann, Elisabeth, 1916–

Religiöses Buch und christlicher Buchhandel; eine Untersuchung des Instituts für Demoskopie Allensbach im Auftrage der Vereinigung Evangelischer Buchhändler und der Vereinigung des Katholischen Buchhandels ₍von₎ Elisabeth Noelle-Neumann ₍und₎ Gerhard Schmidtchen. Hamburg, Verlag für Buchmarkt-Forschung, 1969.

190 p. illus. 21 cm. (Schriften zur Buchmarkt-Forschung, 18)

1. Religious literature—Publication and distribution.   I. Schmidtchen, Gerhard, 1925–   joint author.   II. Institut für Demoskopie.   III. Vereinigung Evangelischer Buchhändler.   IV. Vereinigung des Katholischen Buchhandels.   V. Title.   (Series)   *

Z319.S3   Nr. 18   73–431374

Personal m. e. h. with a personal and three corporate a. e. tracings

Bible. *N. T. German.   Zink.   Selections.   1968.*

Das muss man von Jesus Christus wissen; die Berichte des Neuen Testaments zusammengefasst, neu angeordnet und übertragen von Jörg Zink. ₍1. Aufl. Gütersloh₎ Gütersloher Verlagshaus G. Mohn ₍1968₎

168 p. illus. 19 cm. (Gütersloher Taschenausgaben, 42)

Based on J. Zink's translation of the New Testament published in Stuttgart in 1965.

1. Jesus Christ—Biog.—Sources, Biblical.   I. Zink, Jörg, ed.   II. Title.

BS2561

Library

Uniform title m. e. h. with personal a. e. tracing

Latin American newspapers in United States libraries; a union list compiled in the Serial Division, Library of Congress, by Steven M. Charno. Austin, Published for the Conference on Latin American History by the University of Texas Press ₍1969, ᶜ1968₎

xiv, 619 p. 27 cm. (Conference on Latin American History. Publications, no. 2) 20.00   **

Bibliography: p. ₍611₎–619.

1. Spanish American newspapers—Bibliography—Union lists. 2. Brazilian newspapers — Bibliography — Union lists. 3. Libraries — U. S.   I. Charno, Steven M.   II. U. S. Library of Congress. Serial Division.   III. Conference on Latin American History.   (Series)

Real title m. e. h. with a personal and two corporate a. e. tracings

* Under the 1972 policy referred to in the first footnote on page 16, the series tracing would be "VI. Series."

** Under the 1972 policy referred to in the first footnote on page 16, the series tracing would be "IV. Series."

We shall study later on the specific AA rules for many of these situation.

EXERCISE

(1) Now "overtype" the following card set. The top card is the main entry card.

Fox, Harold George, 1896–
    The Canadian law of copyright and industrial designs,
by Harold G. Fox.   2d ed.   Toronto, Carswell Co., 1967.

lxii, 848 p.   25 cm.   unpriced

(C 68–417)

1st ed. published in 1944 under title: The Canadian law of copy-
right.
Includes legislation.
Bibliographical footnotes.

1. Copyright—Canada.   2. Design protection—Canada.   ɪ. Canada.   Laws, statutes, etc.   ɪɪ. Title.

327

Fox, Harold George, 1896–
    The Canadian law of copyright and industrial designs,
by Harold G. Fox.   2d ed.   Toronto, Carswell Co., 1967.

Fox, Harold George, 1896–
    The Canadian law of copyright and industrial designs,
by Harold G. Fox.   2d ed.   Toronto, Carswell Co., 1967.

Fox, Harold George, 1896–
    The Canadian law of copyright and industrial designs,
by Harold G. Fox.   2d ed.   Toronto, Carswell Co., 1967.

Fox, Harold George, 1896–
    The Canadian law of copyright and industrial designs,
by Harold G. Fox.   2d ed.   Toronto, Carswell Co., 1967.

Answer yes, or no, to the following questions:

Is it possible for the name of a corporate body to become a main entry heading? (2) _____

Is it possible for a form heading to become an added entry heading? (3) _____

Transcription Without Roman Numeral Tracing

You will recall from page 17 that not every name that is transcribed descriptively receives a Roman numeral added entry tracing.* Here are two more examples:

```
    Mitchell, Robert Cameron.
        A comprehensive bibliography of modern African
    religious movements.  Compiled by Robert Cameron
    Mitchell [and] Harold W. Turner, with the assistance
    of Hans-Jürgen Greschat.  [Evanston, Ill., North-
    western University Press, 1966]
        xiv, 132 p.  28 cm.
        On cover:  A bibliography of modern African
    religious movements.
        1. Africa--Religion--Bibl.  I. Turner, Harold
    W., joint author.  II. Title.  III. Title: A bibli-
    ography of modern African religious movements.
```

Receives no
added entry
tracing

```
    Metcalf, Keyes DeWitt, 1889-
        Planning academic and research library buildings
    [by] Keyes D. Metcalf.  New York, McGraw-Hill Book
    Co. [1965]
        xv, 431 p.  illus.  29 cm.
        "Sponsored by the Association of Research Li-
    braries and the Association of College and Research
    Libraries under a grant by the Council on Library
    Resources."
        "Selective annotated bibliography":  p. 403-411.
        1. Library architecture.  2. Libraries, Univer-
    sity and college.  I. Association of Research Li-
    braries.  II. Association of College and Research
    Libraries.  III.              Title.
```

Received no
added entry
tracing

* Explained on pages 12 and 16.

This is done because a name may be quite useful in the description—for example giving credit to a person for a relatively small contribution, or giving the reader a more complete impression of the work—and still not be needed as an access point, or approach* to a work. The AA rules according to which the above examples were constructed assume that few, if any, readers would look for such works under people or organizations making the contributions of Hans Jürgen Greschat or the Council on Library Resources.** This is debatable, of course, and once we start to study the rules in detail you will find that they give you leeway in such matters. For now, let us just recall that it is possible to transcribe a name without making a Roman numeral added entry tracing for it.

"JUSTIFYING" AN ADDED ENTRY HEADING

Conversely, you will note that Roman numeral tracings are made only for persons, organizations, legal concepts, etc. that have been mentioned previously somewhere in the entry.

EXERCISE

Can you find on pages 42 to 44 any Roman numeral tracings (this volume does not deal with Arabic numeral tracings***) for anything that has not been previously put into the description?

---

* Mentioned on page 26.

** For the concept "transcription without added entry tracings because of the *number* of individuals involved," see pages 240-241.

*** Explained on page 16.

This technique is called "justifying" an added entry heading since, by including the name in the description we typically include the contribution, such as "With illustrations by . . ." or "With a chapter on. . . by. . . ." The reader of the added entry card should be able to see at a glance why a book is listed under a name.

COULD THE
READER OF
THIS ADDED ENTRY
KNOW WHY IT
IS LISTED
UNDER
RANDALL?

NOT THIS

```
        Randall, David Anton, 1905-
   Indiana.  University.  Lilly Library.
        Three centuries of American poetry;  an exhibi-
   tion of original paintings [at] the Lilly Library,
   Indiana University.  [Bloomington, 1965]
        viii, 30, 6 p.  facsims.  28 cm.


        1. American poetry--Bibl.--Catalogs.  2. Amer-
   ican literature--Bibl.--First editions.  I. Randall
   David Anton, 1906-      II. Title.
```

BUT THIS

```
        Randall, David Anton, 1905-
   Indiana.  University.  Lilly Library.
        Three centuries of American poetry;  an exhibi-
   tion of original paintings [at] the Lilly Library,
   Indiana University.  [Bloomington, 1965]
        viii, 30, 6 p.  facsims.  28 cm.
        Contents.--Introduction, by J. A. Robbins.--
   Notes on rarity, by D. A. Randall.--Catalog of the
   exhibition.
        1. American poetry--Bibl.--Catalogs.  2. Amer-
   ican literature--Bibl.--First editions.  I. Randall,
   David Anton, 1906-      II. Title.
```

EXERCISE

Making a tracing at the bottom of an entry is called to "trace" a name. For the reader's convenience we transcribe all names for which we plan to make a Roman numeral tracing, but we need not (please fill in) _____ all names that we have transcribed.

CHAPTER TWO

CHOICE OF ENTRY HEADINGS: SELECTED EXAMPLES

HIGHLIGHTS

Some Typical Entry Heading Situations.

Most books are the work of one author, and the title page tells usually clearly who it is. If two or more authors write a book jointly, one of them (typically, but not always) receives the main entry heading and the other an added entry heading. In some cases, the book's creator edited or compiled, rather than wrote it. Other books are written by one person with some support, or special contribution, from one or more others. Typically, the person primarily responsible for the major part of a book receives the main entry heading. For example, in a book consisting primarily of one artist's illustrations, with some comments by a writer, the artist rather than than writer receives the main entry heading, and the writer receives an added entry heading.

Still another situation is the work that has been recast, or changed from its original form: A translation, an adaptation, a dramatization, etc. All these situations will be discussed in detail in subsequent chapters.

How Many Entry Headings Should Be Made For One Book?

When we think of one *book,* we can say, it should be listed in a catalog under (that is, entry headings should be made for), whomever had a major role in creating that book: The author, or illustrator, or whatever other role our standard defines as "significant" or "major."

But when we think of the entire catalog and the *catalog user,* we can ask, even if an illustrator had a major supporting role in creating a particular book, are my patrons apt to look for a work by the name of its illustrator? Or, conversely, suppose Mr. X, who is well known in my community, had only a tiny part in helping to create a book, are my readers not apt to look up his name anyway?

What is good for one book need not be good for an entire catalog and its users. The Anglo-American Cataloging Rules give directions and guidelines and often permit the cataloger to exercise his judgment in such matters.

CHOICE OF ENTRY HEADINGS: SELECTED EXAMPLES

For most books the choice of entry heading(s) is no problem. Most books, especially fiction, are the work of one author, and the title page* tells clearly who it is. A somewhat different situation, of one author with one contributor, is illustrated on page 28.

Two Authors

Below is an example of a book written jointly by two authors.**

The UNIVERSITY LIBRARY

THE ORGANIZATION, ADMINISTRATION, AND FUNCTIONS OF ACADEMIC LIBRARIES

By LOUIS ROUND WILSON
and MAURICE F. TAUBER

Second Edition, 1956

COLUMBIA UNIVERSITY PRESS, NEW YORK

EXERCISE

Although we have not yet studied the rules in detail, can you tell which of these names will be used for the main entry heading?

---

* Title page: A page or a double page spread at the beginning of a book giving its title, author or authors (if acknowledged), usually its publisher, and often its place and date of publication. Typically, it also includes a number of other items of information: the edition number, the names of other contributors to the work such as illustrators, translators, or editors, and sometimes even an apt quotation. Several title pages are illustrated on the following pages.

** The distinction between a contributor and a joint author was mentioned on page 20.

The principal author is, typically, the first one named on the title page, Louis Round Wilson, given in the heading as Wilson, Louis Round.

MAIN
ENTRY

> **Wilson, Louis Round,** 1876–
> The university library; the organization, administration, and functions of academic libraries, by Louis Round Wilson and Maurice F. Tauber. 2d ed. New York, Columbia University Press, 1956.
>
> xiii, 641 p. diagrs., tables. 24 cm. (Columbia University studies in library service, no. 8)
>
> Includes bibliographies.
>
> 1. Libraries, University and college. ɪ. Tauber, Maurice Falcolm, 1908– joint author. (Series)
>
> Z675.U5W745 1956   027.7   55—11184
>
> Library of Congress   ₍66g²1₎

Since the title page implies that Mr. Tauber was the joint author, he deserves an added entry heading. Please "overtype" on the following added entry card his name as traced on the above card.

JOINT
AUTHOR
ADDED
ENTRY

1.

> **Wilson, Louis Round,** 1876–
> The university library; the organization, administration, and functions of academic libraries, by Louis Round Wilson and Maurice F. Tauber. 2d ed. New York, Columbia University Press, 1956.
>
> xiii, 641 p. diagrs., tables. 24 cm. (Columbia University studies library service, no. 8)

Now, as long as we have a chance, let's go off on a tangent and "overtype" the series added entry heading on the card below. (In case of doubt, refer to pages 17 and 19.)

SERIES
ADDED
ENTRY

2.

> **Wilson, Louis Round,** 1876–
> The university library; the organization, administration, and functions of academic libraries, by Louis Round Wilson and Maurice F. Tauber. 2d ed. New York, Columbia University Press, 1956.
>
> xiii, 641 p. diagrs., tables. 24 cm. (Columbia University studies library service, no. 9)

Editors

The situation can become more complicated. For example, sometimes an "author" did not literally write a book, but simply edited and compiled it out of many different bits of information. Nevertheless, he is responsible for this particular intellectual package and is, therefore, considered the author.

The Agitator

A Collection
of
Diverse Opinions
from America's
Not-so-Popular
Press

Edited by
◇ Donald L. Rice

A 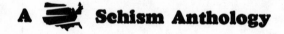 Schism Anthology

American
Library
Association

Chicago 1972

◇ Rice, Donald L   comp.
    The agitator; a collection of diverse opinions
from America's not-so-popular press, edited by
Donald L. Rice. Chicago, American Library Association, 1972.
    xxxi, 430 p. illus. 21 cm. (A Schism anthol-
ogy)
    Articles compiled from Schism, v. 1-2, 1970-71.
    1. U. S. Social conditions--1960-   --Addres-
ses, essays, lectures. 2. U. S.--Economic condi-
tions--1961-   --Addresses, essays, lectures.
3. U. S.--Race question--Addresses, essays, lectures.
I. Schism. II. Title. III. Series.

Sometimes the editor has a lesser role and merely gathers or adjusts one author's original writing. In the following example Emily Dickinson wrote all of these letters and is, thus, their author. Mabel Loomis Todd merely collected and introduced them to the public.

LETTERS

OF

EMILY DICKINSON

EDITED BY

Mabel Loomis Todd

NEW AND ENLARGED EDITION

HARPER & BROTHERS PUBLISHERS
NEW YORK AND LONDON
1 9 3 1

EXERCISE

For whom would you make the main entry heading in this example?

(1) _____

For whom the added entry heading? (2) _____

Text and Illustrations

You can see that, when more than one person contribute to a work the questions of selecting a logical main entry heading and suitable added entry heading often become entwined. For example, a book of reproductions of an artist's paintings may also contain some textual explanations by another person.

PIERRE AUGUSTE

RENOIR

(1 8 4 1 – 1 9 1 9)

text by

MILTON S. FOX

Editor, The Pocket Library of Great Art

published by HARRY N. ABRAMS, INC., *in association with* POCKET BOOKS, INC., *New York*

Examination of the above book would show that it is mostly a collection of reproductions of Pierre Renoir's paintings. Thus, the main entry heading is not the man who wrote the text but the artist:

Renoir, Pierre Auguste, 1841-1919.

Milton S. Fox receives an added entry heading, as contributor. This is quite the opposite of the usual situation in which the author of the text is the one primarily responsible for the work, as in the following example.

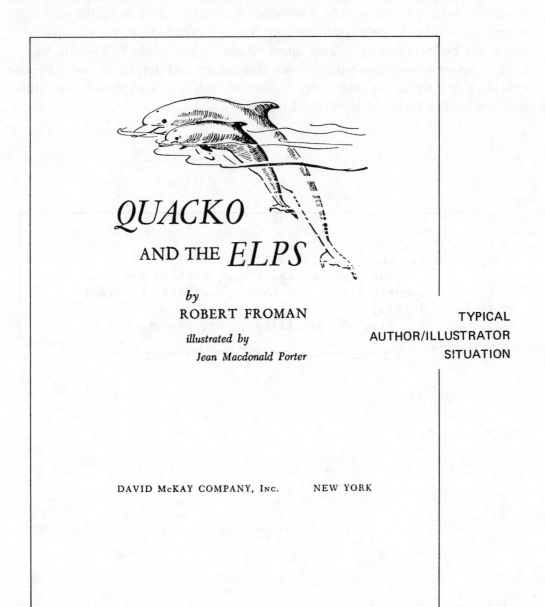

QUACKO
AND THE *ELPS*

by
ROBERT FROMAN

illustrated by
Jean Macdonald Porter

TYPICAL
AUTHOR/ILLUSTRATOR
SITUATION

DAVID McKAY COMPANY, Inc.   NEW YORK

Changed Works

A different, but equally interesting situation exists when one author re-writes, or somehow changes, another author's work. For example, one writer may revise slightly another writer's novel to make it suitable for children. Or, a dramatist may recast completely another writer's novel and turn it into a play.* Or, in the example below, the Bible—ordinarily entered under "Bible"** was retold by Hendrik Van Loon in his own words and with his own elaborations and details, so that it became virtually a new work. The main entry heading for this new work is thus the author who created this particular intellectual package.

```
Van Loon, Hendrik Willem, 1882-1944.
    The story of the Bible, written and drawn by
Hendrik Willem Van Loon.  New York, Liveright
[c1923]
    xix, 452 p.  illus., map, plates.  23 cm.
```

* For example, Owen and Donald Davis dramatized Edith Wharton's novel *Ethan Frome* into a play under the same title.

** For examples of typical main entry headings for actual Bibles see page 34.

FURTHER WESTWARD 65

was heavy on their minds. It was a terrible thing to have sold their brother Joseph to the foreign slave-trader. Now, apparently, they were about to lose their second brother. What would their father Jacob say when he heard of this?

They implored Joseph to be merciful. But he refused. He had overheard their conversation. He was greatly pleased at their repentance. The last thirty years seemed to have taught his brothers a stern lesson. But he was not yet certain. He must try them once more before he could forgive them for what they had done unto him when he was young.

And so it was decided that Simeon should stay behind as a hostage, while the others went back to get Benjamin.

This proved no easy task. Jacob was heart-broken. But his family was hungry, his servants were dying, and there was no seed-grain for next year. And so he was forced to give in. Benjamin and the other brothers returned to Egypt and Jacob remained alone.

The last time, they had been arrested as soon as they had crossed the frontier. Now, however, all the officials were most polite. The brothers were straightway taken to the palace of the Governor. There they were given rooms and were entertained in royal fashion.

They did not quite like this.

After all, they were not exactly beggars. They were poor, but they had come prepared to pay for whatever they got. They did not want charity. But when they offered their gold in exchange for grain, they were told that they could have all they wanted for nothing and when they insisted upon paying they found that the money had been returned to them and had been hidden in their sacks.

They were talking about this strange occurrence that night when they were resting after the heat of the day's journey.

The Story of The Bible

Written and Drawn by
Hendrik Willem Van Loon
and Published by
Boni & Liveright~New York

In our subsequent detailed study of the AA we shall overview the whole range of possibilities for changed works, from works that have undergone no change in intellectual content, such as literal translations, to works that have been virtually recreated, such as the last example.

INTELLECTUAL RESPONSIBILITY FOR A WORK vs "IS THIS CATEGORY OR THIS PERSON USEFUL AS A HEADING IN MY CATALOG?"

We can look at entry headings from two angles. Let us use the concept of translators as an example.

(1) We can look at entry headings from the principle of intellectual responsibility for the **book** being cataloged: The book is listed under whomever helped significantly in creating this intellectual package. This requires some kind of a standard as to what is a significant contribution to a book. For example, do translators contribute enough to a work to warrant an added entry?

(2) We can look at entry headings also from the vantagepoint of the **catalog** into which these entries are to be filed:

(a) By category: If one of the "creators" is a translator, are readers apt to look for a work by the name of a translator?

(b) By person: Regardless of what Mr. X contributed to a work, if he did anything at all for a book we are cataloging, is he someone my readers should find in our catalog?

WHAT ADDED
ENTRIES ARE
USEFUL FOR
THIS BOOK
IN MY
CATALOG?

INTRODUCTION TO THE GREAT RELIGIONS

JEAN DANIELOU, S.J.

ANDRE RETIF, S.J.

JOSEPH HOURS, S.J.

FRANCOIS HOUANG

MAURICE QUEGUINER, P.F.M.

R. P. DUNOYER, P.F.M.

R. P. DEMANN

GASTON FESSARD, S.J.

Translated by Albert J. La Mothe, Jr.

FIDES PUBLISHERS, INC.
NOTRE DAME, INDIANA

Introduction to the great religions [by] Jean
  Danielou [and others] Translated by Albert
  J. La Mothe, Jr. Notre Dame, Ind., Fides
  Publishers [1964]

The *Anglo-American Cataloging Rules,* based on experience and thoughtful consideration, give directives and guidelines on what are considered under normal circumstances to be reasonable main and added entry approaches, both from the vantagepoint of the book being cataloged, and from the vantagepoint of the catalog in which it will be listed. They recognize that one approach may serve most readers well for one given situation such as a "one author" situation while other situations, such as "author unknown," or "a collection of independent works bound together" may require a different approach, or several different approaches. The AA base many of their directives on what is to be done in a given situation.

EXERCISE

In Chapter 7 you will learn the details of examining a book for entry heading work. Now take the first step in this process: Examine the title pages on the next few pages and match them with the situations listed below.

Entry headings situations illustrated by the title pages shown below: Please fill in.

1. A one author situation:

_____

2. A two authors situation:

_____

3. A four editors situation:

_____

4. A one author and one other contributor situation:

_____

5. A many authors and two editors situation:

_____

6. A corporate author situation:

_____

EXAMPLE:
A one author situation:
Chemical publications.

CHEMICAL PUBLICATIONS
THEIR NATURE AND USE

fourth edition

M. G. MELLON, Ph.D., Sc.D.
PROFESSOR EMERITUS
OF ANALYTICAL CHEMISTRY
PURDUE UNIVERSITY

McGraw-Hill Book Company
NEW YORK, ST. LOUIS, SAN FRANCISCO, TORONTO, LONDON, SYDNEY

PUNCHED CARDS

THEIR APPLICATIONS TO SCIENCE AND INDUSTRY

SECOND EDITION

Edited By

ROBERT S. CASEY
W. A. Sheaffer Pen Co.
Fort Madison, Iowa

JAMES W. PERRY
Center for Documentation and Communication Research
Western Reserve University
Cleveland, Ohio

MADELINE M. BERRY
National Science Foundation
Washington, D. C.

And

ALLEN KENT
Center for Documentation and Communication Research
Western Reserve University
Cleveland, Ohio

REINHOLD PUBLISHING CORPORATION
NEW YORK
CHAPMAN & HALL, LTD., LONDON

QUACKO AND THE *ELPS*

by
ROBERT FROMAN

illustrated by
Jean Macdonald Porter

DAVID McKAY COMPANY, INC.   NEW YORK

Strawberry Girl

written and illustrated

by

LOIS LENSKI

J. B. LIPPINCOTT COMPANY
Philadelphia and New York

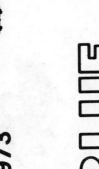

The State of Wisconsin
1973

BLUE BOOK

Published Biennially
In Odd–Numbered Years

Compiled By
Wisconsin Legislative
Reference Bureau

Distributed by
Department of Administration
Document Sales & Distribution
202 S. Thornton Ave.
Madison, Wisconsin 53702

Price:

Soft cover $1.00
Hard cover $2.00

SPACE EXPLORATION

Edited by

Donald P. LeGalley

TRW Space Technology Laboratories
Space Technology Center
Redondo Beach

John W. McKee

General Electric Company—TEMPO
Santa Barbara

Robert M. L. Baker, Jr.
Herbert C. Corben
Paul Dergarabedian
Manfred Eimer
Louis B. C. Fong
A. Donald Goedeke
Maxwell W. Hunter, II
William W. Kellogg
Lewis Larmore
Donald P. LeGalley
Colin J. Maiden
John L. Mason
Robert E. Roberson
Morris Tepper
Robert M. Wood

McGRAW-HILL BOOK COMPANY

New York, San Francisco, Toronto, London

AN INTRODUCTION TO
Medieval Europe
300-1500

JAMES WESTFALL THOMPSON

SIDNEY HELLMAN EHRMAN PROFESSOR OF EUROPEAN HISTORY
THE UNIVERSITY OF CALIFORNIA

&

EDGAR NATHANIEL JOHNSON

ASSOCIATE PROFESSOR OF HISTORY, THE UNIVERSITY OF NEBRASKA

W · W · NORTON & COMPANY · INC ·

PUBLISHERS · NEW YORK

CHAPTER THREE

FORM OF ENTRY HEADINGS: BASIC POLICIES

HIGHLIGHTS

Consistency and Distinction: Once the main and added entry headings have been selected for a book, each heading must be recorded in a form that (1) causes all books that are listed under one name to be listed next to each other in the catalog, so that the reader has an easy overview (Consistency); (2) distinguishes each name from all other names used as entry headings in the catalog (Distinction). Sometimes, this requires changing the form of a name from that used on a title page. Consistency is achieved by using only one form and degree of fullness for a name whenever it is used as a heading in a particular catalog; distinction is achieved by distinguishing otherwise identical names by dates or other devices.

A special case is the author who writes sometimes under a pseudonym and sometimes under his real name. For some libraries, it may be best to list each of this person's books under the name under which it was written, with "see-also" references referring both ways. For other libraries, it may be best to list all of this person's books under his real name, with a "see-reference" from the assumed name.

Cross-references: Two types exist: the see-reference and the see-also reference. See-references refer, at least in a card catalog, from a name-form that is *not* used as a heading to the form that *is* used as a heading. See-also references are used when both forms of a name are used as entry headings.

Printed bibliographies and book catalogs often contain see-references referring from one name to another, for example, from the name of a book's illustrator to that of its author. This saves space and expense (these printed tools often give the full entry only once, under the main entry heading) and works well, since printed bibliographies and book catalogs are published as separate volumes and, once published, are finished. But card catalogs are open-ended, and we dare not say, "For the book that Mr. A. illustrated, look under Mr. B's (the author's) name," for tomorrow we may have to add another catalog card for another book that Mr. A. illustrated, but that was written by Mr. C.

Authority Cards: To permit, within one catalog, consistency and uniqueness in entry headings, the cataloger uses the *Anglo-American Cataloging Rules* to set up a standard for each name that is used as an entry heading, and follows this standard consistently. In many libraries, he records this standard in a separate card file, the name authority file, or authority file. Typically housed in the catalog department for the use of the librarians, it records, on a separate card for each name, the exact form in which the name is always used as an entry heading in the public catalog, and the cross-references that have been made to it, if any.

The sequence of steps through which authority cards are set up is described on text pages 90 and 91. Besides the form of name and the record of (that is, the tracings of) any cross-references made to it, a name authority card typically contains the brief title of the book or books from which the name was taken, and often a statement that the name does not conflict with (that is, is not very similar to) any other name already in the catalog.

Tracings: This term has two meanings: on a unit card, a tracing is a record of the headings under which additional copies of the unit card are filed. On a name authority card, a tracing is a record of the words or names from which cross-references are to be made to the standard recorded on the authority card's first line.

CONSISTENCY AND DISTINCTION FOR ENTRY HEADINGS

While we use basically a name as completely as given on the title page of the book being cataloged, we must sometimes change the title-page-name to (1) get all books that are listed under that name in our catalog to be listed next to each other, and (2) to distinguish each name from all other names used as entry headings in the catalog. This is done to give the reader an easy overview of works listed under any one name. We use two techniques:

(1) We stick within one catalog to one form of a name whenever it is used as a heading, even though the books themselves often use different forms. The title pages of her different books may list an author as Mary Elizabeth Lewis, Mary Lewis, and Mary E. Lewis. But the entry headings must be uniform. Once we have begun using a name as entry heading in a catalog we either keep on using the same form for future books by the same author, or we (rarely) change the old headings to conform to new information. The filing effect of using one form for one name is shown on pages 24 and 39.

(2) We make sure that different names used as entry headings look different. Typically, names on title pages consist of forename, middle initial and surname. Distinction of identical-looking names is made typically by adding to the title page form the author's middle name and/or dates of birth and death. The precise rules on this are presented in subsequent chapters. Here is an example of two books apparently written by the same person. The title pages give the following information:

H. Taylor – Medical radiestesia.
H. Taylor – The future of Sarah Lawrence College.

The difference in subject matter implies that this is not the same person although one cannot tell by the name. To distinguish the two authors from each other we add to the title page information whatever additional relevant information we can find in reference works that makes these two name look different.* In this case it is

Taylor, Harold Bourne   – Medical radiestesia.
Taylor, Harold, 1914   – The future of Sarah Lawrence College.

If we had not found all of this information it would have sufficed to use, for example,

Taylor, Harold B   – Medical radiestesia.
Taylor, Harold   – The future of Sarah Lawrence College.

* We shall discuss later on how to do this.

EXERCISE

Please fill in the following questions.

To achieve consistency and distinction among entry headings, we sometimes must record a name that is used as an entry heading more or less completely than it is given on the title page of the book being cataloged. But, basically, we use a name as completely as given on (fill in)

(1)_____

   When recording a name as main or added entry heading we try to achieve two results:

(2) a. _____

b. _____

_____

   How do we try to achieve these results?   (3) a._____

_____

b. _____

_____

REASONS FOR MAINTAINING ONE DEGREE OF FULLNESS FOR ONE NAME

To understand why it is necessary to maintain one entry heading form for one name, let us see what is apt to happen if we used always the name as completely or as incompletely as given on the title page.

You have just purchased two books by Mr. Peter Egon Blackwell. This author is new to your library. The title page of one book lists his name as P. E. Blackwell, the title page of the other book as Peter Egon Blackwell. If you use in each case the form of name used in the book you are cataloging, your cards would be filed in the catalog as follows:

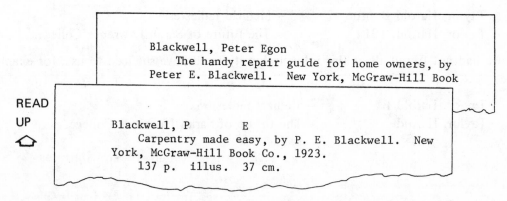

READ
UP

Blackwell, Peter Egon
   The handy repair guide for home owners, by
Peter E. Blackwell. New York, McGraw-Hill Book

Blackwell, P   E
   Carpentry made easy, by P. E. Blackwell. New
York, McGraw-Hill Book Co., 1923.
   137 p. illus. 37 cm.

Cards are filed by their first line, and in filing, we put initials before a word beginning with the same letter—P before Peter—so that Mr. Blackwell's books are listed right next to each other in the catalog according to the principle that books entered under one name should be listed next to each other to give the reader an easy overview.

The difficulty arises when we get books by other P. E. Blackwells. Then Peter's books can easily become separated like this:

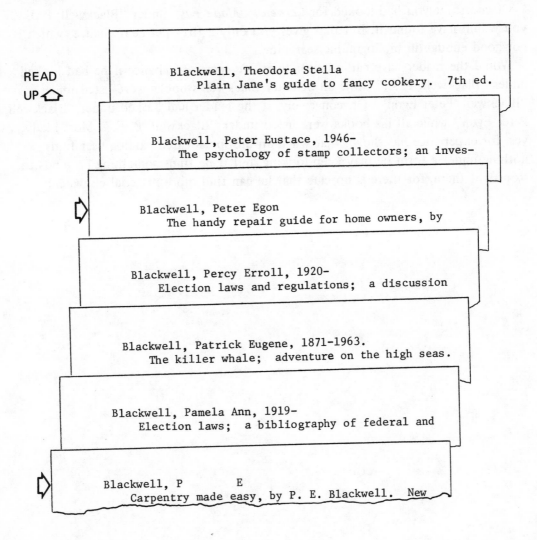

This possibility may seem remote, but in a large catalog it can happen easily. Furthermore, each of these people may have written half a dozen books, thus separating our Peter Egon Blackwell's two books even further. This is bad because it reduces the catalog's effectiveness: Most readers will automatically stop searching for a book if they do not find it with the author's other books.

If you want Peter Blackwell's *Carpentry Made Easy* and look in the catalog under Blackwell, Peter, you find listed only his *The Handy Repair Guide* or Peter Eustace Blackwell's *The Psychology of Stamp Collectors*. In front and behind the entries for Blackwell, Peter are entries with different forenames, so you are bound to assume that you can stop your search. The library does not seem to have Peter Blackwell's *Carpentry Made Easy* because our alphabetical system of filing separated it with irrelevant names from the place where you looked.

Of course, if you had looked for *Carpentry Made Easy* under "Blackwell, P. E.," you would have found it. But that gives you only a fifty per cent chance, which is not good enough in bibliographic searching.

Would the reader have had a better than fifty per cent chance if he had looked under "Blackwell, P. E." while all of Peter Blackwell's books were listed under "Blackwell, Peter Egon"? Or, conversely, if the reader had looked under "Blackwell, Peter Egon" while all his books were listed under "Blackwell, P. E."? Most likely, yes, for experience has shown that when an unsophisticated catalog user finds nothing under a form he may keep looking, but if he finds something he tends to stop right there, for there is no clue that he can find more material elsewhere.

AUTHORS WITH MORE THAN ONE NAME

But what about authors who write under more than one name? There we encounter not only the problem of how much to put into the entry heading but which of these different names to select as entry heading. The author Ray Stannard Baker wrote some works under his own name, like this:

Woodrow Wilson

LIFE AND LETTERS

Youth

1 8 5 6 — 1 8 9 0

BY

RAY STANNARD BAKER

━━◆━━

Garden City, New York

DOUBLEDAY, PAGE & CO.

1 9 2 7

Books which did not deal with historical matters he wrote under the pseudonym David Grayson.

BOOKS BY RAY
STANNARD BAKER
WRITTEN UNDER
THE PSEUDONYM,
DAVID GRAYSON

ADVENTURES IN FRIENDSHIP

By
DAVID GRAYSON
Author of "Adventures in Contentment"

Illustrated by
THOMAS FOGARTY

Garden City   New York
Doubleday, Page & Company
1910

Should each book be listed under the name under which it was written? Should all his books be listed only under his real name? Should they be listed under both names?

A strong case can be made for saying, "The reader will look under the name under which Mr. Baker wrote each book." If a book is listed in the reviews, and exhibited in stores, under the name "Baker," readers will tend to look for it under "Baker," whereas the book which is written and advertised under the name "Grayson" will most often be looked for in the catalog under "Grayson."

A catalog built on this principle would look like this:

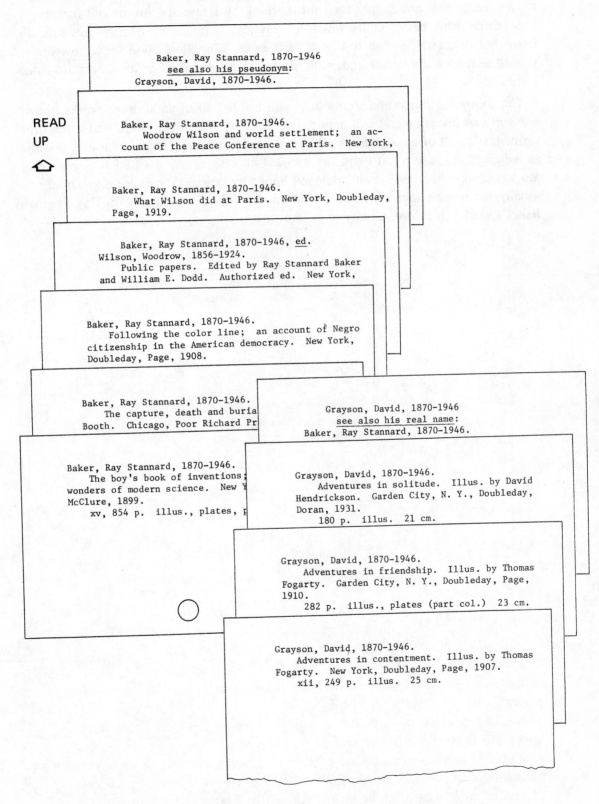

READ UP

Baker, Ray Stannard, 1870-1946
see also his pseudonym:
Grayson, David, 1870-1946.

Baker, Ray Stannard, 1870-1946.
Woodrow Wilson and world settlement; an account of the Peace Conference at Paris. New York,

Baker, Ray Stannard, 1870-1946.
What Wilson did at Paris. New York, Doubleday, Page, 1919.

Baker, Ray Stannard, 1870-1946, ed.
Wilson, Woodrow, 1856-1924.
Public papers. Edited by Ray Stannard Baker and William E. Dodd. Authorized ed. New York,

Baker, Ray Stannard, 1870-1946.
Following the color line; an account of Negro citizenship in the American democracy. New York, Doubleday, Page, 1908.

Baker, Ray Stannard, 1870-1946.
The capture, death and buria[l of] Booth. Chicago, Poor Richard Pr[...]

Baker, Ray Stannard, 1870-1946.
The boy's book of inventions[...] wonders of modern science. New Y[...] McClure, 1899.
xv, 854 p. illus., plates, [...]

Grayson, David, 1870-1946
see also his real name:
Baker, Ray Stannard, 1870-1946.

Grayson, David, 1870-1946.
Adventures in solitude. Illus. by David Hendrickson. Garden City, N. Y., Doubleday, Doran, 1931.
180 p. illus. 21 cm.

Grayson, David, 1870-1946.
Adventures in friendship. Illus. by Thomas Fogarty. Garden City, N. Y., Doubleday, Page, 1910.
282 p. illus., plates (part col.) 23 cm.

Grayson, David, 1870-1946.
Adventures in contentment. Illus. by Thomas Fogarty. New York, Doubleday, Page, 1907.
xii, 249 p. illus. 25 cm.

For the reader who is looking for a **specific book** whose author and title he **knows,** the above approach works well, and the AA permit it although they do not encourage it. But school and public library patrons especially, often will not look for a specific title but simply for another book by a **favority author** and have no idea of the other names under which he may also write. Many readers thus need to know both names. The two top cards in the preceding illustration show how the AA guide the reader who looks under one name to the other, when his works are listed separately.

The following illustration shows how you can list all of an author's works under one form of his name and still help the reader who happens to look under the other form. Listing all of an author's works under one form of his name is useful because, as indicated on page 67, it helps the user get an easy overview of what is available. Most academic libraries list all cataloged books by one author under one name, usually the name under which he is best known. The catalog cards for Ray Stannard Baker's works therefore, usually look like this:

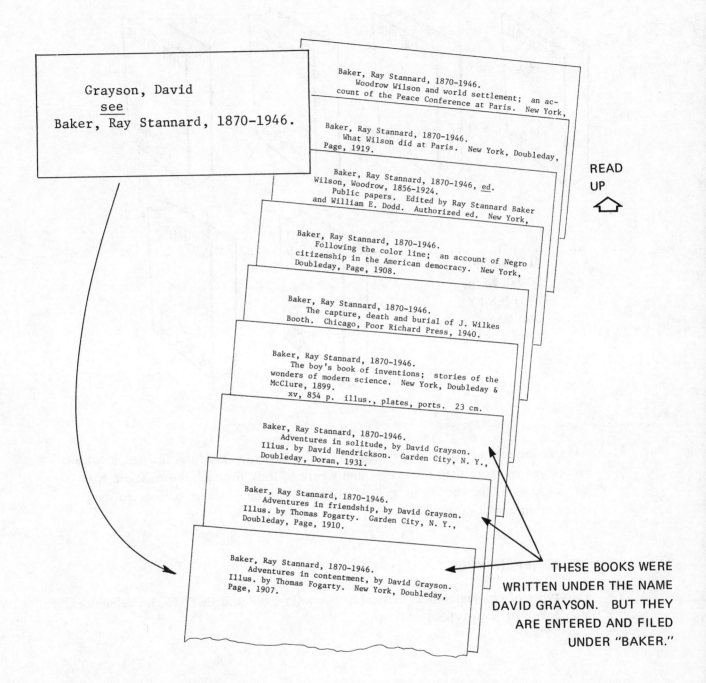

This method is particularly useful with authors who write the same type of book under different names, like John Creasey.

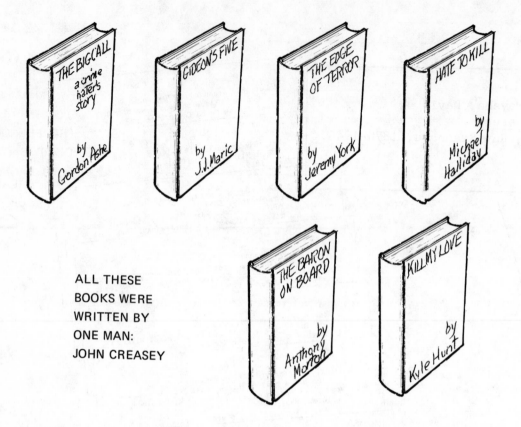

ALL THESE
BOOKS WERE
WRITTEN BY
ONE MAN:
JOHN CREASEY

Later on, you will learn the specific AA rules for entry headings for people who are known by more than one name, and where to look for such information. Now let us examine how the library guides a patron from one form of a name to the other by means of cross-references.

CROSS-REFERENCES

Two types of cross-references exist: The 'see-reference'' and the "see-also reference.'' You have met both types.

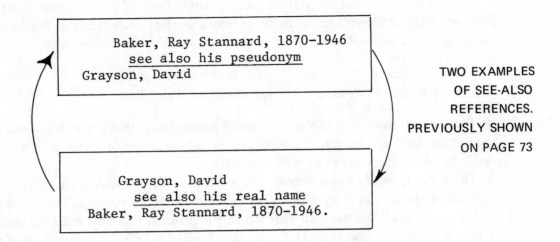

TWO EXAMPLES
OF SEE-ALSO
REFERENCES.
PREVIOUSLY SHOWN
ON PAGE 73

Another possible form for a "see-also reference" is the following, but you will notice that it does not tell the reader as much.

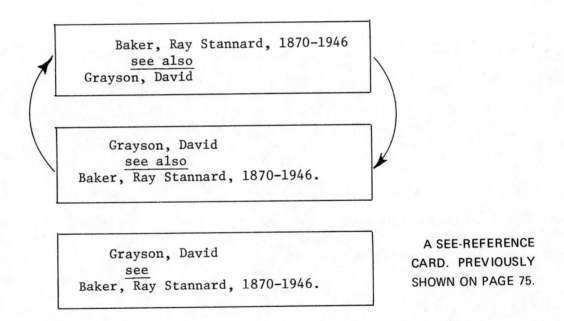

A SEE-REFERENCE
CARD. PREVIOUSLY
SHOWN ON PAGE 75.

See-references refer from a form of a name that is not used as a heading to the form that is used as a heading, as in the example on page 75. It may help you to remember this if you read the complete card like this: [For works by or about] Grayson, David _see_ [instead under] Baker, Ray Stannard, 1870-1946.

See-references are not made from every possible form of a name; only from those that are really different* from the form that is used as entry heading. Beginners sometimes get cross-reference-happy and try to make cross-references as

Blackwell, P   E   <u>see</u> Blackwell, Peter Egon
Blackwell, Peter E   <u>see</u> Blackwell, Peter Egon

Reflection will show that this policy would drown the entries in an ocean of cross-references. Only in very unusual situations do we make cross-references from a name with initials to the same name with forenames.

The other type of cross-reference, the see-also reference, is used when both forms of a name are used as entry heading, as in the example on page 73. See-also references can be read like this: [In addition to the material that you will find under] Grayson, David <u>see also</u> [under] Baker, Ray Stannard, 1870-1946 [where you will find more material].

---

* "Different" means that there is no possible alphabetical connection between the two forms, so that the cross-reference card and the entry heading to which it refers are filed quite far apart, as on page 75.

EXERCISE

Two types of cross-references exist: One type refers from a form of a name under which a reader might reasonably look to the form (1) _____

This type of cross-reference is called a (2) _____

The other type is used when both forms of a name are used as entry headings and is called a

(3) _____

The Filing of Cross-References

Like entries, cross-references are filed by their first line. Therefore, the see-reference on page 75 is filed under the letter "G," like this:

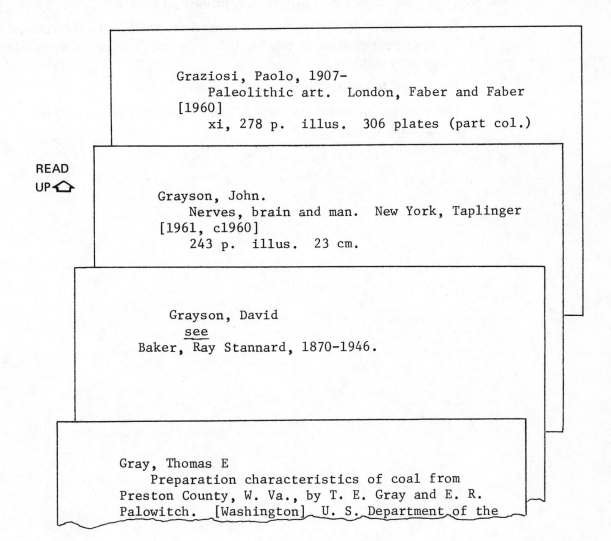

See-also references have, of course, the same first line as the entries for the same name. See page 73 for two examples. The officially preferred method is to file the see-also reference ahead of the first entry with the same name. But the opposite method, in which the see-also reference is the last card in that particular group, as shown on page 73, is also frequently used. Either method seems defensible and useful.

How to Make Cross-Reference Cards

Later on you will learn the policies according to which cross-reference cards are made in specific situations. Now you will learn the technique. Individual libraries differ in the details of spacing or underlining cross-reference cards, but in the basics they are alike. For purposes of this text the following pattern is used which is in line with our basic catalog card pattern as explained on page 409

The first line of text is the form of name **from** which you refer. (Do not use closing punctuation on this line unless the last forename is represented by an initial.)

The second line of text is the action: Underline it.*

The third line of text is the form of name **to** which you refer, which typically includes date(s).

---

* On printed cards this line is usually printed in italics. In typewritten text italics are usually shown by means of underlining.

On a handwritten cross-reference card (which is used only for practice, never nowadays in a catalog)

> The first line of text begins at the **second** indention, on the line below the red horizontal line;
>
> The second line of text begins immediately below, at the (unmarked) **third** indention;
>
> The third line of text begins immediately below this, at the **first** indention.

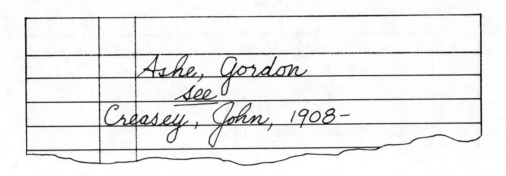

On a typed cross-reference card

> The first line of text begins on the **4th line** of the card at the second indention, that is, at the **12th typewriter space** from the left edge of the card;
>
> The second line of text begins immediately below, at the third indention, that is, at the **14th typewriter space** from the left edge of the card;
>
> The third line of text begins immediately below, at the first indention, that is, the **8th typewriter space** from the left edge of the card.

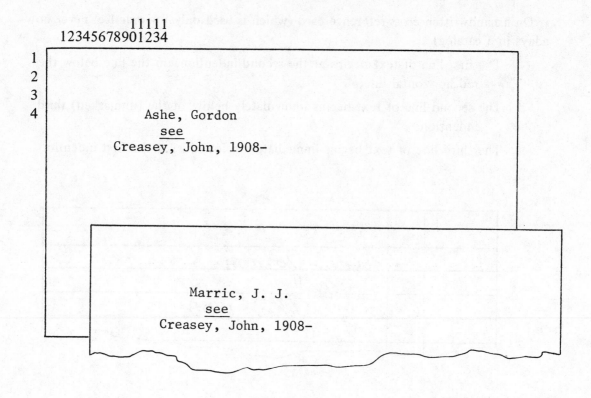

```
        11111
  12345678901234
```

Ashe, Gordon
        see
Creasey, John, 1908-

Marric, J. J.
        see
Creasey, John, 1908-

EXERCISE

On the basis of the facts given below try your hand at making see-reference cards, following the exact pattern you have just learned.

1. Nevil Shute Norway, who lived from 1899 to 1960, wrote all his books under the name Nevil Shute. The library enters his books under the name

Shute, Nevil, 1899-1960.

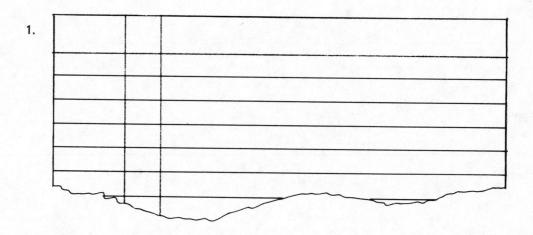

2. Benjamin Maisler, who was born in 1906, has changed his name to Benjamin Mazar. The library enters his books under the name

Mazar, Benjamin, 1906-

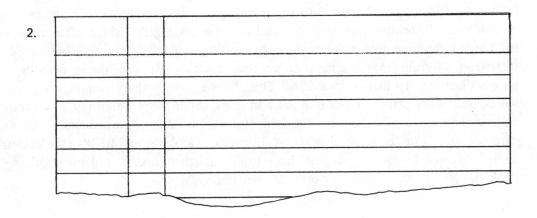

3. William Anthony Parker White, born in 1911, writes most of his works under the pseudonym Anthony Boucher. Until about 1942 he also used the pseudonym H. H. Holmes. The library enters his books under the name

Boucher, Anthony, 1911-

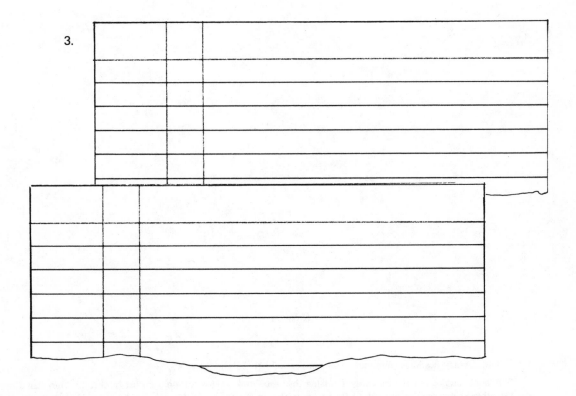

In a Card Catalog Cross-References Stick to One Person

Note that a see-reference in a card catalog refers from one form of a name to another form of the same name. It does not refer from one person to another person. For example, a see-reference in a card catalog does not refer from a name used as an added entry heading* to the name that is used as the main entry heading, or vice versa. In printed bibliographies and in book catalogs,** which often give the full entry only once, under the main entry heading, you will often find see-references referring from one name to another, for example from the name of a book's illustrator to that of its author. This is done to save space and expense and works well, since printed bibliographies and book catalogs are published as separate volumes and, once published, are finished. But card catalogs are open-ended and you dare not say, "For the book that Mr. A. illustrated, look under Mr. B's (the author's name," because tomorrow you may have to add another catalog card for another book the Mr. A. illustrated, but that was written by Mr. C.

---

* Added entry headings were mentioned on pages 20 to 26 and 42 to 48.

** A book catalog is not necessarily a catalog that lists books. (Most catalogs do list books, but they can also list other things such as filmstrips.) Rather, a catalog in the form of a book.

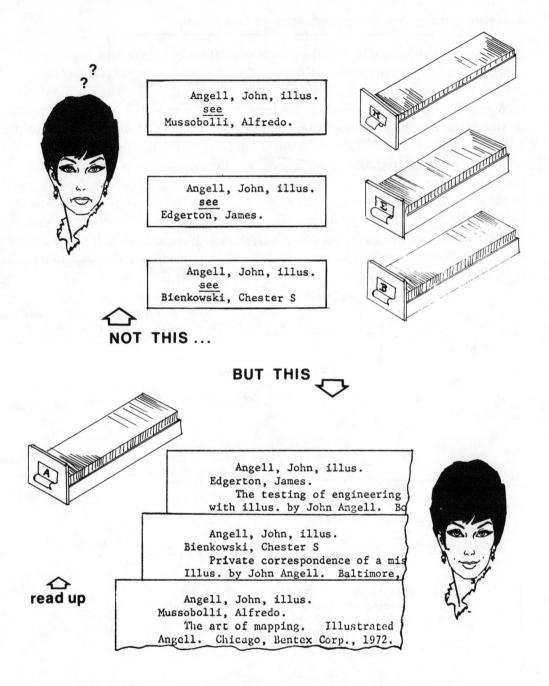

In the following fictitious example you are looking at four different sections of a card catalog. You see here the names of two people who wrote some books under their real names and some books under their pseudonyms. Follow the arrows and you will see that (1) each see-reference sticks to one person. In this particular case, each pseudonym refers to its own real name, not to the name of the other person. (2) regardless of which approach the patron uses, regardless of which of the names the reader knows or remembers, he will be led to the one place in the catalog, to the precise entry heading under which that author's works are listed.

Kimball, Alice, 1937-
     The nature of matter; physical theory from
Thales to Fermi. Boston, C. S. Allnutt Pub Co.,

Kent, Waldo
     see
Paxton, Edward, 1923-

Keller, John, 1831-1907.
     The spirit of the law; or, The state and the
individual in today's society. Baltimore, Marginal

Paxton, Edward, 1923-
     Winter sports as a means of recharging one's
batteries, by Waldo Kent. With illus. by C. R.

READ
UP

Paxton, Edward, 1923-
     The story of sleighing in the hills of North
Dakota, by E. Paxton. Boston, Snoflake Pub. Co.,

Paxton, Edward, 1923-
     History of skating, by Waldo Kent [and] Alex
Dykes. New York, Cold Press, 1967.

Dykes, Alex
     see
Saunders, Felix A   1916-

Diller, Felicia Alice, 1883-1961.
     Optimization of stainless steel melting prac-
tice by means of dynamic programming, by F. A.

Schlemmer, Daniel, 1931-
     Die Geschichte der Frühzeit in grossen Europä-

Saunders, Felix A   1916-
     Legal aspects of sports reporting, by Felix A.

Saunders, Felix A   1916-
Paxton, Edward, 1923-
     History of skating, by Waldo Kent [and] Alex
Dykes. New York, Cold Press, 1967.

EXERCISE

You will need to examine the preceding diagram to answer the following questions.

Kent and Dykes wrote one book jointly. Which book is it?

(1) _____

List the entry headings under which it is listed.

(2) _____

Why is it listed under more than one name? (3) _____

_____

Can you tell, by looking at the see-reference cards, that "Kent, Waldo" is a pseudonymn for "Paxton, Edward"? (4) _____

Which book(s) did Edward Paxton write under his real name?

(5) _____

Can the catalog user find this entry even if he only knows Mr. Paxton's pseudonym, "Kent, Waldo"? (6) _____

Which book(s) did Edward Paxton write under his pseudonym?

(7) _____

Now let us ask you a question for which you have not yet read an answer! When we are so interested in a reader's convenience and in giving him an easy overview of what is available,* why do we only make a see-reference from one form of a name to the other instead of using a main entry heading for one form, an added entry heading for the other, and thus listing each of his books under both forms of his name? (8)_____

_____

_____

_____

_____

How many cards would you need in the catalog for Edward Paxton, if you listed his books under both forms of his name? (9) _____.

How many cards would you need in the catalog for Felix A. Saunders if you listed his books under both forms of his name? (10) _____.

For both authors together, you would thus need a total of (11) _____cards, whereas with the other method, as illustrated, we need only (12)_____ cards.

* This concept was touched on pages 67 and 74.

Two Concepts

It may be useful at this stage to summarize two concepts that seem opposed if they are not looked at jointly:

(1) We make a complete entry for a book under each person who had a significant share in creating its intellectual content. (See pages 12 and 23 to 26.) In a card catalog, we do not make a cross-reference from one of these people to the other because that could lead to complications. (See page 84.)

(2) But if one of these people happens to be known by more than one name, we do not make a complete entry under each of his names. Instead, we list the book under one of his names and make a cross-reference from the other (see pages 73 to 76, and page 84) because that permits an overview in one place of all that is available by that person, and because it saves space, work, and money. (See answers to questions 87-8 to 87-12.)

The diagram on page 86 shows how these two concepts work together.

AUTHORITY CARDS

A name that is used as an entry heading is given basically as completely as it is given on the title page of the book being cataloged. (See page 67.) Most of the time, "John C. Wedemeyer," listed on the title page, is reproduced as the entry heading "Wedemeyer, John C   ." However, there are three situations in which we cannot accept the title page format automatically.

EXERCISE

To firm these situations in your mind, re-read pages 67 and 71 to 76, and fill in the three typical situations under which the cataloger must somehow change the title page form of a name before it can become an entry heading.

(1) _____

_____

(2) _____

_____

(3) _____

_____

_____

The purpose of changing the title page format when necessary is to achieve the two results previously mentioned on page 67: Within any one catalog each entry heading must be consistent and unique.

A fourth situation may not require the cataloger to change the title page form or fullness of a name, but still requires a decision: When more than one word could be the filing element in a name:

        Should Menno ter Braak
            be entered as   Braak, Menno ter
            or as   ter Braak, Menno ?

        Should Francis Russell, the seond Earl of Bedford
            be entered as   Russel, Francis, 2d Earl of Bedford
            or as   Bedford, Francis Russell, 2d Earl of   ?

        Should Leónidas Amezúa de Calderón y Murillo
            be entered as   Murillo, Leónidas Amezúa de Calderón y
            or as   Calderón y Murillo, Leónidas Amezúa de
            or as   Amezúa de Calderón y Murillo, Leónidas ?

The entry heading decision affects where, and how easily, such names can be found in the catalog, and what cross-references will be needed.

To permit within one catalog consistency and uniqueness in entry headings, the cataloger uses the *Anglo-American Cataloging Rules* to set up a standard for each name that is used as an entry heading, and follows this standard consistently. In many libraries, he records this standard in a separate card file, the name authority file, or authority file. This file of authority cards is not part of the public catalog since it is a working file for the use of the librarians. It serves as a quick reference to names and the form of names that exist already in the library's public catalog, and to the see-references that have been made. Since it is usually housed in the catalog department it eliminates the necessity for catalogers of going to the public catalog to check names against entry headings already listed in the catalog each time a book is added to the collection.

Sequence of Steps

Name decisions, authority cards, and cross-references are the product of a specific sequence of steps that generally works as shown in the following diagram. Examine this diagram step by step, please, and note also where we are apt to find name information.

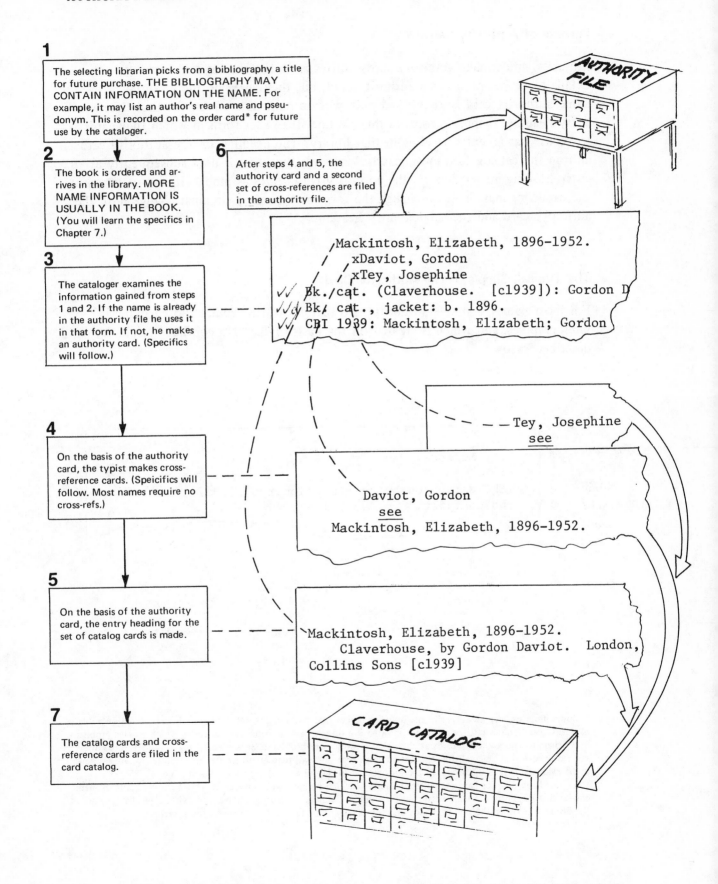

1

The selecting librarian picks from a bibliography a title for future purchase. THE BIBLIOGRAPHY MAY CONTAIN INFORMATION ON THE NAME. For example, it may list an author's real name and pseudonym. This is recorded on the order card* for future use by the cataloger.

2

The book is ordered and arrives in the library. MORE NAME INFORMATION IS USUALLY IN THE BOOK. (You will learn the specifics in Chapter 7.)

3

The cataloger examines the information gained from steps 1 and 2. If the name is already in the authority file he uses it in that form. If not, he makes an authority card. (Specifics will follow.)

4

On the basis of the authority card, the typist makes cross-reference cards. (Speicifics will follow. Most names require no cross-refs.)

5

On the basis of the authority card, the entry heading for the set of catalog cards is made.

6

After steps 4 and 5, the authority card and a second set of cross-references are filed in the authority file.

7

The catalog cards and cross-reference cards are filed in the card catalog.

Mackintosh, Elizabeth, 1896–1952.
    xDaviot, Gordon
    xTey, Josephine
√√ Bk. cat. (Claverhouse. [c1939]): Gordon D
√√ Bk. cat., jacket: b. 1896.
√√ CBI 1939: Mackintosh, Elizabeth; Gordon

        Tey, Josephine
        see

        Daviot, Gordon
        see
    Mackintosh, Elizabeth, 1896–1952.

Mackintosh, Elizabeth, 1896–1952.
    Claverhouse, by Gordon Daviot. London,
Collins Sons [c1939]

* Order card: A working card for recording bibliographical and price information used in ordering a book. From it, the actual book order is prepared that is mailed to the vendor.

Purpose of Authority Cards

Libraries which make authority cards* differ as to the spacing and some of the details to be put on a name authority card, but they agree on the essentials: A name authority card is established only when a name is used for the first time as an entry heading. It must record, in the top line, the exact form in which that name is to be used as an entry heading in that library: The headings on the authority card and on the catalog card must match. Whenever the name is used subsequently as an entry heading in that library, the authority card serves as model. If, for some reason, the cataloger must later on change the form of the name, he must change both the authority card and the catalog entry heading.

The Typical, Simple, Name Authority Card

For most names, a simple authority card suffices which requires no checking in bibliographies, and which is created on the basis of the "No conflict" principle, described below.

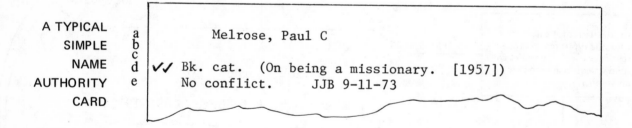

A TYPICAL SIMPLE NAME AUTHORITY CARD

a
b
c
d
e

Melrose, Paul C

✓✓ Bk. cat. (On being a missionary.   [1957])
No conflict.   JJB 9-11-73

* Some libraries keep an authority file only for names that require cross-references, such as prefixed or noble names. Other libraries put the authority information on the back of some catalog cards, which creates problems. Still others use no authority cards at all, which creates more problems. Besides, omitting authority cards does not really save time since all the verification steps that you will read about shortly must be taken anyway, even if the evidence is then discarded. In the long run, it is helpful to keep a name authority file.

A few large libraries have an "Official Catalog" which includes authority cards. It is basically a file of main entries that duplicate the main entries in the "Public Catalog." It is for staff use and exists typically only when the distance between the public catalog and the catalog department is uneconomically great.

Line a records the standard, that is, the exact form in which that name is to be used as an entry heading in that library's catalog. (Role designations, such as "joint author," or "ed." (for "editor") are omitted from authority cards, since one individual may fulfill different roles in different books.)

Lines b and c are left blank for tracing (that is, recording) any see-references that need to be made later on. (Most of the time, they stay blank.)

Line d means: The book being cataloged ("Bk. cat."), which has the title *On being a missionary,** and whose date is recorded on the catalog card as [1957], gives the name with the degree of fullness indicated in line a. The book gives no indication, nor does the order card, that this is in any way a problematical name.

Line e means: The name was checked in our name authority file (or, if none exists, in our catalog) and is not so similar to an already established name that a conflict could arise. This is a "No conflict" situation. That statement is followed by the cataloger's initials and the date of the decision.

(If, for example, the authority file had already contained an entry heading for "Melrose, Paul Charles," or for "Melrose, Paul C   1949-   " a potential conflict situation would have existed. The cataloger would then have to check in bibliographies whether one or more persons were involved, to keep all headings consistent and unique.** Even if no "Melrose" had been previously entered in the catalog, the likelihood of a *future* conflict would be great if the new entry heading had an initial instead of the first forename, such as "Melrose, P   Charles." Then, too, it would have behooved the cataloger to check further in bibliographies to try to discover the first forename.)

If a "No conflict" situation exists, simple names are entered in the catalog nowadays as completely as given in the book being cataloged, without further checking in bibliographies. (See also page 89.)

More Complicated Name Authority Cards

For more difficult names, more authority work is required which is reflected in more complex authority cards. Compound surnames, names with prefixes, names of people who write under pseudonyms, and corporate bodies are among this group.*** The following example is a name authority card for an author who wrote under a pseudonym. This card was made on July 5, 1940.

---

* When a main entry heading is being established, as here, only the book's brief title and date are needed for line d. When an added entry is being established, the brief main entry heading of the book being cataloged is also needed. For examples of the latter, see the second and sixth cards on page 219. This stylistic difference does not affect the entry heading being established but is to aid in retrieving the source book, if needed later on.

** This was mentioned on page 67.

*** Examples of such names are on pages 71 to 72, 76, and 89.

```
a  │          Mackintosh, Elizabeth, 1896-                    NAME AUTHORITY
b  │             xDaviot, Gordon                                 CARD THAT
c  │                                                         RESULTED FROM
d  │✓✓ Bk. cat. (Claverhouse.  [c1939]): Gordon Daviot.      SOME CHECKING
e  │✓✓d Bk. cat., jacket: b. 1896.                              IN A BIBLIO-
f  │✓✓ CBI 1939: Mackintosh, Elizabeth; Gordon Daviot, pseud.    GRAPHY.
   │                                   EBG 7-5-40
```

Line a records the standard, that is, the exact form in which that name is to be used as an entry heading in that library.

Line b traces, that is, records, a see-reference that is made from a form of the name not used as heading, to the form under which the name will be found in the catalog. (Specific instructions on what to do with cross-reference tracings begin on page 100.)

Line c is left blank for a possible future additional see-reference tracing.

Lind d indicates that the book being cataloged ("Bk. cat."), which has the title *Claverhouse,* and whose date was recorded on the catalog card as [c1939], gave the name as Gordon Daviot.

Line e indicates that the book jacket provides additional information, the date of birth, 1896.

In 1940, when this name was established, catalogers searched always in bibliographies to verify, or to complete, name information.* Therefore, the cataloger checked this name in the *Cumulative Book Index* (CBI).** There, he found proof that Gordon Daviot is the pseudonym of Elizabeth Mackintosh. This is recorded on **Line f.**

The last item is the cataloger's initials and the date of the decision.

---

* The Library of Congress, and many other libraries, officially abandoned this policy in 1949 and adopted the "No conflict" policy. (See pages 92-93.)

** The *Cumulative Book Index* (generally referred to as the "CBI") is a bibliography of new trade books published in the English language. It is published monthly, with longer cumulations.

This authority card may have served as authority for many a book over many years. But finally, in 1953, the cataloger received a book by Josephine Tey which, for some reason, he checked in the CBI, where he found that this was a new pseudonym of Elizabeth Mackintosh. Checking further in the *National Union Catalog* (NUC)* he found also the author's date of death. He recorded the new information on the authority card, changed the entry heading on it and on all catalog cards filed under that name, and prepared a second cross-reference from the newly discovered pseudonym to the entry heading.**

a	Mackintosh, Elizabeth, 1896-
b	xDaviot, Gordon
c	xTey, Josephine
d	✓✓ Bk. cat. (Claverhouse. [c1939]): Gordon Daviot.
e	✓✓ᴅ Bk. cat., jacket: b. 1896.
f	✓✓ CBI 1939: Mackintosh, Elizabeth; Gordon Daviot, pseud.
g	EBG 7-5-40
h	✓ᴅ CBI 1943-48: Josephine Tey, pseud.
i	✓ᴅ NUC 1948-52: d. 1952. JR 7-9-53

THE SAME NAME
AUTHORITY
CARD THIRTEEN
YEARS LATER

* The *National Union Catalog* is a union catalog of books and other items recently cataloged by the Library of Congress and about one thousand other United States and Canadian libraries. It is published monthly in book form and cululates for periods of up to twenty years.

** Much of the technical work, such as changing the entry headings on catalog cards, or typing cross-references, can be done by assistants.

How Name Authority Cards Are Made

The following is a more detailed breakdown of Step 3 on page 91. Please review this step before proceeding.

Name authority cards are apt to be made in an order somewhat like this:

A. **The facts are gathered** and jotted down on the workslip.*

AUTHORITY
INFORMATION
ON A WORK-
SLIP

B. **The facts are interpreted** according to the AA. You will learn the specifics of interpretation later on. In cases like the above, both the AA and its predecessor chose the author's real name as entry heading.** Thus, the decision to use "Mackintosh" as entry heading, and the pseudonyms as cross-references.

C. **The decision is recorded** on top of the authority card (Line a), the necessary cross-references are traced (lines b-c), and the facts on which the decision is based are also recorded in a sort of shorthand (lines d-i). Many local versions exist, of which the following is fairly common:

✓ One checkmark means: The name was found in some form in the reference tool listed.

✓✓ Two checkmarks mean: The name and the title of the book (any edition) were found in the reference tool listed.

d The letter "d" means: One or more of the person's dates wer found, as indicated.

° A small circle means: The tool listed does not have this name.

(It is useful to indicate unsuccessful searches, too, to avoid re-checking the same tool later on.)

* A temporary record of bibliographical information. Most frequently, a record on which the cataloger constructs an entry, along with supplemental information, from which the typist prepares a stencil master for duplication. It may range from an ordinary P-slip to a preprinted, highly organized, 5" x 8" sheet of paper. A model for one kind of workslip is on page 412.

** The predecessors of our current AA are discussed briefly in Chapter 5.

When recording the facts (lines d-i) an attempt is made to be brief but precise, and to avoid unnecessary repetition. But it is essential to record every new fact and its source.

D. **The necessary cross-references are typed twice:** One set for the catalog and one set for the authority file.

The following illustration shows the relationship between a name authority card, a series of main entry cards for the same heading, and cross-reference cards leading to that heading. (See also page 91.)

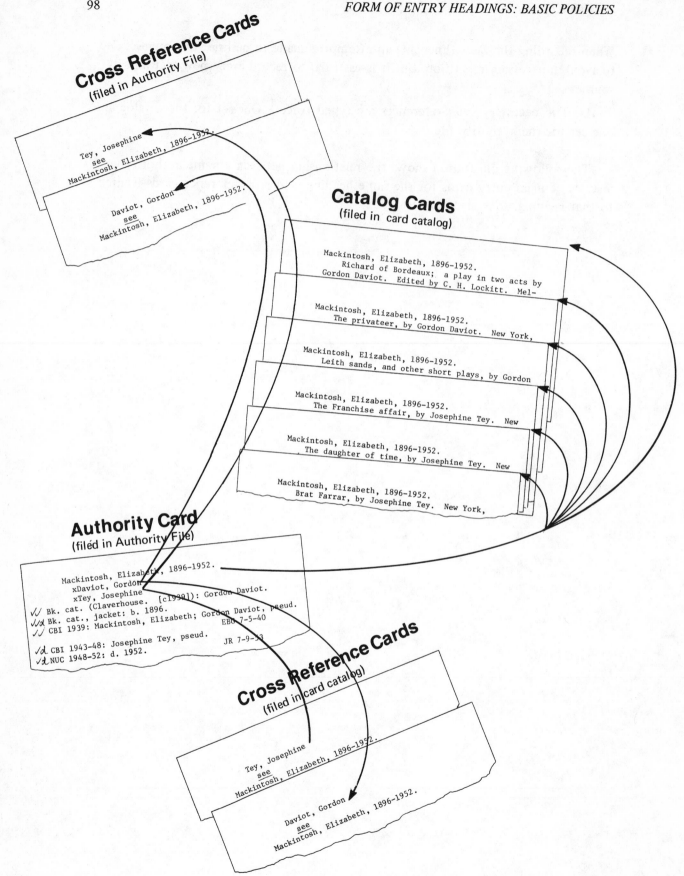

Cross Reference Cards
(filed in Authority File)

Tey, Josephine
    see
Mackintosh, Elizabeth, 1896-1952.

Daviot, Gordon
    see
Mackintosh, Elizabeth, 1896-1952.

Catalog Cards
(filed in card catalog)

Mackintosh, Elizabeth, 1896-1952.
    Richard of Bordeaux; a play in two acts by
Gordon Daviot. Edited by C. H. Lockitt. Mel-

Mackintosh, Elizabeth, 1896-1952.
    The privateer, by Gordon Daviot. New York,

Mackintosh, Elizabeth, 1896-1952.
    Leith sands, and other short plays, by Gordon

Mackintosh, Elizabeth, 1896-1952.
    The Franchise affair, by Josephine Tey. New

Mackintosh, Elizabeth, 1896-1952.
    The daughter of time, by Josephine Tey. New

Mackintosh, Elizabeth, 1896-1952.
    Brat Farrar, by Josephine Tey. New York,

Authority Card
(filed in Authority File)

Mackintosh, Elizabeth, 1896-1952.
    xDaviot, Gordon
    xTey, Josephine
✓✓ Bk. cat. (Claverhouse. [c1939]): Gordon Daviot.
✓✓ Bk. cat., jacket: b. 1896.
✓✓ CBI 1939: Mackintosh, Elizabeth; Gordon Daviot, pseud.
                                        EBG 7-5-40
✓✓ CBI 1943-48: Josephine Tey, pseud.   JR 7-9-53
✓✓ NUC 1948-52: d. 1952.

Cross Reference Cards
(filed in card catalog)

Tey, Josephine
    see
Mackintosh, Elizabeth, 1896-1952.

Daviot, Gordon
    see
Mackintosh, Elizabeth, 1896-1952.

How to Make a Cross-Reference from a Cross-Reference Tracing

Typically, it is the typist's job to make a cross-reference on the basis of a cross-reference tracing. But since the cataloger must normally train the typist in this technical aspect of making cross-references, an exercise seems in order. And, although it sounds implausible, a precise knowledge of what the symbols "x" and "xx" signify is indispensable to the professional librarian who wishes to be able to understand with facility the subject relationships shown in most subject authority lists.*

The authority card in the preceding illustration shows the officially established entry heading (Mackintosh, Elizabeth, 1896-1952), followed by two tracings (xDaviot, Gordon; xTey, Josephine). The term "tracing" has two meanings: On a unit card, a tracing is a record that shows under what headings additional copies of that unit card are to be filed. (See pages 12 to 15.) On an authority card, a tracing is a record of the words or names from which cross-references are to be made. "x" means, "**make a see-**reference from the following term to the official heading," "xx" means, "**Make a see-also** reference from the following term to the official heading."

* A subject authority list is a list of subject headings (mentioned on pages 5, and 12 to 20) that are suitable for use in a library. Shows typically the cross-references that should be made to and from each heading.

EXERCISE

Study the preceding illustration to see how the see-reference cards came to be made, and then
make see-references for the following names, using the indentions you learned on pages 80 to 83.

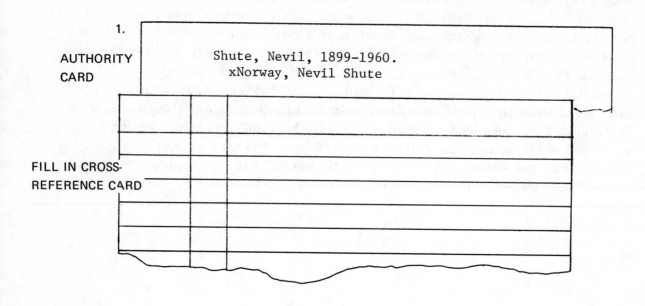

1.

AUTHORITY
CARD

Shute, Nevil, 1899–1960.
    xNorway, Nevil Shute

FILL IN CROSS-
REFERENCE CARD

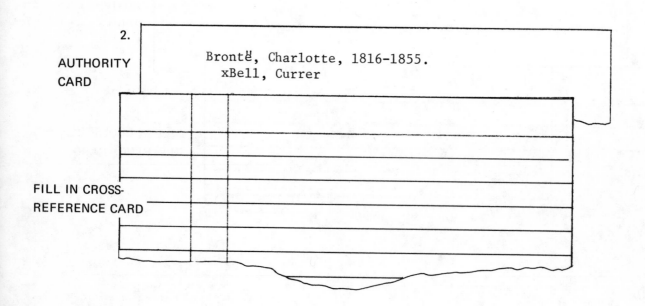

2.

AUTHORITY
CARD

Brontë, Charlotte, 1816–1855.
    xBell, Currer

FILL IN CROSS-
REFERENCE CARD

3.

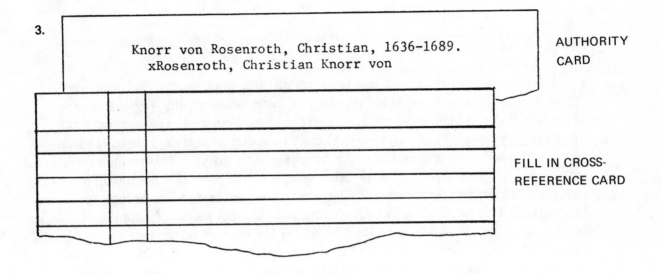

Knorr von Rosenroth, Christian, 1636-1689.
xRosenroth, Christian Knorr von

AUTHORITY
CARD

FILL IN CROSS-
REFERENCE CARD

4.

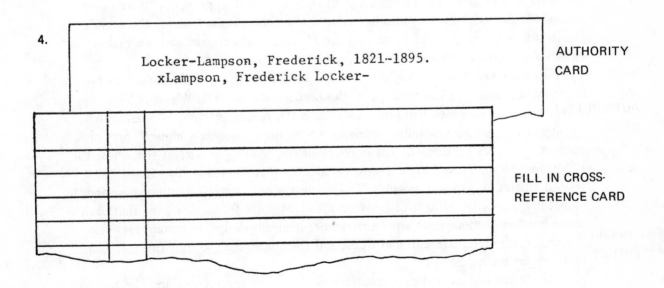

Locker-Lampson, Frederick, 1821--1895.
xLampson, Frederick Locker-

AUTHORITY
CARD

FILL IN CROSS-
REFERENCE CARD

PART B: THE CATALOGING PROCESS

CHAPTER FOUR   **CONCEPTS AND GUIDELINES: A SUMMARY OF AACR INTENT**

HIGHLIGHTS

For decisions on both the choice and the form of entry headings the cataloger turns to the commonly accepted national standard for entry headings, the *Anglo-American Cataloging Rules* (AACR, most often indicated as AA). Four basic concepts express the central tendency of these rules with respect to choice of entry headings: (1) The concept of intellectual responsibility. ("Who created this work?") This permits entry under author, editor, organization, or other creator of the book's content. (2) The concept of the user's approaches. ("Under what names are readers apt to look for this work?") This permits, for example, added entries under names of people and organizations that did *not* help create a book. (3) The concept of the user's convenience. ("What would help the user find this item?") If a work's authorship is diffuse or unknown, this permits entry under the book's real title or under stylized substitutes for the unknown author, that effectively cause different versions of a book, or related material, to be listed next to each other in the catalog. It permits making cross-references from a name-form that was not used as a heading to the one that *was* used as a heading. (4) The concept of the reasonable approach. ("How many entries for this book is the optimum number?") This permits limiting the number of entries for any one book to those that are likely to be used, rather than making entries for all names that could conceivably be used.

Two basic concepts express the AACR's central tendency with respect to form of entry headings: (5) The concept of the best known name. ("Which of this person's names, or which form of his name, is the reader apt to use in his search?") "Best known" means generally, the name which the author uses himself, or which is given in reference sources. (6) The concept of the heading as part of the whole file. ("Will this heading cause the entry to be filed so that the reader can find it, and related entries, as easily as possible?") This means one degree of fullness for one name; it means cross-references between different name-forms; it means that each name must be distinct from any other name; it means designing certain classes of headings (corporate, conventional titles, and form headings) so that the entries are grouped for easiest overview.

The difficulties created by the differences between the present and the former codes will be discussed in detail in Chapter 18.

CONCEPTS AND GUIDELINES

For decision on both the choice of entry headings* and the form of entry headings** the cataloger turns to the commonly accepted national standard for entry headings, the *Anglo-American Cataloging Rules* (AACR). With respect to choice of entry headings, the central tendency of these rules can be expressed as four basic concepts:

(1) **The concept of intellectual responsibility.** (*"Who created this work?"*) Whenever possible, enter a work under the person or organization primarily responsible for its intellectual content.*** Make added entries for other persons or organizations that contributed significantly to it.†

(2) **The concept of the user's approaches.** (*"Under what names are readers apt to look for this work?"*) We really know still too little about how users approach entries, but we do know that the approach of even one reader to the same book may vary from time to time.

To some extent, the concept of intellectual responsibility is used because it is hoped that it overlaps the concept of the user's approach; that it tends to match the approaches which most readers will use instinctively or which they can be taught to use.

The concept of the user's approaches demands that books be listed at times under headings that do not indicate intellectual responsibility. For example, the book's title is a likely approach to a book and thus becomes typically an added entry heading. And if a book belongs to a series, catalogers make an added entry heading under the name of the series if they feel that enough readers are apt to use that approach. Under this concept a book sometimes receives an added entry under the name of a person or organization that did not help to create it but who can be though of in connection with it, such as the sponsor of an institute. Note, on page 43, the entry on "Air turbulence." Its second Roman numeral tracing is for the (non-commercial) publisher. This is most unusual but, given the subject matter of this publication, and the subject interest of the Aviation Safety Center, it is quite useful that the Center be an access point to this particular publication. Knowledgeable readers are apt to think of one in connection with the other.

Should all non-commercial publishers become Roman numeral added entry tracings for their publications? Definitely not. The question of how far to go will be discussed shortly.

---

   * This concept was discussed on pages 5, 26, and 50-64.

  ** See pages 67-76.

 *** See pages 28-32.

   † See pages 12, 26, and 25-26.

EXERCISE

Please study now the other entries on pages 43 and 44, and list below any other Roman numeral tracings for persons or organizations that seem **not** to have been intellectually responsible for that particular work._____

_____

_____

_____

_____

_____

(3) **The concept of the user's convenience.** (*"What would help the user find this item?"*) If no person or organization can be effectively identified as the author, that is, if a work's authorship is diffuse, indeterminate, or unknown, use a heading that either comes naturally to the user's mind, or that he can be taught effectively, and that brings, if possible, related material together just as the concept of intellectual responsibility brings all works of one author together.

For some types of materials it is felt that the user's convenience is best served by entering a book under its real title as it appears on the title page.* For other types, a conventional form of the title** or even a stylized substitute for the author, that is, a form heading,*** are considered most helpful.

These three concepts—Intellectual responsibility, User's approaches, User's convenience—tend to blend at times. For example, the technique of using added entries can fall into all three concepts: Added entries are used because often more than one person or organization had a major share in creating a book; because the user's needs and, thus, approaches, tend to vary and thus tend to make him approach one book at different times from more than one angle; and because multiple listing is obviously more convenient to the user than listing under only one heading.

The technique of using cross-references† can fall under the concept of the user's approaches and that of the user's convenience. Users are apt to approach a pseudonymous author under either name, and it is obviously more convenient if the catalog indicates under which name the entries are listed.

* See pages 32-33.

** As illustrated on pages 34-37.

*** See pages 37-39.

† See pages 76-85.

(4) **The concept of the reasonable approach.** (*"How many entries is the optimum number for this book for my patrons?"*) The concepts of the user's approaches and the user's convenience could tempt one to provide innumerable entry headings for any one book on the theory that somebody, at some time, could need that particular name as an approach to a particular book.* While undoubtedly true, this philosophy would not be worth the cost, for it would require making many very rarely used added entry headings, possibly at the expense of other library activities. It would also make the catalog harder to use, for it would probably double its size and thus bloat it with these seldom used added entries, making the frequently demanded entries harder to find.

Following this philosophy, we might have 21 entries for Robert Frost in a catalog with perhaps 9 entries for his works, 7 entries for prefaces that he wrote for other people's books, and 5 entries for books for which he furnished the motto. Yet the reader, who 99 out of 100 times would only want Robert Frost's poems, would have to go through all 21 entries to find the 9 books of his poetry which the library owns.

Thus, catalogers and bibliographers try to make entries only for approaches that are apt to be fairly frequent: the reasonable approach. No catalog, no index in a book, no bibliography can or should provide every conceivable approach, or answer every conceivable question. But it should provide those approaches which will serve many of its users much of the time. This requires judgment on the part of the cataloger and on the part of the framers of the AA. This is one of the factors that make cataloging an art rather than an exact science. As you get acquainted with the specific rules you will find that the AA give you a chance to exercise your judgment, to make more or fewer added entries for any one work depending on your estimate of the needs of your clientele.

EXERCISE

Can you think of a situation in which, for example, it would be very useful to make an added entry for a book's illustrator? (1) _____

_____

_____

Or, a situation in which it would not be particularly necessary to make an added entry for a book's illustrator? (2) _____

_____

_____

---

* For example, for the writer of the preface, for the person to whom a book is dedicated, for the printer, for the bindery, for the poet who was quoted on the title page, for the research assistant, etc.

Few serious difficulties arise in the choice-of-entry-heading sector, for in it the AA provide enough safety valves to permit a cataloger to provide whatever multiple approaches he deems useful for his library and his patrons. But the form-of-entry-headings sector faces problems, partly because people do not always use, and are not always called by, precisely the same name, and partly because names prepared according to the current AA must sometimes be interfiled into catalogs created according to our previous code, the *A.L.A Cataloging Rules for Author and Title Entries.* (ALA)*

The central tendency of the AA with respect to form-of-entry-headings can be expressed as two basic concepts:

(5) **The concept of the best known name.** (*"Which of this person's names is the reader apt to use in his search?"*) For persons known by several names** the AA prefer, in general, entry under the form of a name that is apt to be best known to the public.

For a person, this form may be a name with initials instead of regular forenames, it may be the real name, a pseudonym, a nickname, a title of nobility, a married woman's maiden surname, or any other name. For an organization, the best known name may be a real, official name, a short form of the real name, or even a nickname.

$$?\quad\begin{array}{l}\text{Stendhal}\qquad\qquad\text{[the pseudonym]}\\\text{or}\\\text{Beyle, Marie Henri }\;\text{[the real name]}\end{array}$$

$$?\quad\begin{array}{l}\text{Eden, Anthony}\qquad\text{[most commonly known name]}\\\text{or}\\\text{Eden, Robert Anthony}\qquad\text{[complete original name]}\\\text{or}\\\text{Avon, Robert Anthony Eden, Earl of}\qquad\text{[complete later name]}\end{array}$$

$$?\quad\begin{array}{l}\text{American Documentation Institute}\qquad\text{[original name]}\\\text{or}\\\text{American Society for Information Science}\qquad\text{[new name]}\\\text{or}\\\text{A.S.I.S.}\qquad\text{[frequently used initials]}\end{array}$$

---

* *A.L.A. Cataloging Rules for Author and Title Entries.* Prepared by the Division of Cataloging and Classification of the American Library Association. 2d ed., edited by Clara Beetle. Chicago, American Library Association, 1949.

** This concept was touched on pages 71-76.

The concept of using the best known name makes sense, but it also causes complications, because for many people known by more than one name it is difficult to decide which name is best known. For example, many sophisticated readers know that Mark Twain is the pseudonym for Samuel Clemens and are apt to look under either form. Some women authors are as well known under their maiden name as under their married name, for example Clare Booth who became Mrs. Clare Booth Luce. A few writers use many pseudonyms, any one of which is well known to some readers. John Creasey, mentioned on page 76, is an example. Still others are as well known under their real name for one type of work as under their assumed name for another type of work. Ray Stannard Baker, mentioned on pages 71-75, is an example.

Therefore, the AA define what is meant by "best known" and specify, in effect: If in doubt, use the name which the author generally uses himself in his works, or use the name as given in reference sources, or use the latest form of his name.* The specific applications of this tendency you will learn later on.

The guideline of using the name which the author generally uses himself in his works (see preceding paragraph) also causes complications because even authors who have no pseudonym do not always record their names in their books with the same degree of fullness.** Therefore, the AA expand this guideline further and say, in effect: Use the fullest form the writer himself has used (for example, forenames instead of initials) if you can find it without much searching, and if necessary to distinguish a new name from a similar one already used as a heading in your catalog.*** In practice, this causes the cataloger almost always to follow the fullest form of name used prominently in the first work and library happens to receive by an author.

---

* For readers who look under the "other" name (the one not selected as entry heading) a cross-reference is made that leads to the name that is used as entry heading. See also pages 82 to 93.

Bell, Currer
see
Bronte, Charlotte, 1816-1855.

** See also page 67.

*** See page 93.

If the title page*   reads: J. P. Mulgawany

But the book jacket**   reads: James Peter Mulgawany, born in 1902

Use as entry heading automatically: Mulgawany, James Peter, 1902-

If the new name conflicts with an existing entry heading, a still fuller form of name is sought.***

Berger, Robert, 1933 (July 8)–
    All about antiquing and restoring furniture. **New York,** Hawthorn Books [1971]
        viii, 181 p. illus. 24 cm. $5.95

THE LIBRARY OF CONGRESS, WHICH PRODUCED THIS CARD, OBVIOUSLY ALREADY HAD ANOTHER MAN WITH THE SAME NAME AND YEAR AS AN ENTRY HEADING.

* Title page: A page, or a double page spread at the beginning of a book giving its title, author or authors (if acknowledged), usually its publisher, and often its place and date of publication. Typically, it includes also a number of other items of information: the edition number, the names of other contributors to the work such as illustrators, translators or editors, and sometimes even an apt quotation.

** The book jacket, or jacket, is the printed or unprinted paper cover placed around a bound book. In addition to the author's name and the title, it often contains information about the author, his other works, favorable comments about the book (what has come to be known as the publisher's "blurb"), an indication of the contents, or advertising notices for selected other books put out by the same publisher.

*** For additional situations, in which the cataloger cannot follow the title page form of name, see page 89. 97.

(6) **The concept of the heading as part of the whole file.** (*"Will this entry heading cause the entry to be filed effectively?"*) To be effective—to help the user find entries with some confidence—all entry headings for one name must be uniform, so that all the library's books by one person or organization are listed together.* Or, if it is decided to use different entry heading forms for one person, then each form must be consistent within itself, and see-also references must be made between them.** Different degrees of fullness for one entry heading can too easily seem to refer to different people and can reduce the reader's chances of finding entries.† The name must also be distinguishable from (that is, differ from) all other names used as headings in the catalog,†† lest the user assume that two identical headings that represent different authors list the works of one author.

To be effective, entry headings must also be designed with the filing arrangement in mind. (See page 98.) Especially corporate entry headings, conventional titles, and form headings are partly designed to result in an effective file arrangement, for example by grouping entries for many sub-units of an organization next to the parent organization. For examples, see the illustrations on pages 31, 36, and 39.

Differences Between ALA and AACR

Difficulties arise when one considers a heading as part of a whole file, because the heading must be interfiled with others already in the catalog, which were most likely constructed according to our earlier code, the ALA Rules. The same name, when constructed according to our present code, may differ considerably from the form it received when constructed according to the former code, and often would file quite differently. Here are some examples.

NAMES CONSTRUCTED ACCORDING TO THE *A.L.A. CATALOGING RULES FOR AUTHOR AND TITLE ENTRIES,* WHICH WERE USED FROM 1949 TO JANUARY 1967.	THE SAME NAMES CONSTRUCTED ACCORDING TO THE *ANGLO-AMERICAN CATALOGING RULES* WHICH CAME IN FORCE IN FEBRUARY 1967.
Hardenberg, Friedrich, *freiherr* von, 1772-1801.	Novalis, 1772-1801. [pseudonym of the German novelist von Hardenberg]
Karl V, *Emperor of Germany,* 1500-1558.	Charles V, *Emperor of Germany,* 1500-1558.
Horatius Flaccus, Quintus.	Horace.
Wodehouse, Pelham Grenville.	Wodehouse, P. G.

* See page 67.

** For an example, see the file of cards on page 73.

† See pages 68-70.

†† See page 67.

While the differences between the former and the present code are not always as great as the above examples indicate, they do exist. The ALA Code tended to use as entry heading a person's or organization's real and full name; the present code tends to use the name that is most frequently used, or that is best known.* What should libraries do that already have books by von Hardenberg when they get another one by him? Should they recatalog their old books to conform to the new rules, in order to keep all of an author's works under one form of name? Recataloging is expensive and takes time away from that needed for cataloging new books. In practice, most libraries will probably follow the lead of the Library of Congress, which sells cards to many libraries. It has adopted a policy known as "superimposition" in applying the new rules. This means that it will leave most existing entry headings as they are and will follow the new code only for works, people, and organizations that are new to its catalogs.** Therefore, you will learn in this text how to work with the new code but will, in the last chapter, also learn how the former code handled the same situation.

* "Best known" does not necessarily mean "well known by everybody." It means the form of name that a knowledgeable or sophisticated reader is apt to know, or the form of name that is used in a bibliography or book review or reference work.

* U.S. Library of Congress. Processing Department. *Cataloging Service Bulletin 79.* Washington, D.C., 1967, page 1.

Try to learn by heart the names of the six basic concepts, and what they stand for. Since they do represent the central tendencies of the AA they will help you in difficult situations, when you will have to make decisions on the basis of conflicting evidence, or when the specific rules permit you alternative solutions. In doubtful bibliographic situations it is always best to act on the basis of central guidelines.

The six basic concepts are like the three corners of a triangle, three aspects of one unit.

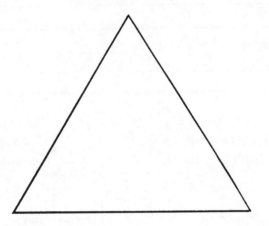

**CHOICE OF ENTRY HEADINGS
ON THE BASIS OF**
Intellectual responsibility
User's approaches
User's convenience
Reasonable approach

**SELECTION OF A NAME FOR
PEOPLE OR ORGANIZATIONS
KNOWN BY MORE THAN ONE NAME**

**THE HEADING AS PART
OF THE WHOLE FILE
(THE FORM OF THE HEADING)**

EXERCISE

Below is an expansion of the preceding diagram. To help you review, fill in the various concepts (not necessarily the words but the ideas) contained in the "Six basic concepts." Feel free to refer back to the text while doing this. Some concepts are filled in as examples.

CHOICE OF ENTRY HEADINGS
ON THE BASIS OF:

INTELLECTUAL RESPONSIBILITY:

Enter a work [that is, make the main entry] under the person or organization that is responsible for the intellectual content of a work.

Make added entries for _____

USER'S APPROACHES:

_____

_____

USER'S CONVENIENCE:

_____

_____

REASONABLE APPROACH:

_____

_____

SELECTION OF A NAME FOR	**THE HEADING AS PART**
PEOPLE OR ORGANIZATIONS	**OF THE WHOLE FILE**
KNOWN BY MORE THAN ONE NAME	**(THE FORM OF THE HEADING)**

Use the name most patrons are most likely to know, the best known name.

DIFFICULTIES ARE: _____

_____

_____

IF IN DOUBT, USE: _____

_____

_____

MAKE SEE-REFERENCES _____

_____

_____

(1) Use one form for one name; or, if you use different entry headings for one person, then

_____

_____

(2) _____

_____

_____

_____

(3) _____

_____

_____

CHAPTER FIVE

THE ANGLO-AMERICAN CATALOGING RULES: HISTORY AND TECHNICAL ASPECTS

HIGHLIGHTS

History: The present entry heading code is the result of evolution. This chapter contains a chronology of the most important, nationally accepted, English language codes, of which the following are major milestones:

1841: The British Museum Code of 91 Rules, chiefly by Sir Anthony Panizzi, the first major code, influenced

1876: Charles Ammi Cutter's *Rules for a Dictionary Catalog.* This is the basis of all subsequent English language codes, and of many conventions covering all aspects of cataloging.

1908: Cooperative effort of the British and American library associations, resulting in *Catalog Rules: Author and Title Entries,* considered the first Anglo-American code.

1949: The American Library Association issued, without coordinating with British standards, a separate entry heading code (*A.L.A. Cataloging Rules for Author and Title Entries*), and the Library of Congress issued one for descriptive cataloging. Both codes differed relatively little from the 1908 Rules.

1967: The *AACR*; a combined English, American, and Canadian code, initially with major differences between the British and the North American versions with respect to corporate bodies. Most of these differences have by now been resolved in favor of British precedent. Once again includes description. Also includes rules for many non-book materials.

While much progress has been made, especially in English speaking countries, towards international standardization, we still have no single standard for entry headings that applies throughout the world, nor even within any one country, nor even within a single library, if one considers the differences bewteen its AA-dictated, home-made catalog as against many of its purchased bibliographies. But the AA is probably the most widely accepted entry heading code in the world and is also the basis for entry headings in many bibliographies. Therefore, it behooves us to know it well. While anyone can grope around in a catalog and find something, one must know its rules and principles, its strengths and omissions, to search effectively in it.

AACR Structure, and How to Use the AACR (AA): The AA is divided into 3 major parts: Entry and Heading; Description; Non-Book Materials. This text deals only with the first part, Entry and Heading. To permit the student to keep his bearings in this mass of rules, this chapter does not yet examine individual rules, but surveys the pattern into which they fall.

The AA Choice-of-entry-headings rules can be grouped into (1) Rules based on the criterion of authorship, ("What authorship situation—such as, a single author—does the book being cataloged represent?"); (2) Rules based on the criterion of the type of work, ("What kind of work—such as a law—is being cataloged?")

The AA Form-of-entry-headings-for-personal-names rules can be grouped into (1) Rules based on the nature of the name, ("What kind of name—such as a compound surname—is involved?"); (2) Rules based on the criterion of language, ("In what language does the person write, or to what language does his name belong?"); (3) Rules based on the criterion of personal status, ("Is this the name of a nobleman?").

In the AA Table of Contents, only the basic rule numbers are listed, such as "3." In the AA text, these rules are further subdivided, such as "3B, 3B1, 3B1a," but only the last element of each rule number is listed with the text, such as "a." To reconstruct the complete rule number, look also at the head of the page where the complete number of the first rule given on the page is listed, such as "3B1a."

When weighing whether or not a rule, such as "3B1a," applies to the book being cataloged, always consider the entire rule, such as "3." Often, several rules must be used jointly. This will be further discussed in subsequent chapters.

HISTORICAL ASPECTS

Codes of entry heading rules, you will find, are almost living things. They are created, they develop, mature, give birth to a new code, and then they are discarded. While this may sound dramatic, it merely shows evolution. As people's library needs change, and as librarians become more familiar with patrons' needs, an existing code is bound to be revised and replaced by a new code which, it is hoped, will give better service. For example, apart from the many local conventions that existed, the first really important code of entry heading rules was developed in 1841 by Sir Anthony Panizzi and others of the British Museum. This famous British Museum Code of 91 rules* served as the basis for the first code that tried to achieve nationwide recognition in the United States, Charles Coffin Jewett's rules of 1852.** While Jewett's rules did not become the official United States code, the 91 rules of the British Museum were also the basis for the first United States code that was nationally accepted, Charles Ammi Cutter's *Rules for a Dictionary Catalog* (1876).† The American Library Association, in turn, prepared a somewhat different code of entry heading rules in 1883†† which was later on printed together with revisions of Cutter's 1876 *Rules*, to form a more or less combined code.††† A new

---

* The *"Rules for the Compilation of the Catalogue"* were printed at the beginning of volume 1 of the British Museum's *Catalogue of Printed Books.* London, 1841.

** Charles Coffin Jewett, *On the Construction of Catalogues of Libraries, and of a General Catalogue.* Washington, D.C., Smithsonian Institution, 1852. (2d ed., 1853, with different title).

† Charles Ammi Cutter, *Rules for a Dictionary Catalog.* Washington, D.C., U.S. Gov't. Print. Off., 1876. (U.S. Bureau of Education, *Special Report on Public Libraries, Part 2.*)

†† American Library Association. Cooperation Committee, *"Condensed Rules for an Author and Title Catalogue," Library Journal* 8:251-254. 1883.

††† Charles Ammi Cutter, *Rules for a Dictionary Catalog.* 3d ed. Washington, D.C., U.S. Gov't. Print. Off., 1891.

edition, prepared in cooperation with the (British) Library Association, appeared in 1908.† This so-called "Anglo-American Code of 1908" was again revised and resulted in 1949 in two separate American codes, one for entry headings†† and one for descriptive cataloging.* The shift from the "1908 Code" to the 1949 entry heading code was relatively easy because most entry headings created according to either code were either identical, or at least sufficiently similar, to permit interfiling the new with the old. Most contemporary American library catalogs still contain mostly entries created according to the two 1949 codes. (See also pages 108-109.)

The present code, the *Anglo-American Cataloging Rules* (AACR or AA) was officially adopted in February 1967. Although it is about seven steps removed from the British Museum *Rules* of 1841, and although it was advertised by its creators as something quite new, one can still see in it traces of many of Sir Anthony Panizzi's ideas of 1841. But it is also the first true revision of the "Anglo-American Code of 1908," and is thus considered to be the second Anglo-American code.

The current AA makes several contributions. Among them are its attempts to standardize the cataloging of the increasing amount of non-book as well as book materials, and the fact that it was created after some attempts to achieve agreement among cataloging codes of many different countries. The principal attempt to create a basis for a super-national code of entry headings was the so-called "Paris Statement of 1961."** The 1967 AA follows the intent of the 1961 Paris statement, with some notable exceptions, and while it was prepared by library associations of three countries (and the Library of Congress) and is undoubtedly used by most English speaking countries, it is not truly international in the sense of standardizing and formalizing the practice of all countries. As a matter of fact, it is published in two different editions, (British text; North American text) which differ in some significant respects. (This text uses the Nort American text as a basis but concentrates on areas common to both texts.)

Many countries have their own cataloging codes for entry headings. Although all these codes differ somewhat, they are often based on each other. Ideally, to achieve inter-library cooperation on an international basis, these entry heading codes should agree so that a book or a name will be listed in every country in such a way that a librarian in another country can find it easily in a printed bibliography. Current efforts are moving in this direction, but we still have a long way to go.

---

† *Catalog Rules: Author and Title Entries,* Compiled by committees of the American Library Association and the (British) Library Association. American ed. Chicago, American Library Association, 1908.

†† *A. L. A. Cataloging Rules for Author and Title Entries.* 2d ed., edited by Clara Beetle. Chicago, American Library Association, 1949.

* U.S. Library of Congress. Descriptive Cataloging Division. *Rules for Descriptive Cataloging.* Washington, D.C., U.S. Gov't. Print. Off., 1949.

** International Conference on Cataloging Principles, Paris, 1961. *Report.* London, 1963.

At least the various national entry heading codes achieve a certain amount of standardization within any one library, and often also within one country. Standardization of entry headings is imperative for efficient communication within and among libraries: Not only for catalogers, but especially for catalog users, including librarians. This the the reason why it is so important for us to learn our standard, the AA.

EXERCISE

Explain briefly what is meant by "standardization of entry headings." (You may have to go back to chapters two and three for some relevant thoughts.) (1) _____

_____

_____

_____

_____

Explain in two or three sentences why standardization of entry headings is important within one library, within one country, and internationally. (2) _____

_____

_____

_____

_____

The AA, based on experience and thoughtful consideration, give guidelines and directives on what main and added entry headings to **select** in a given situation—on what is considered "reasonable" main and added entry approaches—and, once selected, in what **form** to record these entry headings. The rules provide these guidelines for books, periodicals, incunabula,* maps, motion pictures, sheet music, phonorecords, and other so-called "non-book" or "audiovisual" materials. While the rules for each type of material differ, they are based on the same general concepts. Since books form most of the holdings of most libraries, and since, apart from subject headings, most entry headings in catalogs are for personal names, the rest of this text is devoted to books and emphasizes personal name entry headings. This is the type of heading that you will encounter most frequently on the job.

* Incunabula: Books printed before 1501.

HOW TO USE THE AA

The rest of this text contains frequent references to individual rules in the **AA**. To help you use this code, let us examine it briefly. At the moment, you are not yet responsible for learning the content of actual rules, only for the general organization of the book itself. (The next few paragraphs will not make much sense unless you actually examine the **AA** at the same time, as directed.)

Turn to the **Table of "Contents"** in the **AA**. You can see from it that, following the front matter* the book is divided into three major parts:

Part I.   Entry and Heading.
Part II.   Description.
Part III. Non-Book Materials.

Following this central part of the book come several appendices. Note particularly **"Appendix I. Glossary,"** and glance at it. It is very helpful, and even experienced librarians use it often. The AA Glossary should be used in conjunction with the Glossary that is appended to this text, beginning on page 413. Between the two, you should find each significant term explained.

Now turn back to the **AA Table of "Contents."** In it, you will find two columns of numbers. The numbers at the left are the numbers of the cataloging rules; those at the right are page numbers. For example, **"Chapter 1. Entry"** begins on page 9, and **AA Rule number 1** begins on page 11.

This text deals with **AA "Part I. Entry and Heading,"** which is divided into four long chapters. **"Chapter 1. Entry"** contains rules dealing with the choice of entry heading, a concept that was discussed on pages 26, 32, 50 to 58, and 102 to 105. **"Chapter 2. Headings for Persons"** contains rules on the form of entry heading for personal names. This concept was discussed on pages 71 to 82 and 115 to 120. **"Chapter 3. Headings for Corporate Bodies"** contains rules on the form of entry headings for corporate bodies. This concept was touched on pages 29 to 31. **"Chapter 4. Uniform Titles"** contains rules on the choice and the form of entry headings for material that has no author, as well as for other works that can be handled in similar fashion. This concept was touched on pages 33 to 38 and 103.

---

* Front matter of a book: The pages preceding the text, and made up of some or all of the following items, arranged usually in the order listed: Half-title, Frontispiece; Title page; Verso of the title page; Dedication; Preface or Foreword; Table of contents; List of illustrations; Introduction. It very often has no page number at all; but if it is paged, it is apt to be a separate sequence in Roman numerals while the main text is numbered in Arabic numerals.

Criteria for Grouping AA Rules

AA Chapter 1, with its choice-of-entry-headings concept, contains 33 rules* which are grouped under subheadings such as **"General Rules," "Certain Legal Publications,"** etc. Each rule represents a particular choice-of-entry-heading situation. Let us examine the titles of these rules to learn whether the rules fall into a pattern, whether they have some common criteria. (You need not yet turn to the text of the rules. This will come later. But do study the **AA Table of "Contents"** carefully while reading these paragraphs.)

AA Rule 1, for example, is evidently based on the number of authors. So is **AA Rule 3**. On the other hand, **AA Rule 2** is based on the criterion of doubtful or unknown authorship. **AA Rule 4** seems based on the concept of kind-of-authorship. In summary, one general criterion on which several choice-of-entry-heading rules are based is that of authorship: What authorship situation does the book being cataloged represent?

The second general criterion according to which other choice-of-entry-heading rules are framed is that of the type of work: What type of work are you cataloging? For example, **AA Rule 20** deals with a type of work, "Laws" and similar publications.

* The AA Table of "Contents" also shows that AA Rules 34 to 39 do not yet exist. This block of numbers was undoubtedly left blank for future use.

EXERCISE: CHOICE-OF-ENTRY-HEADING RULES

Using only the **AA Table of "Contents"** as a guide, list the rule numbers for **AA Rules 1 through 18,** and **20 through 32** under the heading that seems most appropriate. (**AA Rules 19** and **33** are excluded from this exercise since their titles do not indicate to which group they belong.) A few rules can be listed in both columns.

CRITERION OF AUTHORSHIP:
_____

Examples: 1
               3
_____

Your answer:

_____ _____

_____ _____

_____ _____

_____ _____

_____ _____

_____ _____

_____ _____

_____ _____

CRITERION OF TYPE OF WORK:
_____

Example   20
_____

Your answer:

_____ _____

_____ _____

_____ _____

_____ _____

_____ _____

_____ _____

_____

Turning to Chapter 2 in the **AA Table of "Contents"** you will find that it handles the concept of form-of-entry-heading for personal names by means of 19 rules (**AA Rules 40 to 58**) which are also grouped under subheadings, such as "Choice and Form of Name." (This particular terminology is confusing. It refers to the choice among several names used by one person, such as one person's pseudonym as against his real name.* Thus, it refers not to the **choice** of an entry heading, but to the choice of a **form** of a name that is used as an entry heading.)

 AA Rules 40 to 58 can also be grouped according to several broad criteria. These are:

The nature of the name, as **AA Rule 46B**;

The language in which a name is established, or in which
    the author writes, as **AA Rule 50**;

The person's status, as **AA Rule 46G**.

EXERCISE: FORM-OF-ENTRY-HEADING RULES
FOR PERSONAL NAMES

 Using only the **AA Table of "Contents"** as a guide, list the rule numbers for **AA Rules 41 through 51**, and **54 through 58**, under the heading that seems most appropriate. (**AA Rules 48, 52, and 53** are excluded from this exercise since their titles do not indicate to which group they belong.)

* This was touched on pages 71 to 76, and 86.

CRITERION OF THE NATURE OF THE NAME	CRITERION OF LANGUAGE	CRITERION OF PERSONAL STATUS
Example: 46B	Example: 50	Example: 46G
Your answer:	Your answer:	Your answer:

Now turn in the **AA Table of "Contents"** to **Chapter 3, "Headings for Corporate Bodies."** * It handles the concept of form-of-entry-headings for corporate names by means of 40 rules, **AA Rules 60 to 99**, again grouped under appropriate subheadings. (As in Chapter 2, the subheading "Choice and Form of Name" refers not to the **choice** of an entry heading, but to the choice of one among several possible **forms** of a name that is used as an entry heading.)

AA Rules 60 to 99 can also be grouped according to a few broad criteria, namely:

Rules for corporate bodies in general, that is, rules that
fit most situations, as **AA Rules 60 and 69**;

---

* This concept was touched on pages 29 to 32 and 42 to 44.

> Rules applicable only to specific types of corporate bodies, that is, limited to specific categories, as **AA Rules 92 and 97**.

The same kind of division is also evident in **AA Chapter 4, "Uniform Titles,"** * which deals with the choice and form of entry headings for material that has no author and for other works that can be handled similarly. Thus, **AA Rules 101 and 103** fall among the group of rules applicable to all materials that can be listed under a uniform, or conventional, title instead of an author. On the other hand, **AA Rules 108 and 118** deal with specific types of material that are to be listed under a standardized uniform title.

AA Numbering System

You may have noticed that the **AA Table of "Contents"** lists usually only the basic rule number. However, in the AA text the rules are often subdivided.

In Table of "Contents," AA page xi:	*In text, AA pages 11-12:*
[Rule] 1. Works of single authorship.	[Rule] 1. Works of single authorship.
	A. Enter a work . . .
[Rule] 2. Works by unknown or uncertain authorship, or by unnamed groups.	B. If the publication . . .

* For this concept, see pages 34 to 37.

Some rules are even further subdivided, like **AA Rule 3**, on **AA pages 14-17**, which is divided into subsections

3	3B1	3B1c	3C1
3A	3B1a	3B2	3C2
3B	3B1b	3C	

In the AA text, unfortunately only the last element of each number is usually listed. For example, on **AA page 26**, the AA text lists merely Rule **B**. But at the head of the page you will find reference to the full AA Rule number, **8B**.

Always Consult the Entire Rule

Although you need not learn by heart the content of each rule, you must make it a habit to consider a rule in its entirety before using any part of it. Especially the beginning section of a rule or group of rules (often called "Preliminary note," or "General rule") is useful for learning its intent, general framework, and limitations. For example, if you catalog a book to which you think **AA Rule 3B2** applies, be sure to study carefully **AA Rule 3B2**, plus all other parts of **AA Rule 3B**, plus the "Preliminary note" at the beginning of **AA Rule 3** before making a final decision. As a matter of fact, you will probably also find yourself taking a quick look at **AA Rules 3A and 3C** before cataloging your book according to **AA Rule 3B2**.

Examing a rule in its entirety is necessary because every rule exists within the context of other rules. For example, you must know how many possible pigeon holes the AA contain for a "shared authorship" situation before you can decide which pigeon hole is best suited to the book you are cataloging. Put another way, the use of a code of rules demands that you match the situation given by the book you are cataloging with the rule, or group of rules, that most nearly matches that given situation.

The AA Index

To find the rule, or rules, that best matches a given situation, you can check either the AA Table of "Contents" or the AA "Index." While experienced catalogers sometimes prefer to use the Table of "Contents," the "Index" is probably more helpful for the beginner. Either method takes practice; either method requires getting used to the terminology.

Now browse through the captions in the AA Index. Most refer to specific concepts, that is, specific sub-rules or paragraphs, such as

Alumni organizations, **71A**

whereas the AA Table of Contents lists the same rule only under the much broader, and really meaningless term

71. Related bodies.

Since the AA Index usually refers to specific concepts it is usually more helpful than the AA Table of Contents when searching for a rule that fits a specific entry heading situation, that is, when you know precisely what you are looking for. But note that the AA Index also lists broad concepts and sometimes refers to whole blocks of rules, as

Government bodies,   **78-86.**
Legal publications,   **20-26.**

This is helpful when you cannot define, or cannot find in the AA Index, a specific situation.

Now look at the rule numbers to which the AA "Index" refers. We know from the AA Table of "Contents" that the highest number for an entry heading rule is **AA Rule 126.** But the AA Index refers also to much higher numbers, since it is a combined index to all three parts of the AA:*

Part I.   Entry and Heading: Rules 1 to 126
Part II.   Description: Rules 130-191
Part III. Non-Book Materials: Rules 200 to 272.

Each caption in the AA Index refers to a cataloging situation, either an entry heading situation, or a descriptive cataloging situation, or a non-book-material situation. Often the wording of the caption indicates precisely which aspect is meant. For example,

Addresses by chiefs of state, etc., **17C.**

implies that an entry heading situation is mean,** whereas

Appendices in contents note, **149A4**

implies that a descriptive cataloging situation is meant.** But when the wording of the caption does not indicate clearly whether the rule cited describes an entry head-

* See also page 118.

** It may not be obvious if you have not studied descriptive cataloging principles and specifics.

ing situation, or a descriptive situation, or a non-book-material situation, the number of the rule can serve as a guide. For example, the wording

Academic degrees, **147C**

does not indicate whether one is supposed to do something with academic degrees in an entry heading or in the descriptive part of the entry. But since **AA Rule 147C** falls within Rules 130 and 191, it can only deal with a descriptive situation.

Notice also the indentions in the AA Index. They imply, of course, that each indented caption is one aspect of the larger, unindented caption listed above. For example,

Change of name
corporate bodies, **68**
persons, **41**
places in imprint, **139E**

should read as follows:

If you have a corporate-body-entry-heading situation where the corporate body has changed its name, consult **AA Rule 68**.

If you have a personal-name-entry-heading situation where the individual concerned has changed his name, consult **AA Rule 41**.

If you have a descriptive cataloging situation where the name of a place of publication has been changed, consult **AA Rule 139E**.

EXERCISE

(The purpose of this exercise is to show that some rules are listed in the AA Index more than once, but not under all the words that you may think of.) With reference to the preceding example (Change of name), check in the AA Index whether you can find references to AA Rules 68, or 41, or 139E under different captions, such as

Personal names
change of.

(1) _____

_____

_____

THE FIRST FEW RULES

Turn to the beginning of AA Chapter 1 (on page 9) and read the first paragraph, "Main and added entries."

EXERCISE

Did the paragraph indicate that the individual rules are essentially rules for main entry headings? (1)___(Yes)___(No)___

Did the paragraph also indicate that the individual rules indicate what added entry headings to make in a given situation? (2) ____(Yes)_____(No)_____

Did the paragraph also give you permission to make additional added entry headings if you felt it desirable for your library? (3) ____(Yes)_____(No)_____

Now turn to **AA Rule 33** (pages 70-72) and browse through this rule. You need not memorize its details, but you should be acquainted with it in general terms:

> Whenever you use a rule in AA Chapter 1 (that is, a choice-of-entry-heading rule) for a book that has more than one author or contributor, use it in conjunction with **AA Rule 33**.

If you wonder why, turn back to pages 25 to 26, where it is explained why the cataloger should always think of the whole cluster of entry headings that are needed for one book.

Now read the second footnote on AA page 9. It confirms what you have learned in Chapter 2 of this text. The following cards represent typical examples.

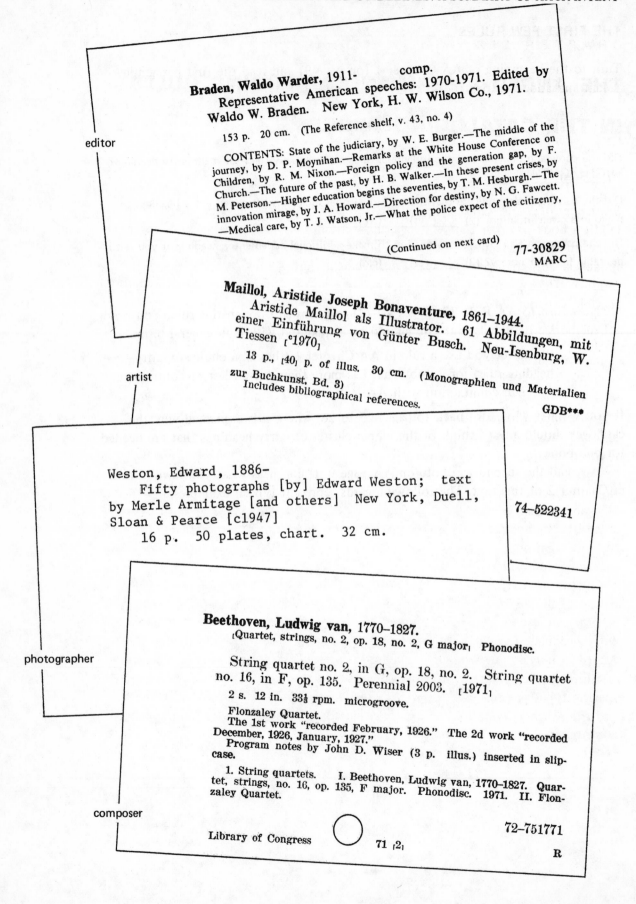

editor

Braden, Waldo Warder, 1911-   comp.
Representative American speeches: 1970-1971. Edited by
Waldo W. Braden. New York, H. W. Wilson Co., 1971.

153 p. 20 cm. (The Reference shelf, v. 43, no. 4)

CONTENTS: State of the judiciary, by W. E. Burger.—The middle of the
journey, by D. P. Moynihan.—Remarks at the White House Conference on
Children, by R. M. Nixon.—Foreign policy and the generation gap, by F.
Church.—The future of the past, by H. B. Walker.—In these present crises, by
M. Peterson.—Higher education begins the seventies, by T. M. Hesburgh.—The
innovation mirage, by J. A. Howard.—Direction for destiny, by N. G. Fawcett.
—Medical care, by T. J. Watson, Jr.—What the police expect of the citizenry,

(Continued on next card)   77-30829
                                      MARC

artist

Maillol, Aristide Joseph Bonaventure, 1861–1944.
Aristide Maillol als Illustrator. 61 Abbildungen, mit
einer Einführung von Günter Busch. Neu-Isenburg, W.
Tiessen [ᶜ1970]

13 p., [40] p. of illus. 30 cm. (Monographien und Materialien
zur Buchkunst, Bd. 3)
Includes bibliographical references.

                                      GDB***

photographer

Weston, Edward, 1886–
    Fifty photographs [by] Edward Weston; text
by Merle Armitage [and others] New York, Duell,
Sloan & Pearce [c1947]   74–522341
    16 p. 50 plates, chart. 32 cm.

composer

Beethoven, Ludwig van, 1770–1827.
    [Quartet, strings, no. 2, op. 18, no. 2, G major] Phonodisc.

String quartet no. 2, in G, op. 18, no. 2. String quartet
no. 16, in F, op. 135. Perennial 2003. [1971]

2 s. 12 in. 33⅓ rpm. microgroove.

Flonzaley Quartet.
    The 1st work "recorded February, 1926." The 2d work "recorded
December, 1926, January, 1927."
    Program notes by John D. Wiser (3 p. illus.) inserted in slip-
case.

    1. String quartets.   I. Beethoven, Ludwig van, 1770–1827. Quar-
tet, strings, no. 16, op. 135, F major. Phonodisc. 1971. II. Flonzaley Quartet.

Library of Congress   71 [2]   72–751771

                                      R

CHAPTER SIX

THE ANGLO-AMERICAN CATALOGING RULES
IN THE CATALOGING PROCESS

HIGHLIGHTS

Sequences of Steps: Cataloging consists of many sequences of steps, designed to (1) fit a book or other library item effectively into an existing collection, and (2) to make up multiple records for it, so that it can be found through different approaches. This chapter treats the several sequences of steps that are designed to produce effective entry headings. Many variations of sequences are possible, and, on the job, experienced personnel typically handle several sequences simultaneously/ intermittently.

On pages 130-131 is a synopsis-table of all entry heading sequences, A through F. A more detailed breakdown of sequences A and B, the Choice-of-Entry-Headings sequences, is on pages 134-135; of Sequences C-F, the Form-of-Entry-Heading sequences, on page 142.

Using and combining the AA Rules: Some AA Rules are explicit and can be used automatically, others require the cataloger to make a judgment, such as, "Is this a literal translation or not?" A major purpose of this chapter is to introduce the reader, by means of illustrations and exercises, to the careful study and interpretation of selected AA rules. Cataloging rules should be read carefully, interpreted literally, and studied in the context of other rules. The examples that go with the rules should be studied carefully, for they clarify and, sometimes, even expand the text of the rule. This chapter also illustrates how different AA rules must be used in conjunction, for example, on pages 133, 140 and 148.

Clusters of AA Rules: In addition to clustering AA rules by the criteria (1) of the nature of the name, (2) of language, and (3) of personal status, as done in Chapter 5, they can also be grouped according to the *answers* they provide to questions on entry headings: (A) Which of one person's names to select, how thoroughly to record it, how to resolve variant spellings (Khruschev, Khrushchev, Chruschtschow, or Khrouchtchev?), how to distinguish it from other names; (B) What to do with specific types of name situations (for example, persons known only by forename and title, such as Pope Paul V); (C) In what function did an "added entry person" contribute?

Cataloging consists of many sequences of steps that are designed to (1) fit a book or other library item effectively into an existing collection, and (2) to make up multiple records for it, so that it can be found through different approaches.* One sequence of steps gets a book cataloged descriptively,** another sequence gets it physically prepared with charge-out card, plastic wrap, and ownership symbol. This chapter is concerned with the sequences of steps that result in effective entry headings for a book. No one perfect sequence exists: The library's physical layout, its equipment, the working habits of its staff, the librarian's administrative policies, and many other factors cause each library to have its own variations of sequences. Furthermore, experienced catalogers typically handle several of these sequences simultaneously/intermittently to save time and effort. For learning purposes it is best, however, to treat each sequence separately. The following synopsis is fairly typical of entry heading work. Don't let it throw you. It is largely a summary of much that you have read so far.

SYNOPSIS OF THE COMPLETE SEQUENCES OF STEPS USED FOR ENTRY HEADING WORK IN ORIGINAL CATALOGING***

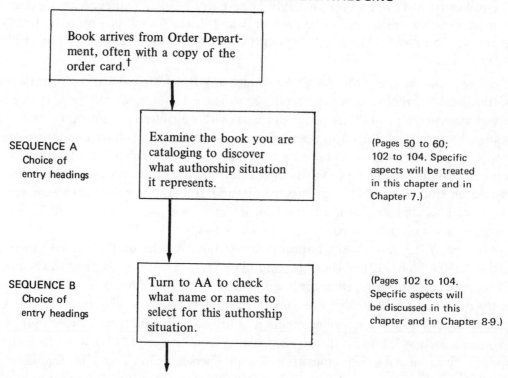

Book arrives from Order Department, often with a copy of the order card.†

SEQUENCE A
Choice of
entry headings

Examine the book you are cataloging to discover what authorship situation it represents.

(Pages 50 to 60; 102 to 104. Specific aspects will be treated in this chapter and in Chapter 7.)

SEQUENCE B
Choice of
entry headings

Turn to AA to check what name or names to select for this authorship situation.

(Pages 102 to 104. Specific aspects will be discussed in this chapter and in Chapter 8-9.)

---

* This was mentioned on pages 1 and 5.

** This topic was treated in volume one of this text.

*** Obviously, when cataloging with Library of Congress cards (see pages 8 to 9) your sequence of steps, and thought processes, would be quite different. You would then, essentially, have to (1) Compare the book you are cataloging with the set of cards received from the Library of Congress to make sure they match; (This aspect is sub-professional, but the following aspects require professional judgment and are often neglected by libraries that like to have their "L.C. cataloging" done entirely by sub-professionals for reasons of immediate economy.) (2) Make sure that the various entry headings the Library of Congress has used for that particular book do not conflict with any already in your catalog; (3) Provide cross-references for names and subject headings as needed; (4) Use the Library of Congress call number, or complete the Dewey Decimal call number, making sure that it does not conflict with one already in your shelflist.

† Order card: A working card for recording bibliographical and price information used in ordering a book. From it, the actual book order is prepared that is mailed to the vendor.

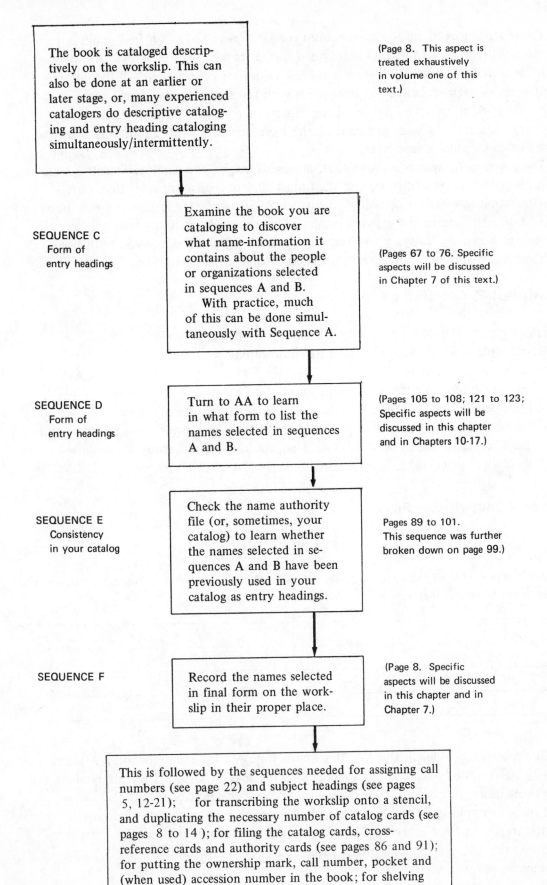

The book is cataloged descriptively on the workslip. This can also be done at an earlier or later stage, or, many experienced catalogers do descriptive cataloging and entry heading cataloging simultaneously/intermittently.

(Page 8. This aspect is treated exhaustively in volume one of this text.)

SEQUENCE C
Form of
entry headings

Examine the book you are cataloging to discover what name-information it contains about the people or organizations selected in sequences A and B.
    With practice, much of this can be done simultaneously with Sequence A.

(Pages 67 to 76. Specific aspects will be discussed in Chapter 7 of this text.)

SEQUENCE D
Form of
entry headings

Turn to AA to learn in what form to list the names selected in sequences A and B.

(Pages 105 to 108; 121 to 123; Specific aspects will be discussed in this chapter and in Chapters 10-17.)

SEQUENCE E
Consistency
in your catalog

Check the name authority file (or, sometimes, your catalog) to learn whether the names selected in sequences A and B have been previously used in your catalog as entry headings.

Pages 89 to 101. This sequence was further broken down on page 99.)

SEQUENCE F

Record the names selected in final form on the workslip in their proper place.

(Page 8. Specific aspects will be discussed in this chapter and in Chapter 7.)

This is followed by the sequences needed for assigning call numbers (see page 22) and subject headings (see pages 5, 12-21);   for transcribing the workslip onto a stencil, and duplicating the necessary number of catalog cards (see pages 8 to 14); for filing the catalog cards, cross-reference cards and authority cards (see pages 86 and 91); for putting the ownership mark, call number, pocket and (when used) accession number in the book; for shelving the book.

These sequences of steps may seem unnecessarily involved upon first reading, particularly when you will find on future pages further breakdowns of several of these sequences. Indeed, on the job, one is usually no longer conscious of all the component parts of each sequence but does them with the sureness that comes from experience, skipping some, intermingling others, or reversing the sequences as the occasion demands. As you read further, the logic behind all this admittedly intricate series of steps will become clear.

The diagramatic synopsis shows that, at several stages, the cataloger meets a situation (Sequence A; Sequence C) and then must find one or more rules that match that situation as closely as possible (Sequence B; Sequence D) so that the new book will fit effectively into the existing catalog. This is somewhat like a lawyer's preparing for a case by studying the Statutes and earlier judicial decisions. Both tasks demand the fitting of a new, given, situation into an existing standard.*

READ RULES CAREFULLY

Cataloging rules should be read with the following thoughts in mind:

Read a rule carefully to understand its full meaning.

Interpret a rule literally. This means, each word in a rule counts. The rule may tell you to **do** something, or that you **may** do something, or that one of two possible solutions is **preferred**. These words carry definite meaning.

Remember that many, but not all, rules handle only one aspect of a situation and are often only one of several possible pigeon holes. Thus, study a rule in the context of other rules, as explained on page 124 of this text.

Choice-of-Entry-Heading Rules

EXERCISE

Turn to a typical choice-of-entry-heading rule, **AA Rule 1A.** Read it carefully, and then jot down below words or phrases that indicate this rule's scope and limitations. _____

_____

_____

_____

_____

_____

Like most other rules in the AA, this one is followed by examples (on AA pages 11-12). Always study the examples along with the text of a rule. They always illustrate, sometimes clarify, and sometimes even expand the text of a rule. But note that these examples do not follow the AA descriptive cataloging rules, but are limited to the parts of an entry that are essential to illustrate a particular entry heading rule. This is explained in the paragraph "Form of examples," on AA page 10. Please read it.

---

* This was also touched on page 124.

EXERCISE

For another example of a choice-of-entry-heading rule, turn to **AA Rule 15A,** read it carefully, and then fill in the answers.

What kinds of translations does the rule cover? (1) _____

What kinds of translations does the rule exclude? (2) _____

For whom should entry headings be made? (3) _____

_____

_____

The author may be (4) _____

_____

Now combine your knowledge of **AA Rules 1A and 15A,** and indicate the main entry heading and added entry heading (if needed) for the following book:

(Although the book itself does not indicate it, you know that the author is Jean Milquetost.)

THE CATALOGER'S FOLLY

a poem

by

****

A literal translation from the French by

Herbert M. Powell

The main entry should be under

(5) _____

An added entry (6) (should) (should not)

be made.

If it should be made, it should be

under (7) _____

You will often need to combine your knowledge of different rules in order to apply any one of them meaningfully, as with the above example.

While studying **AA Rules 1A** and **15A,** did you notice that **AA Rule 1A** is explicit and gives no alternatives but that **AA Rule 15A** requires the cataloger to make a value jugement? "If the translation involves adaptation . . . treat it [not as a translation but] as an adaptation . . . ." In other words, the cataloger must decide whether or not a translation is literal.* Several similar rules exist which give the cataloger some leeway on the basis of his judgment. Making in such cases the most appropriate decision—selecting a group of entry headings that will be most useful to the user of a particular book—calls for experience as well as an understanding of each rule as part of a whole. Future chapters will acquaint you with some of the techniques helpful for making valid decisions.

CHOICE-OF-ENTRY-HEADING SEQUENCES

Having examined two typical choice-of-entry-heading rules let us now study the technique of applying such rules. Following is a more detailed breakdown of sequences A and B as shown on page 145, the sequences used when choosing entry headings for a book.

* The book being cataloged will often indicate this, like the fictitious example above.

CHOICE-OF-ENTRY-HEADING SEQUENCES: BREAKDOWN OF SEQUENCES A AND B FROM PAGES 130-131

SEQUENCE A
STEP 1

> Examine the book you are cataloging to discover what choice-of-main-entry-heading situation it represents.

SEQUENCE B
STEP 2

> Find this situation (or one as close to it as possible) in the AA Index. (See pages 124-126.)

STEP 3

> Turn to the text of the rule or rules you found listed in the AA Index and study it completely to learn whether it applies to the book you are cataloging. (See page 124.)

STEP 4

> Do descriptive cataloging on the work-slip, including tentative listing of the main entry heading. (Tentative because you still need to check the form of the main entry heading.) At this point, your workslip might look like this:

Smith, H   Samuel
Gardening for amateurs, by H. Samuel Smith and Priscilla Wellington-Spade. 2d ed. London, Methuen, 1966.
     xii, 311 p.   illus.   25 cm.

ALTERNATIVES

> (Many catalogers prefer to do tentative descriptive cataloging earlier, say, following STEP 1, sometimes recording the entry at first without a heading. Some libraries have sub-professional employees do tentative descriptive cataloging, preferably by typewriter, preceding or following STEP 1.)

STEP 5

> When more than one author or contributor
> is involved, check **AA Rule 33** for
> guidelines on selecting added entry headings.

STEP 6

> List on the workslip in tentative form
> the name(s) selected as added entry heading(s).
> (Tentative because you still need to check
> the form of the added entry heading(s).)
> At this point, your workslip might look
> like this:

Smith, H   Samuel
    Gardening for amateurs, by H.
Samuel Smith and Priscilla Wellington-
Spade. 2d ed. London, Methuen,
1966.
    xii, 311 p.   illus. 25 cm.

I. Wellington-Spade, Priscilla

This sequence of steps may seem involved upon first reading and, since the example represents a simple and obvious cataloging situation, the sequence may seem unnecessarily complicated. Admittedly, for this book, an experienced cataloger would go through steps 1-3 and 5 in a few seconds, without having to consult the AA. But many books are not as simple as the above example, and for our purposes it seems necessary to be conscious of the different steps. With practice you, too, can go through them quickly and automatically.

Once you have fixed the above sequence in your mind, go on to the following, more detailed, analysis which shows how this sequence of steps might work in a typical situation. Consult the AA while studying this analysis.

APPLICATION OF THE CHOICE-OF-ENTRY-HEADINGS SEQUENCES A AND B TO A TYPICAL SITUATION*

SEQUENCE A   STEP 1

The book you are cataloging represents the following situation:
Shared authorship—
2 authors—
the wording on the title page indicated clearly who the principal author is and who the other (joint) author is.

SEQUENCE B   STEP 2

The Index to the AA leads you from the term "Shared authorship" to **AA Rules 3 and 33B.**

STEP 3

Turning to the text of AA Rule 3 you find that the Preliminary note indicates that AA Rule 3 is *probably* useful for your given situation. But it also mentions **AA Rules 17, 8A, 13, 16, 4, and 5** for specific situations.

Turning to **AA Rules 17, 8A, 13, 16, 4 and 5** you find that none of them applies to your particular book. (Your book is *not* issued by a corporate body, it is *not* prepared jointly by a writer and an artist, etc.)

Thus you proceed with **AA Rule 3** and read **AA Rule 3A.** This *seems* to fit your given situation exactly, but for safety's sake you read on to **AA Rule 3B** and its subdivisions, and to **AA Rule 3C** and its subdivisions.

None of these rules seem to fit your given situation closely, so you go back to **AA Rule 3A** and decide to use it for your given situation.

Now you can study the names that you have *selected* as main and added entry headings for your book and decide *in what form* to list them. This is the subject of another diagram which you will study soon.

STEP 6

On the workslip you add, in tentative form, as a tracing, the name selected as added entry heading on the basis of **AA Rules 3A and 33B.**

STEP 5

But wait—The Index also referred you to **AA Rule 33B!** Therefore, you turn to **AA Rule 33,** read its "Preliminary note," then read **AA Rule 33B,** and relax because it merely confirms what you already know from reading **AA Rule 3A.** (Note that you should have turned to **AA Rule 33** automatically even if the Index had not referred to it.)**

STEP 4

You do descriptive cataloging on a workslip, unless it was done earlier, adding in tentative form the name selected as main entry heading on the basis of **AA Rule 3A.**

* See also pages 130-131 and 134-135.

** If you do not remember why, re-read page 127.

FORM-OF-ENTRY-HEADING RULES

Now let us examine some typical rules for form-of-entry headings. AA Chapter 2 deals with the form-of-personal-name-entry-headings. Like AA Chapter 1, it consists of text and examples, but footnote number 1, on AA page 73, indicates that the examples are not given in the complete form in which they are to be listed as headings. Thus, the first example in **AA Rule 40** is given as

Shakespeare, William

but as an entry heading it should be given as

Shakespeare, William, 1564-1616.

You will learn in one of the next chapters when and how to add such dates, or similar devices.

On page 122 of this text, you grouped **AA Rules 41-51**, and **54-58** on the basis of three criteria;

> Criterion of the nature of the name;
> Criterion of language;
> Criterion of personal status.

These criteria are valid. But it may help to recognize at this point the additional fact that the rules can also be grouped according to the **answers** they provide to questions on entry headings. Looked at from this point of view, the form-of-entry-headings rules for personal names can be grouped as follows:

A. General guidelines, intended to permeate **AA Rules 40-58**:

  I. **Which of one person's names** should be selected as entry heading if he is known by several names, or if his name consists of several parts, or if he prefers one of his names over the other?
AA Rules 40, 41, 42. 44.

  II. **How completely to record** the name selected, how to resolve variant spellings of one name, and how to distinguish one name from similar ones used as headings?
AA Rules 43, 45, 52, 53.

B. What to do with **specific name situations**, such as surnames with prefixes, forenames used in lieu of surnames, or names that follow social customs different from ours.
AA Rules 46, 47, 48, 49, 50, 51, 54, 55, 56, 57, 58.

C. In what **function** did a person under whom an added entry is made, contribute to a work?
(*"Designation of function in heading,"* **pages 10-11 of the AA.**)

You need not study and memorize the individual rules at this point, but you should be aware of these groups. When confronted with large numbers of different name situations and of specific rules, it helps to remember that the form-of-entry-heading rules can be clustered according to several mutually **not** exclusive catagories:

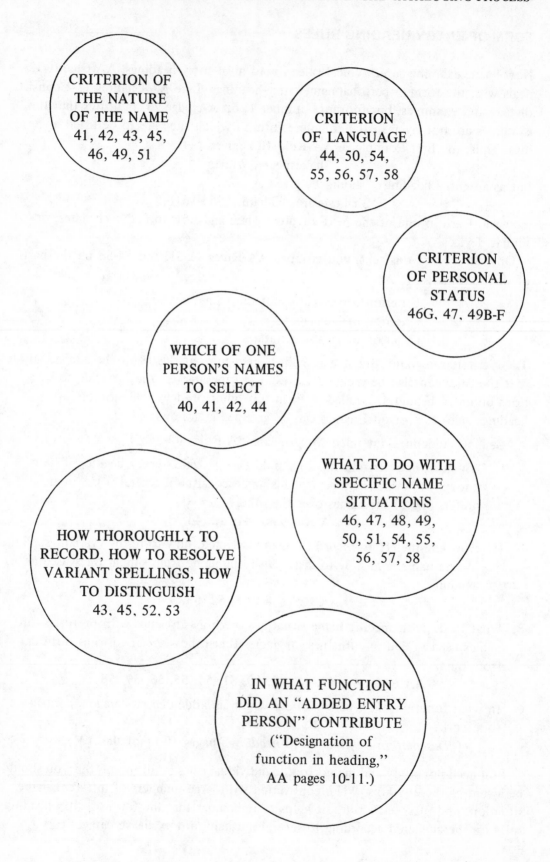

CRITERION OF
THE NATURE
OF THE NAME
41, 42, 43, 45,
46, 49, 51

CRITERION
OF LANGUAGE
44, 50, 54,
55, 56, 57, 58

CRITERION
OF PERSONAL
STATUS
46G, 47, 49B-F

WHICH OF ONE
PERSON'S NAMES
TO SELECT
40, 41, 42, 44

WHAT TO DO WITH
SPECIFIC NAME
SITUATIONS
46, 47, 48, 49,
50, 51, 54, 55,
56, 57, 58

HOW THOROUGHLY TO
RECORD, HOW TO RESOLVE
VARIANT SPELLINGS, HOW
TO DISTINGUISH
43, 45, 52, 53

IN WHAT FUNCTION
DID AN "ADDED ENTRY
PERSON" CONTRIBUTE
("Designation of
function in heading,"
AA pages 10-11.)

To get acquainted with a typical form-of-entry-heading rule, read **AA Rule 46B3a.** This is one of several rules dealing with compound surnames, that is, family names that consist of two or more proper names. Although little known in this country they are not infrequent abroad. In the United States and in Scandinavia, a name such as John Prentice Taylor consists almost always of two forenames and one surname

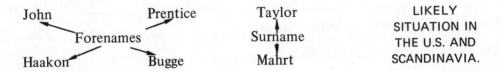

On the other hand, when dealing with foreign names, a middle name that looks like a surname really is almost always the first part of the surname. While the American John Prentice Taylor is apt to be Mr. Taylor, and his book therefore listed under "T," the British John Prentice Taylor is likely to be Mr. Prentice Taylor, and his book will be listed under "P."

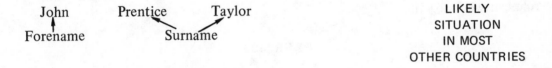

EXERCISE

Read **AA Rule 46B3a,** study the examples, and then answer the following questions.[*]

* The see-reference tracing "x" is explained on AA page 10, and pages 98 to 101 of this text, show how to turn it into a see-reference.

What names does this rule include? (1)_____

_____

_____

Exclusions and limitations are (2)_____

_____

_____

_____

What are the central tendencies of this rule? (3) _____

_____

_____

_____

Should we make see-references? (4) _____

_____

_____

On page 133, you did an exercise designed to show how two choice-of-entry-headings rules work together. Now let us show how a "choice" rule and a "form" rule can work together.

EXERCISE

Combine your knowledge of **AA Rules 1A** and **46B3a** and provide (1) the correct main entry heading and (2) any cross-reference needed for the situation illustrated below. (Ordinarily, you might have to consult reference works to learn the facts that will help you make the necessary decisions. In this imaginary example, the facts are provided.)

Introducing
Problematical Solutions
to Simple
Entry Heading Problems

By

Cecil Dunstan Pawe

Checking on this name you
find that Mr. Cecil Dunstan
Pawe is a British librarian
who is listed in British
reference works under the
letter "D."

The main entry heading is:

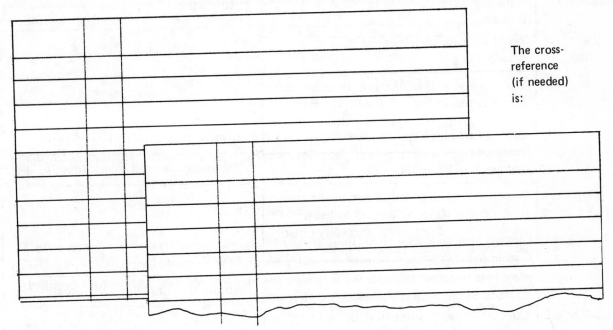

The cross-
reference
(if needed)
is:

The important part of this exercise was that you had to apply first a choice-of-entry-heading rule and then a form-of-entry-heading rule. This is the standard procedure that you will be following, with variations. Sometimes, indeed, you will need to apply more than one "choice" and one "form" rule.

FORM-OF-ENTRY-HEADING-SEQUENCES

On pages 130-131 you saw an overview of sequences A-F, the complete sequences of steps used in entry heading work. On pages 134 to 136 you saw further analyses of sequences A and B, the choice-of-entry-headings sequences. Now you will meet an analysis of sequences C-F, the sequences of steps ordinarily followed for form-of-entry-headings decisions. Don't let the following chart "throw" you. Follow it step by step. It merely shows that you look up a fact and then record it. Then you look up the next fact, record it, and so forth.

FORM-OF-ENTRY-HEADING SEQUENCE: BREAKDOWN OF SEQUENCES C TO FROM PAGE 130-131

STEP 1

SEQUENCE C — For each name selected examine the book you are cataloging to learn what type of name it is, and what facts about the name or the person the book reveals.

STEP 2 — Note any name information in tentative form on the workslip.
(Once you are really experienced, you would then sometimes turn directly to Step 8.)

STEP 3

SEQUENCE D — Find this type of name in the AA Index.

STEP 4 — Turn to the text of the rule or rules you found listed in the AA Index, to learn how to record this type of name and whether to make any see- references.

STEP 5 — Adjust the workslip accordingly.

STEP 6 — If you are dealing with a personal name, look up AA Rules 52 and 53 to learn when to add dates or (if necessary) distinguishing terms to a personal name.

STEP 7 — Adjust the workslip accordingly

STEP 8

SEQUENCE E — Check the name authority file to learn whether this particular name has been previously used as an entry heading in your catalog.

STEP 9a — If yes, make the old and the new agree.

STEP 9b — If not, make a name authority card for the new name. Often, this involves checking reference works.

SEQUENCE F

STEP 10 — Record the name, in final form, on the workslip, in its proper place: Either as the main entry heading, or as a tracing.

With experience you will find that some of these steps can be omitted. Also, you will find that, for main entry headings, in a smoothly running library, some of this work can be done ahead of time, at the time the book is ordered. Remember that this is a learning situation in which you are learning the full thought-and-action sequence. Short cuts can come with experience.

Once you have fixed the above sequence in your mind, go on to the following, more detailed, analysis which shows how this form-of-entry-heading sequence might work in a typical situation. Consult the AA while studying this analysis.

APPLICATION OF THE FORM-OF-ENTRY HEADINGS SEQUENCE TO A TYPICAL SITUATION*

SEQUENCE C

STEP 1

Examination of the book you are cataloging shows that the name with which you are dealing represents the following situation:

A personal author, male, apparently using a compound surname.

The title page lists him as *Cecil Dunstan Pawe,* the jacket** refers to him as *Mr. Dunstan Pawe* and indicates that he is a British librarian and was born in 1946.

STEP 2

You record this name information on the workslip in tentative form. From this information you can later on produce an authority card, if needed.

Dunstan Pawe, Cecil
Introducing problematical solutions to simple entry heading problems. 1st ed. New York,

t.-p.: Cecil Dunstan Pawe
jacket: Brit. lib., Mr. Dunstan Pawe, b. 1946.

* See also pages 130-131 and 142.

** Jacket, or book jacket: The printed or unprinted paper cover placed around a bound book. In addition to the author's name and the title, it often contains information about the author, his other works, favorable comments about the book (what has come to be known as the publisher's "blurb"), an indication of the contents, or advertising notices for selected other books put out by the same publisher.

SEQUENCE D

STEP 3

> The AA Index leads you from the term "Compound sur-names" to **AA Rules 46B** and **121A3**, as well as to the definition on AA page 344.

STEP 4

> Turning to the text of **AA Rule 46B,** you read first through its "Preliminary note," noting that it tells you to apply the sub-rules in the order given.

> **AA Rule 46B1** tells you to use the preferred or estab-lished order of name. According to your information (from STEP 1) this seems to be *Dunstan Pawe.* *

> **AA Rule 46B2** does not concern you since he does not seem to use a hyphen.

> But **AA Rule 46B3a** seems to be the important one for your man, so you study it and its examples carefully.

> **AA Rule 46B3b** you can obviously ignore, and **AA Rule 46B4** also seems not to apply (since the book jacket refers to him as *Mr. Dunstant Pawe, not as Mr. Pawe*). Finally, a quick glance at **AA Rules 46C** through **46E** shows that they also do not apply to your given situa-tion.

STEP 5

> Since your check gave you no additional or different information you need only add to your workslip that a see-reference is needed if the name is new to your cata-log.

> t.p.: Cecil Dunstan Pawe
> jacket: Brt.lib. Mr. Dunstan Pawe, 1946
> x Pawe, Cecil Dunstan

* On pages 89, 102, and 107 you learned that, typically, the book being cataloged is the first (and usually also final) source for name decisions. This will be further illustrated in Chapter 7.

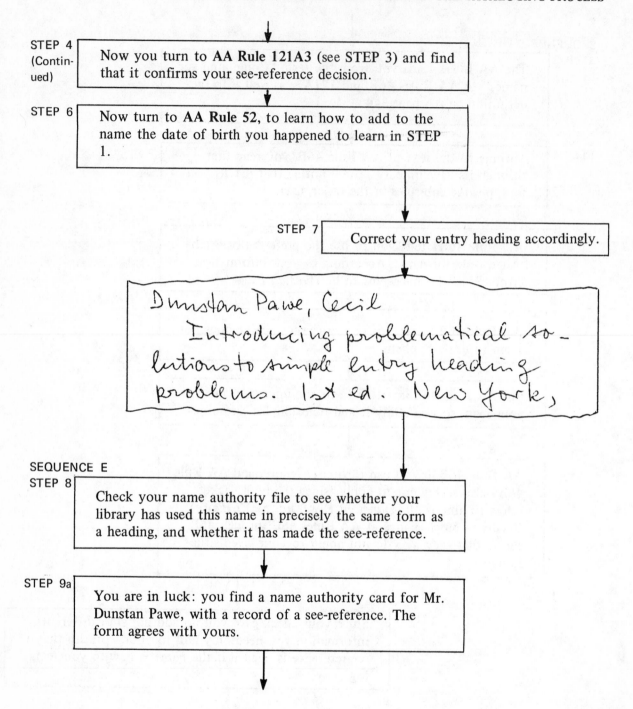

STEP 4
(Contin-
ued)

Now you turn to **AA Rule 121A3** (see STEP 3) and find that it confirms your see-reference decision.

STEP 6

Now turn to **AA Rule 52**, to learn how to add to the name the date of birth you happened to learn in STEP 1.

STEP 7

Correct your entry heading accordingly.

> Dunstan Pawe, Cecil
>   Introducing problematical so-
> lutions to simple entry heading
> problems. 1st ed. New York,

SEQUENCE E
STEP 8

Check your name authority file to see whether your library has used this name in precisely the same form as a heading, and whether it has made the see-reference.

STEP 9a

You are in luck: you find a name authority card for Mr. Dunstan Pawe, with a record of a see-reference. The form agrees with yours.

Dunstan Pawe, Cecil, 1946-
        xPawe, Cecil Dunstan

√√ Bk. cat. (Faceted classification. 1965.)
√√d Bk. cat., jacket: b. 1946.
    No conflict.   RKS 9-7-66

THIS AUTHORITY
CARD WAS ALREADY
IN THE AUTHORITY
FILE

SEQUENCE F
STEP 10

Now a final correction on your workslip, and then you
are ready for subject heading and classification work.
(See page 131, bottom frame.)

t.-p.: Cecil Dunstan Pawe
jacket: Brit. l.b., Mr. Dunstan Pawe, b. 1946.
x Pawe, Cecil Dunstan

This must have seemed an interminably long process. It is, indeed, time consuming. But remember that it takes often far longer to read about a process than to do it. Also, with experience, this process goes faster, and you will be able to omit several steps most of the time, for example STEP 6 in the preceding chart. Finally, with experience, you will learn to handle several names at once. Thus you would, for example, go to the authority file with five or six workslips to check on all of them at once, rather than go five or six separate times.

EXERCISE

To get acquainted with another form-of-entry-heading rule read **AA Rule 42** (ignoring the footnote for the present). Study the examples, and then fill in the following questions.

The rule covers (1) _____

_____

It excluded (2) _____

_____

Authors who always write under one pseudonym are entered under their (3) _____

_____

Authors who use several pseudonyms or pseudonym(s) and their real name are entered under

(4) _____

The intent of **AA Rule 42** seems to be (5) _____

_____

_____

Should you make see-references? (6) _____

_____

   You will have noticed that this rule gives you several alternatives. It requires decisions. For some decisions you will need to consult reference works, but usually the book being cataloged gives sufficient information.*

EXERCISE

Now combine your knowledge of **AA Rules 1A, 42, 46B3a, and 52,** and provide the correct main entry heading and any see-references needed for the following situation. Ordinarily, you would need to consult reference works to learn the facts that will help you make the necessary decisions. In this imaginary example, the facts are provided.

* See pages 89, 102, and 107.

THE NUCLEUS

OF

CATALOGING

By

James Card

Checking up on this name you learn that *James Card* is the pseudonym of *James Edward Spence Penniston,* a British librarian who writes mostly under his real name. British reference works list this name as a compound name. He was born in 1931.

The main entry heading is

The cross-references (if needed) are

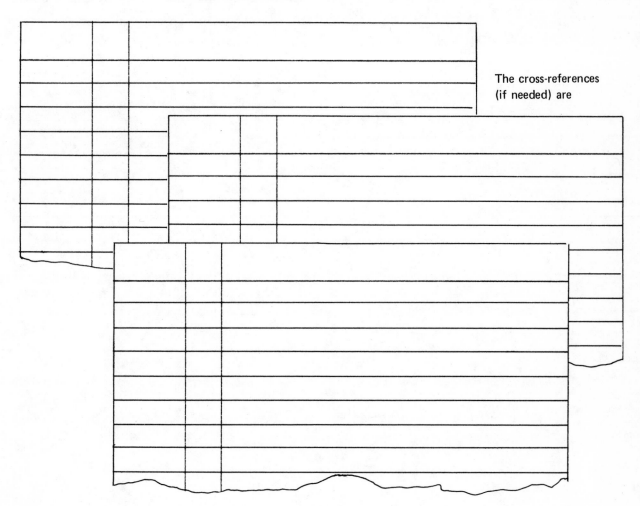

The purpose of this exercise was to give you further practice in applying a combination of rules to one given situation. In this particular case the combination consisted of one "choice" rule and three "form" rules. Together, they answered the following questions:

(1) Under whom is a "one author" situation book listed? (2) If the person whose name was selected as a heading uses a pseudonym once in a while, which of his names shall be used as heading and which as see-reference? (3) If one decides to use the author's real name and this happens to be a compound surname, under which part of his surname should the book be entered? (5) What, if any, cross-reference(s) should be made?

CHAPTER SEVEN

EXAMINING A BOOK FOR ENTRY HEADINGS

HIGHLIGHTS

Experienced catalogers become adept at examining a book simultaneously for all phases of cataloging: Descriptive cataloging, entry headings, subject headings, and classification. This chapter treats one of these examinations: It shows the type of entry heading information for which you are to search and where, in the book you are cataloging, you are most likely to find it. This chapter illustrates in detail Sequences A and C that were described in Chapter 6 on pages 130-131, 134-136, 142, and 144-147.

Sources for Entry Heading Information: The first, the basic, and usually the only, source for entry heading information is the book being cataloged. While some books give, intentionally or otherwise, wrong or misleading entry heading information, this text does not deal with them. Our problem is to find the information and interpret it at face value. In the book, the most useful sources are the title page or a substitute for it, the verso of the title page, the preface, foreword and introduction, and the book jacket. Always start with the title page to check for entry heading information, but then also check all the other sources noted, for they can correct, or round out, the title page information. Additional information from outside sources, such as bibliographies, often travels with the book to the Catalog Department and may also have to be considered.

Title page: Among the authorship situations which a title page may show are single authorship or editorship, and multiple authorship. Type size and phraseology often indicate who the primary author is. Multiple authorship can be truly "shared" or "joint": All individuals mentioned seem to be responsible for the entire book. Or, it can be "multiple," with each individual clearly responsible for a separate section or chapter. In addition, in any one of these situations there can also be "contributors," that is individuals who make either a relatively minor, or a very specialized, contribution.

Title pages sometimes also list names of persons or organizations that did not create the book but still had a significant connection with it, and whose names might thus be needed as entry headings.

Cover, Spine, Half-title: They give sometimes only the author's surname rather than his full name. This can help in establishing the form of a name. They also tend to list only the people primarily responsible. This can help with the choice of a main entry heading. *Verso of the Title Page:* It may give, in the copyright notice, the author's real name, or a fuller form of his name; it may give the names of contributors. But, more often than not, it gives no entry heading information. *Book jacket:* Often contributes biographical and bibliographical information that helps identify an individual. This may be important if someone with an almost identical name is already in your catalog. Typically, it helps with the form rather than the choice of an entry heading. *Caption title and colophon*: Typically do not help in entry heading work. *Preface, Introduction, Text*: Most useful for determining a book's subject matter (which is outside the scope of this volume), but AA wishes us to use them for entry heading work only as a last resort, and only if the other sources listed are clearly insufficient, ambiguous, or contradictory. Especially in the case of corporate authorship the Preface or Foreword may clarify an organization's name or role, thus helping with choice and form of entry heading. *Bibliography and Vita*: Like the Book Jacket, often help with respect to the form of an entry heading.

The last part of this chapter amalgamates the content of Chapters 6 and 7: The reader has a chance to examine a particular book, and to prepare a workslip in the context of the complete entry headings sequences of steps.

The experienced cataloger becomes adept at examining a book simultaneously for all phases of cataloging: Descriptive cataloging, entry headings, subject headings and classification. For learning purposes, however, these processes are best divided into separate sequences of steps. Volume one of this text shows, among other things, how to examine a book for descriptive cataloging. Entry heading work requires a somewhat different, but just as thorough, examination of the book. Therefore, the purpose of this chapter is to show the type of entry heading information for which you are to search and where, in the book you are cataloging, you are most likely to find it.

Please review, on pages 130-131, the synopsis of the entry headings sequences. In the preceding chapter we went hypothetically through sequences A-F of that synopsis.* This chapter examines sequences A and C.

The synopsis on page 130-131 shows that the purpose of examining a book for entry heading work is twofold:

(1) **To find out what authorship situation the book represents** (Sequence A) —is it a book written by one person or is the responsibility shared; is it the product of an organization rather than of a person; is it the text of a law or an adaptation**of an existing work, etc. This will help in the choice of main and added entry headings.

(2) **To find out what name information the book contains about the people or organizations that have been selected as main or added entry headings.** Many books provide facts about these names, such as birth and death dates for persons and location for organizations. These facts, when interpreted according to the AA, will help you to record the selected names in suitable form, and to decide whether or not a name is new to your catalog.***

---

* Shown in greater detail on pages 134-136, 142, and 144-147.

** Adaptation: 1. A rewritten form of a literary work modified for a purpose or use other than that for which the original work was intended. 2. A new version based upon one or more versions of a given work or story. . . (Elizabeth H. Thompson, *A.L.A. Glossary of Library Terms.* Chicago, American Library Association, 1943).

*** The importance of knowing whether or not a name is new to your catalog can be seen from pages 67-70.

FIRST SOURCE: THE BOOK BEING CATALOGED

The basic, and usually only, source for gathering entry heading information about a book is the book itself. Just as the book being cataloged is used as the source for cataloging it descriptively* so it is used as the source for its own entry heading information. This means that you can accept the entry heading information given in the book being cataloged. This is the basic assumption on which this whole chapter rests. Therefore:

When the book indicates that it was
written by Mr. "A" and Mr. "B" . . . . you can assume that it really
                                                                was written by them.

When the book indicates that it was
written by Mr. "C" with the assistance of Mr. "D"you can assume that Mr. "D" really
                                                                only provided assistance.

When the book indicates that it is
an adaptation of another work . . . . you can assume that it really is
                                                                an adaptation.

Conversely, when the book does not
indicate clearly that it is an
adaptation of another work . . . . .you can assume that it is not
                                                                an adaptation.

While some books give, intentionally or otherwise, wrong or misleading entry heading information this text does not deal with them. Our problem will be to find the information and to interpret it at face value.

---

* "The librarian takes the book—cover, spine, title page, text, appendices, bibliographies, indexes, and all—and translates it into an entry." (John J. Boll, *Introduction to Cataloging. Vol. 1: Descriptive Cataloging*. . . New York, McGraw-Hill Book Co. [c1970], p. 53.)

Four Stages of Examination

To learn how the AA wish us to proceed when examining a book for entry heading information, turn to **AA page 9** and read carefully the paragraph entitled "Sources for determining entry."*

EXERCISE

Did you notice that the sources are divided into four groups or stages of examination? List these four stages, or groups, below.

Stage 1: _____

Stage 2: _____

_____

_____

Stage 3: _____

_____

Stage 4: _____

_____

It is unfortunate that the AA omit the book jacket from this list. When one is available, always examine it thoroughly, because it often gives biographical information about the author. It may give his date of birth, or both his birth and death dates. It may list other names under which he has written. It may mention other works which he wrote or to which he contributed. It may tell you enough about him to help you determine whether or not he is the same person as one already listed in your catalog.

It is also unrealistic of the AA to relegate "outside sources" to the last stage. In practice, information from outside sources often travels with the book to the Catalog Department and is the first thing the cataloger sees. If a pseudonym is involved, for example, the Order Department often finds this out from the bibliographies while ordering the book, and forwards this information to the Catalog Department. (See top frame on page 130.)

---

* The terms entry, main entry, and added entry, as customarily defined, are ambiguous because each refers to two different things. (The "Glossary" in the back of the AA gives these standard definitions.) To avoid this confusion, this text distinguishes between an entry (main or added) ad the *complete record* of a bibliographical entity in a catalog or list, and the entry heading (main or added) as the word or words under which an entry is *listed.* According to these definitions, the AA really mean on page 9, "Sources for determining entry *headings.*"

MOST USEFUL SOURCES FOR ENTRY HEADING INFORMATION

For most books you will find most helpful for entry heading work one or more of the following, and I recommend that you always examine them carefully:

- Title page, or a substitute for it;
- Verso of the title page
- Preface, foreword, or introduction
- Book jacket

The **title page*** is a page, or a double page spread at the beginning of a book giving its title, author or authors (if acknowledged), usually its publisher, and often its place and date of publication. Typically, it also includes a number of other items of information: the edition number, the names of other contributors to the work such as illustrators, translators, or editors, and sometimes even an apt quotation. But, except for title, author and publisher, any of these items may be listed instead on the verso of the title page or even in the preface or foreword.

A **substitute for the title page** is any other part of a book that gives its title and, perhaps, also author and publisher when there is no title page. The most common substitute for the title page, especially among paper-covered pamphlets of less than 50 pages, is the **cover**, that is, the front and back halves of the outer shell of a book.

The **verso of the title page** is the back of the title page, which usually lists the date and holders of the copyright. It may also carry the dates and numbers of earlier editions and previous impressions and the name and address of the printer along with other information concerning the production of the book.

The **preface** is an explanatory note written by the author and preceding the text, giving the purpose of the book, its sources, the author's qualifications or his reasons for writing the book, or his acknowledgments to persons who have helped him in the work.

The **foreword** fulfills most of the functions of the preface but is written by someone other than the author.

The **introduction** defines the scope and level of the text, outlines its manner of organization or content, or in some other way provides the reader with perspective on it. It often leads directly into the text proper.

---

* Partly defined on page 50.

The **book jacket, or jacket,** is the printed or unprinted paper cover placed around a bound book. In addition to the author's name and title, it often contains information about the author, his other works, favorable comments about the book (what has come to be known as the publisher's "blurb"), an indication of the contents, or advertising notices for selected other books put out by the same publisher.

These are the most useful sources for entry heading information, but it is worth remembering that many books vary from the above definitions. For example, a book's Introduction may really be its Preface. When checking the physical makeup of books you will find innumerable variations, but this will not cause any difficulties in entry heading work.

Always check for entry heading information all of the sources listed on pages 156 and 157 and, in case of uncertainty, proceed to the other sources you filled in on page 155, because any one of them may be incomplete and even misleading by itself. For example:

The title page may give you the correct author and title of the work—but the preface may indicate that it is an adaptation of another work.

The title page may show that the book is a one-author situation—but its verso may show that the author's name as given on the title page is really a pseudonym.

The title page and preface may give the two joint author's names, using initials for their forenames. —The jacket may add the full forenames of one author and date of birth for the other.

Now let us examine how each stage, and the various sources within each stage, may help the cataloger in entry heading work.

STAGE 1: THE TITLE PAGE OF THE BOOK BEING CATALOGED

Always turn first to the title page for entry heading information. When no title page exists, turn to a substitute, that is, another page that contains similar information. Usually this would be the cover.

The title page will generally list the name of the author and all others who contributed significantly to the intellectual content of the work, whether it be a joint author, or a contributor such as a translator, editor, or illustrator. You have already encountered many different author situations on title pages.

Single Authorship

A typical title page for a "single authorship" situation is on page 71. It represents an ordinary situation with a plain author statement: "By Ray Stannard Baker." Some author statements, like the example on page 61, do not contain the word "by," and the author's name can be below the title, or above, as in the example on page 167. The example below, on the other hand, has no real author statement, but the wording on the title page still shows clearly who the intellectual creator of these poems is.

COLLECTED POEMS
OF ROBERT FROST

NEW YORK
HENRY HOLT AND COMPANY

Pages 52 and 173 show situations in which one person did not literally write the intellectual content but gathered it together. He has, thus, intellectual responsibility for the existence of this particular package, although he is not the creator of its contents. Page 63 (Strawberry Girl) represents a situation in which one person seems responsible for both the text and the illustrations.

Note that we have so far accepted, without question, the facts as stated on the title page. To correct, or round out, the title page information it is necessary to go to other parts of the book. (See page 157.) But we always work on the assumption that the information in the book being cataloged, taken together, can be taken at face value. (See also page 154.)

Multiple Authorship

Several kinds and degrees of multiple authorship situations exist. They range from shared creation of a book's content to the creation of a specific section, or to providing substantial assistance, and are discussed on the following pages. The corresponding AA Rules are discussed in Chapter 8.

Multiple Authorship: Shared Authorship

This concept, also known as joint authorship, covers situations in which several authors share responsibility for a work more or less equally, but their individual responsibility is undefined. One of two authors may have written the first draft and the other revised it; each author may have had primary responsbility for half the book; other kinds of cooperation may have existed, but the book does not indicate this, nor do we really need to know. The person named first on the title page is generally considered the main author—if he were not, his name would not be 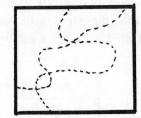 first—and thus generally receives the main entry heading. For an example of a straightforward "two author" situation turn to page 50. Note that, at this stage in the examination of a book, we rely on the wording on the title page of the book being cataloged as the clue that this seems to be a "two authors" situation.

EXERCISE

Please turn to page 64 (An Introduction to Medieval Europe) and answer the following questions: Judging, at this stage, only by the title page, for whom should you make the main entry heading? (1) _____

For whom should you make the added entry heading? (2) _____

_____

Type Size: Sometimes a Clue

The size of the type is sometimes, but not always, a clue that shows what is more or less important, and who played a greater or lesser role. In title transcription,* for example, variations in type size are significant only if they separate phrases.

Business Law

BY THE

Case Method

From a bibliographic standpoint, the variation in type size means nothing in the above example. This is clearly one title, transcribed as: Business law by the case method.

---

* This takes us, for a moment, outside the realm of entry headings. But it should help to create a framework within which we can operate.

The UNIVERSITY LIBRARY

THE ORGANIZATION, ADMINISTRATION, AND

FUNCTIONS OF ACADEMIC LIBRARIES

In the above example the variation in type size, and especially the fact that separate phrases are involved, show that this is a title and subtitle, transcribed as: The university library; the organization, administration and functions of academic libraries.

In author statements, type size is almost always considered a significant clue. Usually, it supports the wording. In the example below, both type size and wording indicate that Edmund W. Janss is the author and thus receives the main entry heading.

By EDMUND W. JANSS

With a Foreword by
Dr. Daniel A. Poling

In the following example, type size is no clue as to who is the main author, but the wording is. Thus, Wilson would become typically the main entry heading, and Tauber the added entry heading.

By LOUIS ROUND WILSON
and MAURICE F. TAUBER

EXERCISE

In this exercise, wording and type size on the title page give conflicting clues. Judging, at this stage, only by the title page, which of these names should become the main entry heading?

(1) _____

Which should become the added entry headings? (2) _____

_____

by
JOHN SMITH
AGNES BAKER
and
JAMES MILLER

A "Three Authors" Situation

Note that in none of the "Shared authorship" situations you have seen so far, does the title page indicate that one author was responsible for one section of the book, and someone else for another. This is what makes them true "joint authorship" situations.

Scientific and Technical Libraries

Their Organization and Administration

Lucille J. Strauss

CHEMISTRY AND PHYSICS LIBRARIAN
THE PENNSYLVANIA STATE UNIVERSITY
UNIVERSITY PARK, PENNSYLVANIA

Irene M. Strieby

CONSULTANT IN ORGANIZATION OF
SPECIAL LIBRARIES AND COMPANY ARCHIVES

Alberta L. Brown

ASSOCIATE PROFESSOR
WESTERN MICHIGAN UNIVERSITY
KALAMAZOO, MICHIGAN

Interscience Publishers

a division of John Wiley and Sons, New York • London • Sydney

Multiple Authorship: Separate Responsibilities

In this situation, one author or editor is responsible for gathering together the complete package, but the various sections or chapters are clearly labeled as the product of different authors. This responsibility is usually not shown on the title page but is typically indicated clearly in the Table of Contents. In the following example, the title page only lists the names of the various authors, but the Table of Contents lists their individual contributions.

EDITOR			
Author 1	Author 2	Author 3	Author 4

INTRODUCTION TO THE GREAT RELIGIONS

JEAN DANIELOU, S.J.

ANDRE RETIF, S.J.

JOSEPH HOURS, S.J.

FRANCOIS HOUANG

MAURICE QUEGUINER, P.F.M.

R. P. DUNOYER, P.F.M.

R. P. DEMANN

GASTON FESSARD, S.J.

Translated by Albert J. La Mothe, Jr.

FIDES PUBLISHERS, INC.
NOTRE DAME, INDIANA

CONTENTS

In the example below, the title page does not even list the names but the table of contents lists names and contributions.

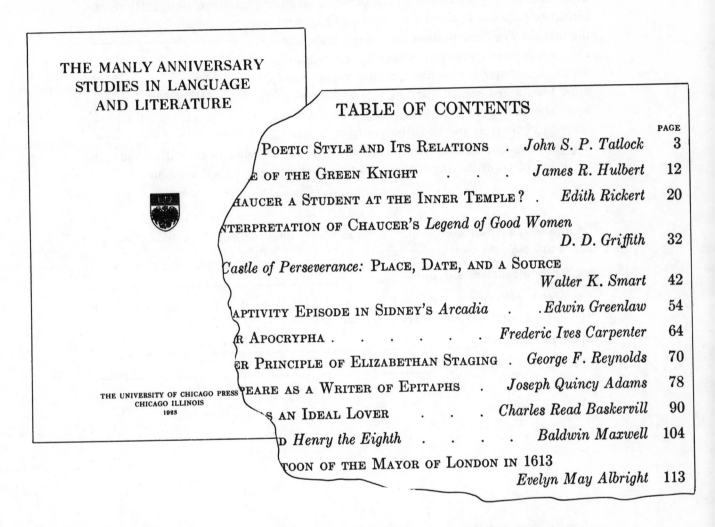

THE MANLY ANNIVERSARY STUDIES IN LANGUAGE AND LITERATURE

THE UNIVERSITY OF CHICAGO PRESS
CHICAGO ILLINOIS
1923

TABLE OF CONTENTS

		PAGE
POETIC STYLE AND ITS RELATIONS .	*John S. P. Tatlock*	3
E OF THE GREEN KNIGHT . . .	*James R. Hulbert*	12
HAUCER A STUDENT AT THE INNER TEMPLE? .	*Edith Rickert*	20
NTERPRETATION OF CHAUCER'S *Legend of Good Women*	*D. D. Griffith*	32
Castle of Perseverance: PLACE, DATE, AND A SOURCE	*Walter K. Smart*	42
APTIVITY EPISODE IN SIDNEY'S *Arcadia* .	*.Edwin Greenlaw*	54
R APOCRYPHA	*Frederic Ives Carpenter*	64
ER PRINCIPLE OF ELIZABETHAN STAGING .	*George F. Reynolds*	70
PEARE AS A WRITER OF EPITAPHS .	*Joseph Quincy Adams*	78
S AN IDEAL LOVER . . .	*Charles Read Baskervill*	90
D *Henry the Eighth*	*Baldwin Maxwell*	104
TOON OF THE MAYOR OF LONDON IN 1613	*Evelyn May Albright*	113

You will learn the entry heading rules for such situations in Chapter 8. Note that the last two examples, on pages 164 to 165, differ from the example on page 173. The examples on pages 164 to 165 illustrate individual contributions created to be presented together. The editor's names are not mentioned on the title pages. Thus, by inference, they seem to have played a relatively minor role in the creation of these works and do not receive the main entry heading. But the work on page 173 consists of many different items, wirtten at various times for other purposes and other publications. The editor's name is mentioned prominently on the title page. By inference, he seems responsible for the work and his name is used as the main entry heading. This seems justified since he culled the editorials from their original sources and brought them together to create this particular work. There are many instances where typography and wording on the title page help us in our initial decisions on the main and added entry headings.

Multiple Authorship: Authors with Contributors*

This concept covers situations in which one or more persons or organizations are primarily responsible for the content while one or more others contributed support-ing matter. The contribution may range from writing the introduction to drawing illustrations, translating or editing the writer's thoughts, assisting the author(s) in some fashion, or actually writing a few chapters of the text. The difference between sharing in the authorship (pages 159 to 165) and contributing to it, is one of

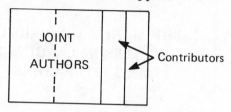

degree. Later on, we shall study the rules that tell us what to do with these differ-ent levels of contribution. Now we just need to recognize their existence.

EXERCISE

On page 55 is a typical example of a "single authorship plus contributor" situation. Judging only by the title page, the contributor's name is (1) _____

and the contribution consists of (2) _____

A somewhat different situation is illustrated below. Judging at this stage only by the title page, indicate who had primary responsibility for this book (3) _____

Who contributed (4) _____

What was the contribution (5) _____

---

* The concept of the contributor as against the joint author was explained on page 20.

LUCRETIA P. HALE

T H E

Complete

Peterkin Papers

With the original illustrations

Introduction by N A N C Y H A L E

HOUGHTON MIFFLIN COMPANY BOSTON

The Riverside Press Cambridge

What authorship situation does the example below represent?

HYDROGEOLOGY

by J. B. Lamarck

translated by Albert V. Carozzi

University of Illinois Press, Urbana, 1964

(Your answer) _____

Notice that the above title page implies by its wording that Albert V. Carozzi translated this text literally. If he had expanded or adapted it in the process of translation, the book would indicate this. Therefore, Lamarck is still the creator of this text even though it uses a new language as its vehicle.

Multiple Authorship: Author(s) with Contributor(s)

A somewhat analogous situation, in which one person created the intellectual content while someone else edited it, is shown at the left.

EXERCISE

On the basis of the title page, who seems to be the author of this work?

(1) _____

_____

The editor is

(2) _____

_____

𝕳eath's 𝕸odern 𝕷anguage 𝕾eries

LE VERRE D'EAU

OU

LES EFFETS ET LES CAUSES

PAR

EUGÈNE SCRIBE

EDITED WITH NOTES AND VOCABULARY

BY

CHARLES A. EGGERT, PH.D.

D. C. HEATH & CO., PUBLISHERS

BOSTON   NEW YORK   CHICAGO

*Understanding
Educational Research*
AN INTRODUCTION

DEOBOLD B. VAN DALEN

Professor of Education, University of Pittsburgh

WITH TWO CHAPTERS BY

WILLIAM J. MEYER

*Associate Professor of Psychology and Education,
University of Pittsburgh*

McGRAW-HILL BOOK COMPANY, INC.   *1962*

New York   San Francisco   Toronto   London

Notice how different the type of contribution is in the example at the left. Judging at this stage only by the title page, who had primary responsibility for this book?

(1) _____

_____

Who contributed?

(2) _____

_____

What was the contribution?

(3) _____

_____

Note that contributors, like authors, are typically listed on the title page. But there are exceptions, as you will soon see.

Other Relationships

Title pages will sometimes also list names of additional persons or organizations that did not create a book but still had a significant connection with it, and whose names might thus be needed as added entry headings.*

PROBLEMS IN UNIVERSITY LIBRARY MANAGEMENT

A Study Conducted by Booz, Allen & Hamilton, Inc., for the Association of Research Libraries and the American Council on Education

Association of Research Libraries
Washington, D. C.

1970

This title page explains the relationship. The preface or foreword, or possibly even the blurb, should give further information in such cases to help you decide whether or not to make added entry headings for the Association of Research Libraries and for the American Council on Education.

* See "The concept of the user's approaches," page 102.

When these names are listed above, or at the head of, the book's title, they typically do **not** explain the organization's role. In such situations it is essential to turn to other parts of the book—most likely the preface or foreword— to learn whether the organization is closely enough connected with this book to justify an added entry heading. In the example below, the cataloger found the explanation on the book's unnumbered page 3, and decided to make an added entry heading for the American Historical Association's Albert J. Beveridge Memorial Fund.*

---

* In case of question, see "Justifying an Added Entry Heading," pages 47-48. See also **AA Rule 33,** especially **33H.** Many research libraries make, by policy, an added entry for a sponsor. But it would have been equally correct to make an added entry merely for the American Historical Association.

The American Historical Association

SOUTHERN EDITORIALS
ON SECESSION

Edited by

DWIGHT LOWELL DUMOND, Ph.D.

ASSISTANT PROFESSOR OF HISTORY

UNIVERSITY OF MICHIGAN

```
Dumond, Dwight Lowell, comp.
     Southern editorials on secession.  New York,
Century Co. [c1931]
     xxxiii, 529 p.  23 cm.
     At head of title:  The American Historical
Association.
     "Prepared and published under the direction of
the American Historical Association from the income
of the Albert J. Beveridge Memorial Fund."--p. [3]
     1. Secession.  2. U. S.--Pol. & gov't.--1857-
1861.  I. American Historical Association.  Albert
J. Beveridge Memorial Fund.  II. Title.  III. Title:
Editorials on          secession.
```

THE CENTURY CO.

NEW YORK   LONDON

EXERCISE

With respect to the names, or phrases, that are listed above the titles, what are the differences between the 3 examples on pages 167, 169, and 173?

The name listed above the title on page 167 is:

(1) _____

The phrase listed above the title on page 169 is:

(2) _____

The name listed above the title on page 173 is:

(3) _____

Perspectives in Reading No. 15

FOLKLORE AND FOLKTALES AROUND THE WORLD

Compiled and Edited by

Ruth Kearney Carlson
California State College at Hayward

Prepared by the IRA Library and Literature Committee

INTERNATIONAL READING ASSOCIATION
Newark, Delaware 19711

Some title pages, although accurate and precise, do raise questions as to who is to be considered for the main entry heading. In such cases, it is also essential to search beyond the title page.

The title page tells much about a book's entry heading situation. Often it is the only part of the book to do so. Therefore, we always check it first, and carefully. But...

EXERCISE

Glance through the preceding sections of this chapter and jot down below four or five reasons why you should always go beyond the title page when searching for entry heading information.

_____

_____

_____

_____

_____

_____

_____

For the reasons you have just indicated, you should always proceed to Stage 2 (see page 155) and examine, in addition to the title page, the book's cover (including its spine*), book jacket, half-title, verso of the title page, caption title, and colophon.

---

* The spine is that part of the book's outer shell (that is, of its cover) which connects the front and back halves of this shell. Also called Backbone or (more correctly) Backstrip.

STAGE 2: "OTHER STATEMENTS OPENLY EXPRESSED." (see AA page 9)

The Book's Cover, Spine, and Half-title

Since they repeat title page information in much abbreviated form, they sometimes
give the author's surname rather than his full name. This can help in establishing the
form of a name. In the example below, the title page gives the full name, implying
that the author's surname is Ingebretsen. The book's spine tells a different story.

TITLE PAGE   SPINE

HERMAN SMITT INGEBRETSEN

EN DIKTER
OG EN HERRE

VILHELM KRAGS LIV
OG DIKTNING

ANNET
OPPLAG

Most likely, then, this is a compound surname (see page 139). To be sure, we should check further in the book being cataloged.*

But remember that clues can also be misleading. The title page below implies that the author's surname is "Du Rietz," but the initial "G" makes one wonder whether this is not also a compound surname, "Einar Du Rietz," although "Einar" is typically a forename. The signature,** at the bottom of the first text page, repeats the title page information and is, thus, no help. But in the text itself, the author refers to himself repeatedly as "Du Rietz," and especailly from the enclosed bibliography we see that "Einar" is really his middle name.***

---

* The correct entry heading form is, in fact, "Smitt Ingebretsen, Herman."

** The signature are the distinguishing letter(s) and/or number(s) printed at the bottom of the first page of each gathering of leaves that form a physical section of the book, to guide the binder in assembling the sections correctly. By extension, the sections themselves.

*** Depding on the amount of information you have available, the correct entry heading form for this name is either "Du Rietz, Gustaf Einar," or "Du Rietz, G   Einar."

ACTA PHYTOGEOGRAPHICA SUECICA. III.

LIFE-FORMS OF TERRESTRIAL FLOWERING PLANTS

BY

G. EINAR DU RIETZ

PRINTED WITH CONTRIBUTION FROM
LÄNGMANSKA KULTURFONDEN

UPPSALA 1931
ALMQVIST & WIKSELLS BOKTRYCKERI-A. B.

Page 1

nad been ... early as by ...)00 B.C.)
(comp. GAMS 1918 pp. 312—314), and the general physiognomic types known as
trees, shrubs, herbs, etc., of course were generally used by the very early botanists. It was, however, ALEXANDER VON HUMBOLDT (1806, comp. WARMING 1908 a
pp. 1—3, DU RIETZ 1921 pp. 13, 37—39), who first drew the attention of the
botanists to the fact that it could be worth while to work out a system of such
purely physiognomic types more purposely, and to the great value of such
physiognomic types for the characterization of the vegetation of different regions.
In his first fundamental paper on the subject, »Ideen zu einer Physiognomik
der Gewächse» (1806), HUMBOLDT described and named 16 »Hauptformen», the
number of which was increased to 19 two years afterwards (1808). These 19

form, die Farenkräuter, die Liliengewächse, die Weidenform, die Myrtengewächse,
die Melastomen- und die Lorbeerform»[1] (comp. DU RIETZ 1921 p. 39). For HUM-
BOLDT these »Hauptformen» were mainly tools for the description of vegetation
physiognomy, and it never occurred to him that there could be anything wrong
in letting a family or a larger taxonomical unit form its own »Hauptform» if
it was really characterized by a definite physiognomy. The »Hauptformen»-system

[1] In the following treatise all quotations in German and French are presented in the original
language, while such in less known languages are translated into English.

1—30830. *G. Einar Du Rietz.*

Bibliography

——, Die ... — Die Wissenschaft, ... Braunschweig 1913.
——, Die Stellung der physiognomischen Ökologie, — Engler's Botan. Jahrbücher,
52. Leipzig und Berlin 1914.
——, Pflanzengeographische Ökologie. — Abderhalden's Handbuch der biologischen
Arbeitsmetoden, Abt. XI, Teil 4. Berlin und Wien 1928.
DU RIETZ, G. E., Zur methodologischen Grundlage der modernen Pflanzensoziologie.
— Diss. Upsala 1921.
——, Studien über die Helianthemum oelandicum-Assoziationen auf Öland. —
Svensk Bot. Tidskr., 17. Stockholm 1923 (a).
——, Einige Beobachtungen und Betrachtungen über Pflanzengesellschaften in Nie-
derösterreich und den Kleinen Karpathen. — Österreich. Bot. Zeitschr.
1923. Wien 1923 (b).
——, De svenska Helianthemum-arterna. — Bot. Not. 1923. Lund 1923 (c).
——, Studien über die Vegetation der Alpen, mit derjenigen Skandinaviens ver-
glichen. — Veröffentl. Geobot. Inst. Rübel in Zürich. Zürich 1924.
——, Gotländische Vegetationsstudien. — Svenska Växtsociologiska Sällskapets Hand-
lingar, 2. Upsala 1925 (a).
——, Zur Kenntnis ...

The title page tends to list names of people primarily and secondarily responsible for a work, but cover, spine, and half-title tend to list only the people **primarily** responsible. This may help with the **choice** of a main entry heading.

The Verso of the Title Page:

The verso of the title page will occasionally give more information about a name listed on the title page, and/or list names of additional people or organizations responsible for the book's intellectual content. It will also give much information that does **not** aid in entry heading work. When checking the verso of a title page for entry heading information, it is as important to know what to ignore as it is to know what to use.

For entry heading purposes, it is usually safe to ignore the copyright notice* if the name given in it is that of the publisher. . .

McGRAW-HILL BOOK COMPANY, INC.   *1962*

New York   San Francisco   Toronto   London

PUBLISHER'S
NAME ON
TITLE PAGE
IS THE SAME AS
COPYRIGHT
CLAIMANT ON
VERSO OF
TITLE PAGE.
NO NEW
INFORMATION.

UNDERSTANDING EDUCATIONAL RESEARCH

Copyright © 1962 by the McGraw-Hill Book Company, Inc. Printed in the United States of America. All rights reserved. This book, or parts thereof, may not be reproduced in any form without permission of the publishers. *Library of Congress Catalog Card Number 61-13172*

IV

66880

---

* Copyright notice: A statement, ususally on the verso of the title page, indicating who has the exclusive right to reproduce and sell a work. Includes the date this right was registered.

. . . or if the corporate name in the copyright notice is neither that of the author, nor of the publisher.

◁ TITLE PAGE

The Taxonomy, Ecology, and Distribution
of the Gramineae
Growing in the State Without Cultivation

COPYRIGHT NOTICE
ON VERSO OF TITLE
PAGE PROVIDES NO
NEW ENTRY HEADING
INFORMATION
⬇

GRASSES OF WISCONSIN
NORMAN C. FASSETT

COPYRIGHT 1951 BY THE REGENTS OF THE UNIVERSITY OF WISCONSIN

PRINTED IN THE UNITED STATES OF AMERICA BY CUSHING-MALLOY, INCORPORATED

with an essay
The Vegetation of Wisconsin
by John T. Curtis

THE UNIVERSITY OF WISCONSIN PRESS

Sometimes, the name of the copyright claimant is that of the author, given in identical form as on the title page. This also provides no new entry heading information. But it is nice to know that it does not contradict the title page.

YANKEE SI!

The Story of Dr. J. Calvitt Clarke
and his 36,000 Children

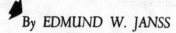

By EDMUND W. JANSS

With a Foreword by
Dr. Daniel A. Poling

TITLE PAGE

**VERSO OF THE TITLE
PAGE. COPYRIGHT
NOTICE PROVIDES NO
NEW ENTRY HEADING
INFORMATION**

But sometimes, the copyright notice will provide important additional information.

EXERCISE

What new information, that conflicts with title page information, do the copyright notices of the
following two examples provide?

THE YEAR
THE YANKEES
LOST
THE PENNANT

A NOVEL BY

DOUGLASS WALLOP

TITLE PAGE

(1) _____

_____

_____

VERSO

COPYRIGHT, 1954, BY JOHN DOUGLASS WALLOP

VILLAGE
DIARY

BY 'MISS READ'

TITLE PAGE

(2) _____

_____

_____

VERSO

Copyright © 1957 by Dora Jessie Saint
All rights reserved including the right to
reproduce this book or parts thereof in any form
Library of Congress Catalog Card Number: 57-9983
Second Printing
The Riverside Press
Cambridge · Massachusetts
Printed in the U. S. A.

How does the last example differ from that shown on page 181? Why can you ignore the copyright statement shown on page 181 but not the copyright statement shown at the bottom of page 183? (1) _____

_____

_____

_____

_____

Sometimes, the verso of the title page, or some other part of the book, will give the names and contributions of people or organizations not mentioned on the title page. In that case it is important to decide whether, according to the AA (and especially according to **AA Rule 33**) these additional names should receive entry headings.

EXERCISE

For the following example, indicate what new name you should at least consider as possible added entry headings, as a result of checking the verso of the title page. (2) _____

_____

EAST PRUSSIAN DIARY

A Journal of Faith
1945-1947

by

COUNT HANS von LEHNDORFF

With an Introduction

by

CONSTANTINE FITZGIBBON

TITLE PAGE

VERSO

First published in Germany by Biederstein Verlag Muenchen
Second Impression
© 1963 FOR ENGLISH TRANSLATION BY
OSWALD WOLFF (PUBLISHERS) LTD., LONDON

Translated by
VIOLET M. MACDONALD

The verso of the title page, and the other pages of the front matter sometimes carry special notices. Indicate below whether you would consider making added entry headings because of any of the following notices:

The lyrics to "When You Were Young and Ugly," page 197, are reprinted by permission of the copyright owner, Gladstone Music, Inc., Scotia, N.Y.

(1) _____ Yes _____ No

Your reason: _____

_____

_____

_____

TO FRANCES LOCKWOOD CLEASBY

One of the generation that will study science in the new manner. [Note: The book is by John Charles Cleasby.]

(2) _____ Yes _____ No

Your reason: _____

_____

_____

_____

Four chapters in this book are based on lectures delivered at Oriole College. In transporting them from oral to written form, I am indebted to Miss Violet Cardinal, who has also contributed the three chapters on "Nesting Habits of Emotionally Disturbed Birds."

THEODORE S. DUCKWORTH

[Note: The title of Mr. Duckworth's book is, *The Psychology of Birds.*]

(3) _____ Yes _____ No

Your reason: _____

_____

_____

_____

© Copyright: 1964, Fides Publishers, Inc.
Notre Dame, Indiana

Nihil Obstat: Louis J. Putz, C.S.C.
University of Notre Dame

Imprimatur: Leo A. Pursley, D.D.
Bishop of Fort Wayne-South Bend

Published originally in France by
CERCLE ST. JEAN-BAPTISTE,
12 Rue St. J.B. De LaSalle, Paris.

Library of Congress Catalog Card Number: 64-16499

(4) _____ Yes _____ No

Your reason: _____

_____

_____

_____

TITLE PAGE

HOOVER INSTITUTION STUDIES

COMMUNIST CHINA

The Politics of Student Opposition

Translated, with an Introduction, by

DENNIS J. DOOLIN

**The Hoover Institution
on War, Revolution, and Peace
Stanford University
1964**

(5) _____ Yes _____ No

Your reason: _____

_____

_____

_____

VERSO

The Hoover Institution on War, Revolution, and Peace, founded at Stanford University in 1919 by Herbert Hoover, is a center for advanced study and research on public and international affairs in the twentieth century. The views expressed in its publications are entirely those of the authors and do not necessarily reflect the views of the Hoover Institution.

© 1964 by the Board of Trustees of
the Leland Stanford Junior University

All rights reserved

Library of Congress Catalog Card Number: 64-16879
Printed in the United States of America

When you wonder whether or not to make an added entry heading for a contributor or someone else, the following rule of thumb may help:

> If they didn't contribute quite a bit. . .
> If their names aren't on the title page. . .
> If their names aren't in pretty big letters. . .
> . . . the public is less likely to use their names
> as approaches to the book.

The Book Jacket

By the time you examine the book jacket, you will most likely have decided who the book's intellectual contributors are. But the "blurb," that is, the advertising matter, on the book jacket often gives additional information about these names. (see page 155.)

EXERCISE

Below are illustrated a title page and part of a book jacket. What new information does the book jacket provide that might help in establishing or verifying the author's name?

_____

_____

_____

_____

_____

_____

ATLAS *THE* | *STORY OF A MISSILE*

JOHN L. | *CHAPMAN*

HARPER & BROTHERS, NEW YORK

John L. Chapman was born in Gilby, North Dakota, in 1920. He attended Marshall High School in Minneapolis and later took a B.A. degree in journalism at the University of Minnesota. During World War II, Mr. Chapman served with a USAAF Bomber Squadron in India and China.

Since then he has worked with the Minneapolis *Star and Tribune* as promotion and editorial writer, with Convair-San Diego as an engineering writer, and with Convair-Astronautics on the editorial staff. He knows well and has worked closely with the designers and engineers who produced Atlas, and did considerable additional research for the book, visiting various astronautics field facilities, the headquarters of the Air Force Ballistic Missile Division, the Rocketdyne Field Test Laboratory, and Cape Canaveral.

Mr. Chapman now lives in San Diego with his wife and two small daughters. His favored sport is tennis, and other interests include music, reading, and photography. *Atlas* is his first book, written mostly in his spare time and during vacation; he is also the author of a booklet, *Space Primer*, and of various short stories.

What new information that might be useful in entry heading work does the following blurb provide? _____

_____

_____

_____

**MARRIAGE
IS
A HAPPY CROWD**

**by
Jane Williams**

TITLE PAGE

BOOK JACKET

The Author: Jane Portney Williams
is an amateur photographer
turned magazine writer and novelist. Her most successful work is
Photographic Sinecure, an amusing
account of her own experiences.
She is married and the mother of
six amateur photographers.

JACKET DESIGN/EMILY DRAWSTRING

Note that the book jacket typically helps with the form, rather than the choice, of
an entry heading.

Caption Title

This title appears at the head of each page in many books. It may be the title of a
chapter, changing with each chapter; it may be the title of the whole book, in which
case it is called the "running title;" it may be a combination of both titles, printed

at the head of alternate pages. It is usually an abbreviated title and seldom aids in entry heading work. If the caption title (or, for that matter, the cover title or the title on the spine) differs significantly from the title page title, it can be recorded in a note. (see page 000.) Any of these titles can also become a second title-added-entry-heading, if readers are apt to use it as an approach to the book, or if the book's real title and the assigned subject headings do not seem to give sufficiently good approaches to the book. But make such second title-added-entry-headings only rarely. Many beginners tend to make them more often than really needed. (See "The concept of the reasonable approach," page 104.)

TITLE PAGE TITLE	*CAPTION TITLE*
SHAKESPEARE'S COMEDY OF THE MERCHANT OF VENICE	MERCHANT OF VENICE
HISTORY OF KING JOHN	King John
COLLOQUIUM ON TECHNICAL PRECONDITIONS FOR RETRIEVAL CENTER OPERATIONS	Retrieval Center Operations

Only the last example is a likely candidate for making a note of the caption title, and then making a tracing for it,* because (1) the available subject heading for this concept is not too helpful,** and (2) the caption title claims much more than the title page title, and it is likely that it will become a "popular" approach to that volume.***

---

* See "Justifying an added entry heading," page 47 to 48.

** This is outside the scope of this volume but will be discussed in Volume 3 of this series.

*** This is the kind of assumption that you can make with more confidence once you know your collection, your users, and their needs and ways of handling things.

The Colophon

This is an inscription found at the end of a book, showing the printer's name, the type used, the date and place of printing, and similar matter. Since the colophon focuses on a time and place for the work, it can guide to possible reference sources that may identify an early, rare, and obscure work and its author, when the book itself does not provide such clues. Such works are, however, outside the scope of this text. When cataloging modern books, one can generally ignore the colophon.

STAGE 3: PREFACE; INTRODUCTION; TEXT, ANY OTHER PART OF THE BOOK*

If the sources of the first two stages give insufficient, ambiguous, or contradictory information for entry heading purposes, proceed to the sources of the third stage. They will often confirm, sometimes clarify, and occasionally contradict the title page with respect to responsibility for a book's intellectual content. In case of conflict between the sources of the first two stages and the third stage, it is generally safe to follow the third stage.

---

* Preface, Introduction, or any other part of the book including the text itself, can be most helpful when determining a book's subject matter. But for entry heading purposes, to save time, the AA recommend that catalogers examine preface, introduction, and text only as a last resort.

Preface, Foreword, Introduction:

Many prefaces are signed or initialed by the author. Typically, this adds no new name information.

GRASSES OF WISCONSIN

NORMAN C. FASSETT

Title Page

ACKNOWLEDGMENTS

Most of the illustrations are reproduced from the *Manual of Grasses*, with the addition of interpretive labels. Figure 103 is original; Figures 67 and 353–356 are reproduced from the author's *Manual of Aquatic Plants*, by permission of the publishers, McGraw-Hill Book Company.

The maps are based on specimens examined by the writer, most of them in the herbaria of the University of Wisconsin and

˗˗ə Public M˗˗˗

˗˗ on ecology has been contributed by Dr. John T. ˗˗˗, Professor of Botany at the University of Wisconsin.

The writer is especially grateful to Mr. A. M. Fuller for many loans of material from the Milwaukee Public Museum and to Mr. Jason R. Swallen of the Smithsonian Institution for his opinions concerning several knotty determinations.

N. C. F.

June, 1950

THESE ACKNOWLEDGMENTS ADD NO NEW NAME INFORMATION, BUT THEY ALSO DO NOT CONTRADICT THE TITLE PAGE

Sometimes, these initials are helpful for confirming an impression gained from the title page. (See Answer Book, 162-2.) The following situation, however, is unusual: The title page and the foreword confirm that C. W. Ceram is the author. Yet, both are equally misleading, for this is a pseudonym. The author's real name was Kurt W. Marek.

FOREWORD
TO THE SECOND, REVISED AND ENLARGED EDITION

SINCE THE ORIGINAL German edition of this book was published in 1949, it has been translated into twenty-six languages and read by millions of people, even though I have never permitted a reprint edition to be issued. While *Gods, Graves, and Scholars* was originally written for the widest general reading public, its strict adherence to scientific standards has led long since to its being made required reading for some college courses. University and college libraries often stock as many as ten copies or more in order to be able to satisfy the demand for the book, which my publisher and a number of critics have called a classic.

In the meantime, archæology has marched on. New discoveries have been made, new interpretations advanced, and above all, remarkable new techniques for archæological researches developed. To cover these new developments, I have revised the original edition and concluded the book with a summary of the important new findings and methods. The extensive additions to the original American text have been translated from the German by Sophie Wilkins, to whom I particularly wish to express my appreciation also for her painstaking work in comparing texts and making necessary rearrangements in the revised edition.

Gods, Graves and Scholars was followed by *The Secret of the Hittites: The Discovery of an Ancient Empire* (1956), *The March of Archæology* (1958), a pictorial history of archæology, and *Hands on the Past* (1966), a documentation. Together these four volumes, with their combined total of nearly a thousand bibliographical items and picture sources, constitute the most comprehensive history of archæology ever published for the general reader, containing numerous facts and stories long forgotten even by the specialists, as well as the latest developments and scientific thought in the field.

C. W. C.
July 1967

GODS, GRAVES, AND SCHOLARS

The Story of Archæology

by C. W. CERAM

TRANSLATED FROM THE GERMAN
BY E. B. GARSIDE AND SOPHIE WILKINS

Second, Revised and Substantially
Enlarged Edition

NEW YORK   ALFRED A. KNOPF   1967

In most such situations, the book being cataloged does not give the real name. You would probably have come across it at an earlier stage (see the chart on pages 130-131) in book reviews (during the selection process) or in bibliographies (during the ordering process). Or, if the author had really kept his name a secret, you might not have come across it at all. This is also alright, because **AA Rule 42** and its footnote permit you to use a pseudonym as entry heading if someone uses it consistently, or if you so prefer.

This particular book, however, contains at the end the following biographical note which corrects the name information of the title page and the Foreword.

A NOTE ABOUT THE AUTHOR

C. W. CERAM is a name familiar to everyone interested in archæology. Born in 1915 in Berlin, he was known for many years under his real name, Kurt W. Marek, as a newspaperman, drama critic, and a leading figure in the publishing world. His first book, *Gods, Graves, and Scholars* (1951), now presented in its second edition, brought world fame to its author—it has since achieved great popular and critical success in twenty-six languages—and immeasurably expanded popular interest and concern for the world's archæological heritage. The saving of Abu Simbel, for example, as the result of the outcry against its threatened disappearance at the bottom of the Nile, owes something to the world's having been alerted to the importance of such monuments by the books of C. W. Ceram and those who followed in his footsteps. He has since published *The Secret of the Hittites* (1956), the result of an invitation to participate in two digs in Turkey, uncovering the Hittite past; *The March of Archæology* (1958); in 1961, under his actual name, *Yestermorrow: Notes on Man's Progress;* in 1965, *Archæology of the Cinema;* and in 1966, *Hands on the Past: Pioneer Archæologists Tell Their Own Story.* Mr. Marek lives with his wife and son in Woodstock, New York.

Especially in the case of corporate authorship* the Foreword may give a clearer explanation of the authorship than the title page.

```
STUDY OF INDUSTRIAL HEALTH PRACTICES

                  FOR

        THE IRON AND STEEL INDUSTRY




                April 1953
```

TITLE PAGE

Corporate authors typically publish their own works. Often, their name appears on the title page only as publisher.

```
American Iron and Steel Institute
350 Fifth Avenue
New York 1, N.Y.
```

F O R E W O R D

This volume was prepared by the Committee on Industrial Health of the American Iron and Steel Institute. Its purpose is to make avail to members of the iron and steel industry the results of a stu

And this Preface to Elizabeth Davis Bancroft's *Letters from England*— obviously not written by the book's author—gives much biographical information of which, however, only a fraction is useful for establishing the necessary entry heading. This is typical of such information.

* Corporate authorship was mentioned on pages 29-31 and 42-44.

PREFACE

Elizabeth Davis Bancroft, the writer of these letters, was the youngest child and only daughter of William and Rebecca Morton Davis, and was born at Plymouth, Mass., in October, 1803. She often spoke in later times of what a good preparation for her life abroad were the years she spent at Miss Cushing's school at Hingham, and of her visits to her uncles, Judge Davis and Mr. I. P. Davis of Boston. In 1825 she married Alexander Bliss, a brilliant young lawyer and a junior partner of Daniel Webster. On his death a few years later, her father having died, her mother and brother formed a household with her and her two sons in Winthrop Place, Boston. As a young girl in Plymouth she became a great friend of the future Mrs. Emerson and later of Mr. Emerson and of Mr. and Mrs. Ripley, and through them was much interested in Brook Farm.

In 1838 she married George Bancroft, the historian and statesman, who was then Collector of the Port of Boston and a widower with three children.

They continued to live in Winthrop Place till 1845, when for one year Mr. Bancroft was Secretary of the Navy in Polk's cabinet. While he was in that position the Naval Academy at Annapolis was established; and he played an important part in the earlier stages of the Mexican War. In the fall of 1846 he became Minister to England. It was then that the letters were written from which these extracts have been taken. A number of passages not of general interest have been omitted, without any indications of such omission in the text, but in no case has any change in a sentence been made. Most of the letters are in the form of a diary and were addressed to immediate relatives, and none of them were written for publication; but owing to the standing of Mr. Bancroft as a man of letters, as well as his official station, the writer saw London life under an unusual variety of interesting aspects.

In 1849 Mr. and Mrs. Bancroft returned to this country, and Mr. Bancroft occupied himself with his history until 1868, when he was for seven years Minister to Prussia and the German Empire. At the expiration of that time they took up their residence in Washington, where they lived during the remainder of their lives.

Of these three sources—preface, foreword, introduction—the introduction is least apt to give useful entry heading information since it, typically, deals with the book's subject, whereas preface and foreword are apt to deal with the book's purpose and creators.

The Text and Other Parts of the Book

Only rarely does the cataloger need to consult the actual text for entry heading purposes. But some books contain a few special features that can prove most helpful:

(1) Biographical information about the author, similar to that found on many book jackets.* If given, it is often at the end of the book, sometimes with a heading such as "Vita," or "About the author." An example is on page 195.

(2) A list of the author's other works. This is apt to be printed on the page facing the title page, or on the verso of the bastard title (that is, two pages preceding the title page), or at the very end of the book, or on the book jacket. If the author's name, as given on the title page, is similar, but not identical, to one already in your catalog or authority file, this list may make it possible to check whether both names belong to one and the same person. (See pages 93 and 67-68.) Here is an imaginary example.

* The book jacket was discussed on pages 188-190.

START HERE:

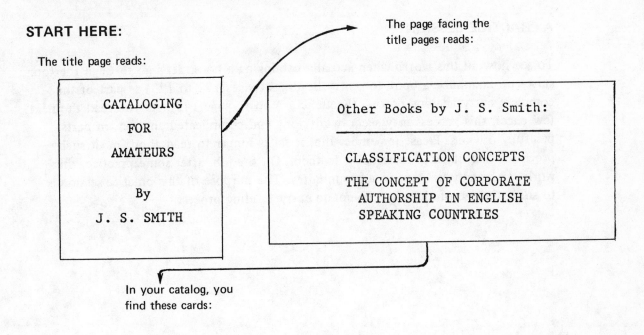

The title page reads:

CATALOGING

FOR

AMATEURS

By

J. S. SMITH

The page facing the
title pages reads:

Other Books by J. S. Smith:

CLASSIFICATION CONCEPTS

THE CONCEPT OF CORPORATE
AUTHORSHIP IN ENGLISH
SPEAKING COUNTRIES

In your catalog, you
find these cards:

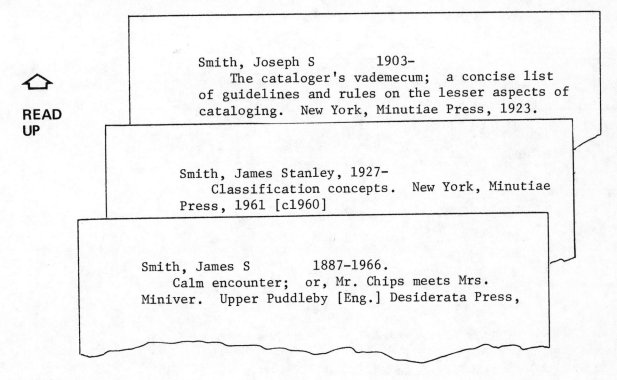

⬆

**READ
UP**

Smith, Joseph S   1903-
    The cataloger's vademecum; a concise list
of guidelines and rules on the lesser aspects of
cataloging. New York, Minutiae Press, 1923.

Smith, James Stanley, 1927-
    Classification concepts. New York, Minutiae
Press, 1961 [c1960]

Smith, James S   1887-1966.
    Calm encounter; or, Mr. Chips meets Mrs.
Miniver. Upper Puddleby [Eng.] Desiderata Press,

E X E R C I S E

On the basis of the above information, fill in below the exact form you would use for the main
entry heading for *Cataloging for amateurs.*

A PRACTICE SESSION

To see how all this works when actually cataloging a book, let's go through the four stages of examining a book for entry headings (pages 172 to 173) as part of the complete entry heading process (Sequences A to F, page 145). As you read the next few pages, this process may seem overly long and complicated and yet, in parts, painfully obvious. Please remember that it takes longer to read about most such processes than it takes to actually do them. On the job, after some practice, this work can usually be done in a few minutes. The purpose of this practice session is to show the use of clues in a complete entry heading process.

Sequence A of the Complete Entry Heading Process
(From pages 130-131)

Examine the book you are cataloging, to discover what authorship situation it represents. This can be done in 4 stages:

Stages 1 & 2 of the Book-Examination Sub-Process
(From page 155)

Examine the title page, or a substitute, and other statements that are openly expressed, such as the cover, half-title, verso of the title page, caption title, or colophon.)

W. MAXWELL REED

and WILFRID S. BRONSON

THE Sea FOR SAM

Revised Edition

Edited by PAUL F. BRANDWEIN

Illustrated with photographs

Harcourt, Brace & World, Inc. NEW YORK

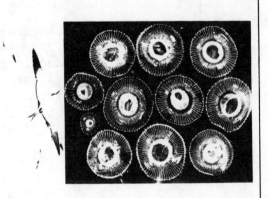

*
TITLE
PAGE
OF THE
BOOK
WE SHALL
CATALOG

Most books can be cataloged descriptively before their choice-of-entry-heading situation has been definitely decided. But some require looking at both aspects simultaneously. From the evidence available so far, either Mr. Brandwein or Messrs. Reed and Bronson could be primarily responsible for *The Sea for Sam*, resulting in quite different descriptions:

If the editor, Paul F. Brandwein, were primarily responsible, his name would become the main entry heading, and the book might be described like this:*

```
[Main entry heading for Brandwein]
     The sea for Sam. Rev. ed., edited by Paul F.
Brandwein.  Illustrated with photos.  New York,
Harcourt, Brace & World [c1960]
     243 p.  illus.  24 cm.

     At head of title:  W. Maxwell Reed and Wilfrid
S. Bronson.
```

But if W. Maxwell Reed and Wilfrid S. Bronson are primarily responsible, the book can be described like this:

```
[Main entry heading for Reed]
     The sea for Sam [by] W. Maxwell Reed and Wil-
frid S. Bronson.  Rev. ed., edited by Paul F.
Brandwein.  Illustrated with photos.  New York,
Harcourt, Brace & World [c1960]
     243 p.  illus.  24 cm.
```

At this stage, we can only guess that W. Maxwell Reed and Wilfrid S. Bronson are primarily responsible for the book's intellectual content.

---

* The specifics of descriptive cataloging are discussed in volume one of this series.

EXERCISE

Where can we find confirmation of this thought? Is the **verso of the title page** of any help?

> *Copyright, 1935, © 1960 by Harcourt, Brace & World, Inc.*
>
> *All rights reserved. No part of this book may be reproduced in any form or by any mechanical means, including mimeograph and tape recorder, without permission in writing from the publisher.*
>
> *D.8.65*
>
> *Library of Congress Catalog Card Number: 59-12826*
> *Printed in the United States of America by The Murray Printing Company*

VERSO OF
TITLE
PAGE

(1) _____ Yes; _____ No

The book's **caption, running,** and **half-titles** list no names that might give a clue. It has no **colophon,** and its cover carries only a symbolic design. The **spine** carries the following information:

---

* From *The Sea for Sam* by W. Maxwell Reed and Wilfrid S. Bronson, copyright 1935,©1960, by Harcourt, Brace and World, Inc.; copyright renewed, 1963 by Philip Reed and Wilfrid S. Bronson, and reproduced by permission of the publisher.

THE SEA FOR SAM   *W. Maxwell Reed & Wilfrid S. Bronson*

Harcourt, Brace & World

EXERCISE

What authorship clue does the spine provide? _____

_____

Stage 3 of the Book-Examination Sub-Process
(From page 155)

Examine preface, introduction, and, if necessary, the text itself.

The book has no **preface** or **introduction** and, as you will soon see, we need not examine its **text** for choice-of-entry-heading decision. But it does have an "Editor's Note."

Editor's Note *

The seas are greater than the land; they are still an untapped resource. *The Sea for Sam* is a story of the sea, its tides and its floods, its deeps and its mountains, its animals and its plants, as well as of its own drama of haven and danger for men who seek out its secrets. Even now work is going on to map the full extent of the geography of the seas and to estimate their true value to man. We are just beginning to understand that almost 90 per cent of the world's food-making — as yet not seriously harvested — goes on in the sea.

The boy Sam first heard the story of the earth's seas from his uncle, W. Maxwell Reed, who cooperated on it with Wilfrid S. Bronson. Over the years, the story found a favorite place with many young people. We have attempted to retain the qualities that made Mr. Reed's story of the sea so appealing, and we have sought the counsel of Christopher W. ** Coates of the New York Aquarium, whose help has been invaluable.

PAUL F. BRANDWEIN

EXERCISE

Does the "Editor's Note" provide a clue on the choice-of-entry-heading? If so, what is the clue?

_____

_____

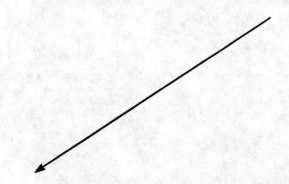

* From *The Sea for Sam* by Maxwell Reed and Wilfrid S. Bronson, copyright 1935, © 1960, by Harcourt, Brace and World, Inc.; copyright renewed, 1963 by Philip Reed and Wilfrid S. Bronson, and reproduced by permission of the publisher.

** Most libraries would not make an added entry heading for Christopher W. Coates. His name is not "openly expressed" elsewhere in the book, and the "Editor's Note" indicates that he gave expert advice rather than actually helped to write the text. See also pages 102 to 104.

Stage 3a of the Book-Examination Sub-Process
(From page 155)

Always examine the book jacket.

Book jackets often contain information that helps with the **form** of a previously selected entry heading.* Since they usually carry the same author statement as the title page, they typically do not contribute to the **choice**-of-entry-heading decision. The following **jacket**, however, is an exception and is more helpful than the title page in the choice-of-entry-heading decision.

* This was discussed on pages 188-190.

** From *The Sea for Sam* by Maxwell Reed and Wilfrid S. Bronson, copyright 1935, © 1960, by Harcourt, Brace & World, Inc.; copyright renewed, 1963 by Philip Reed and Wilfrid S. Bronson, and reproduced by permission of the publisher.

THE PART OF THE BOOK JACKET COVERING THE SPINE

*THE SEA FOR SAM by W. MAXWELL REED and WILFRID S. BRONSON

THE BLURB ON THE BOOK JACKET

*
$4.95

REVISED EDITION

THE SEA FOR SAM

*BY W. MAXWELL REED
AND WILFRID S. BRONSON*

Edited by Paul F. Brandwein

The world's vast and mysterious oceans are slowly beginning to yield their secrets to mankind. In 1935 when *The Sea for Sam* was originally published, very little such information was available to young readers, and the book was immediately recognized as an outstanding contribution in its field. Now,   light of

*
*A HIGHLY ACCLAIMED
SCIENCE SERIES!*

THE EARTH FOR SAM
THE STARS FOR SAM

by W. Maxwell Reed

THE SEA FOR SAM

*by W. Maxwell Reed
and Wilfrid S. Bronson*

REVISED EDITIONS

EDITED BY PAUL F. BRANDWEIN

In a series of three books written in the 1930's, Mr. Reed explained the wonders of the physical world and the universe to his young nephew Sam. As each was pub-   hed, it was a   diate success an

EXERCISE

What clues does the front of the book jacket provide? (1) _____

_____

_____

What clues does the part of the book jacket over the spine provide? (2) _____

_____

_____

What clues does the blurb provide (3) _____

_____

Thus, by going through stages 2 and 3 of the book-examination sub-process, we could resolve the conflicting clues that the title page (stage 1, pages 201 to 202) had given and can tell positively under whom this book should be entered.

EXERCISE

On the basis of your findings indicate below what authorship situation *The Sea for Sam* represents. (4) _____

_____

_____

Which of the two workslips on page 202 describes this book correctly?
(5) The first one: _____; The second one: _____.

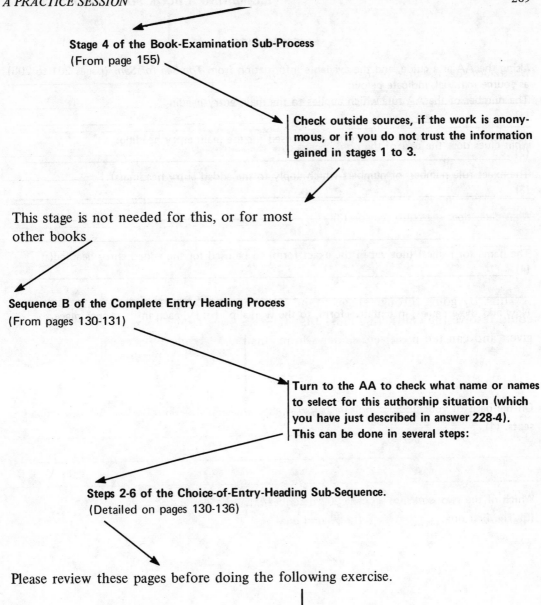

Stage 4 of the Book-Examination Sub-Process
(From page 155)

Check outside sources, if the work is anonymous, or if you do not trust the information gained in stages 1 to 3.

This stage is not needed for this, or for most other books

Sequence B of the Complete Entry Heading Process
(From pages 130-131)

Turn to the AA to check what name or names to select for this authorship situation (which you have just described in answer 228-4). This can be done in several steps:

Steps 2-6 of the Choice-of-Entry-Heading Sub-Sequence.
(Detailed on pages 130-136)

Please review these pages before doing the following exercise.

EXERCISE

Using the AA as a guide, and the available information from *The Sea for Sam* (pages 201 to 208) as source material, indicate below:

The number of the AA rule which applies to the main entry heading:

(1) _____

The name (not yet in the exact form) to be used for the main entry heading:

(2) _____

The exact rule number, or numbers which apply to the added entry heading(s):

(3) _____

_____

_____

The name (or names) (not yet in the exact form) to be used for the added entry heading(s):

(4) _____

_____

Now add these names, in tentative form, to the workslip* below, each in its proper place.

* Workslips were first mentioned on page 8. The example below illustrates a different format. For a complete sample and an explanation see pages 411-412.

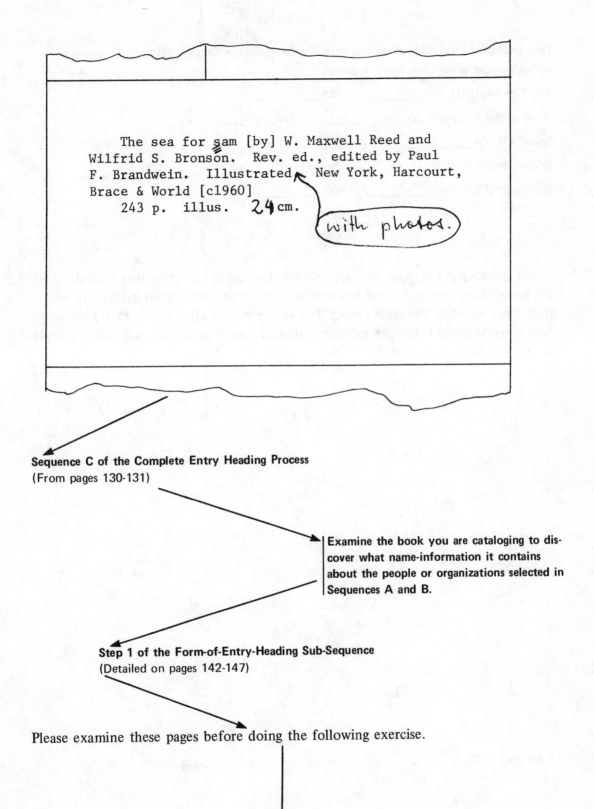

The sea for sam [by] W. Maxwell Reed and
Wilfrid S. Bronson. Rev. ed., edited by Paul
F. Brandwein. Illustrated New York, Harcourt,
Brace & World [c1960]
    243 p. illus. 24 cm.

with photos.

Sequence C of the Complete Entry Heading Process
(From pages 130-131)

Examine the book you are cataloging to discover what name-information it contains
about the people or organizations selected in
Sequences A and B.

Step 1 of the Form-of-Entry-Heading Sub-Sequence
(Detailed on pages 142-147)

Please examine these pages before doing the following exercise.

EXERCISE

Does any part of the book which you have already examined on pages 201 to 107, give the author's or the editor's full name or date(s)?

The Title page? (1) Yes _____ ; No _____ .

Verso of the title page? (2) Yes _____ ; No _____ .

Spine? (3) Yes _____ ; No _____ .

Editor's Note? (4) Yes _____ ; No _____ .

Book jacket? (5) Yes _____ ; No _____ .

   The information at your disposal contains two groups of clues that indicate that the names Reed, Bronson, and Brandwein may already be in your catalog. If so, they must maintain the same form.* The first group of clues shows that *The Sea for Sam* was published before, in another edition. Its authors' names may, thus, already be in your catalog as entry headings.

---

* See pages 67-70.

EXERCISE

List of clues (on pages 201 to 207) that indicate that *The Sea for Sam* was published also in an earlier edition. _____

_____

_____

_____

_____

The second group of clues shows that, even if your library does not own the earlier edition of *The Sea for Sam*, the names Reed and Brandwein may already be listed anyway as entry headings in your catalog, because Mr. Reed wrote other books also, and Mr. Brandwein also edited other books. The list of W. Maxwell Reed's other books, the first clue, is on the page preceding the title page.

by W. Maxwell Reed

THE EARTH FOR SAM

THE STARS FOR SAM

AND THAT'S WHY

THE SKY IS BLUE

AMERICA'S TREASURE

* From *The Sea for Sam* by W. Maxwell Reed and Wilfrid S. Bronson, copyright 1935, ©1960, by Harcourt, Brace & World, Inc.; copyright renewed, 1963 by Philip Reed and Wilfrid S. Bronson, and reproduced by permission of the publisher.

EXERCISE

The second such clue shows that Paul F. Brandwein edited several other books. Where, on pages 201 to 207, do you find such a clue? _____

_____

Step 2 of the Form-of-Entry-Heading Sub-Sequence
(From pages 142-147) §2)

Note the name-information tentatively on the workslip.

The clues and information that catalogers gather are usually noted in much abbreviated form on the workslip, in preparation for Sequence E (see pages 130-131, 142). Everyone develops his own "shorthand" for such notes. Your workslip might look like this at this stage:

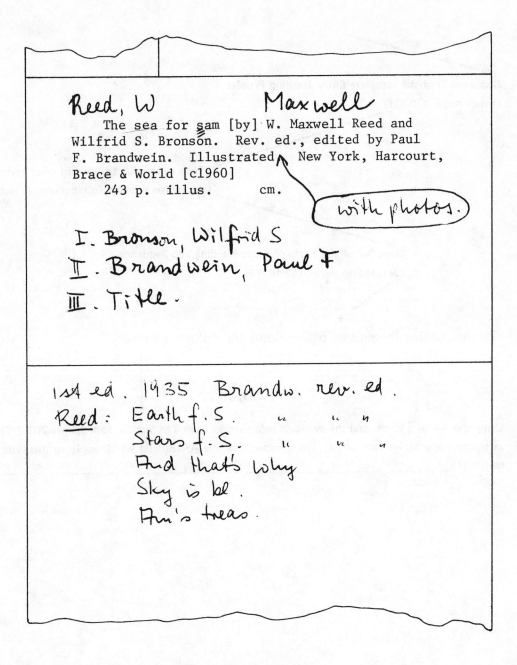

Reed, W   Maxwell
    The sea for sam [by] W. Maxwell Reed and
Wilfrid S. Bronson. Rev. ed., edited by Paul
F. Brandwein. Illustrated New York, Harcourt,
Brace & World [c1960]
    243 p. illus.   cm.

with photos.

I. Bronson, Wilfrid S
II. Brandwein, Paul F
III. Title.

1st ed. 1935 Brandw. rev. ed.
Reed: Earth f. S.   "   " "
       Stars f. S.   "   " "
       And that's why
       Sky is bl.
       An's treas.

(You will soon learn through experience, how much information you need to jot
down, and how much you can trust to your memory.) Note also the title tracing
that is made for most books. (See also page 17.)

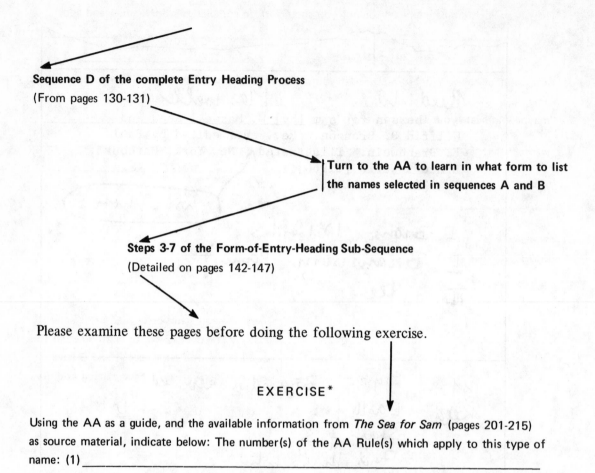

Sequence D of the complete Entry Heading Process
(From pages 130-131)

Turn to the AA to learn in what form to list the names selected in sequences A and B

Steps 3-7 of the Form-of-Entry-Heading Sub-Sequence
(Detailed on pages 142-147)

Please examine these pages before doing the following exercise.

EXERCISE*

Using the AA as a guide, and the available information from *The Sea for Sam* (pages 201-215) as source material, indicate below: The number(s) of the AA Rule(s) which apply to this type of name: (1) _____

* All three names are ordinary English language names which you already know how to list as entry headings. Please go through the following exercise anyway, first to gain practice in using the AA for more difficult situations, and secondly to learn whether such simple names are covered in the AA by one rule, or whether even simple names require gathering together more than one form-of-entry-heading rule.

The rules which indicate whether or not you should try to complete the forenames, and add dates: (2) _____

_____

As a result of checking these rules, must you change on your workslip (page 215) the form of any name? (3)_____ Yes; _____ No; _____ Maybe. If your answer is "yes," or "maybe," indicate your reasons here: (4) _____

_____

_____

Sequence E of the Complete Entry Heading Process
(Form pages 130-131)

Check the name authority file* or, if none exists, check the catalog, to learn whether the names selected in sequences A and B have been previously used in your catalog as entry headings.

Compare now the names on your workslip (page 215) with the names listed below, which appear in your authority file.

---

* Authority cards were discussed on pages 89 to 98. The sequence of steps typically used by creating authority cards is described on page 91.

NAME AUTHORITY FILE*

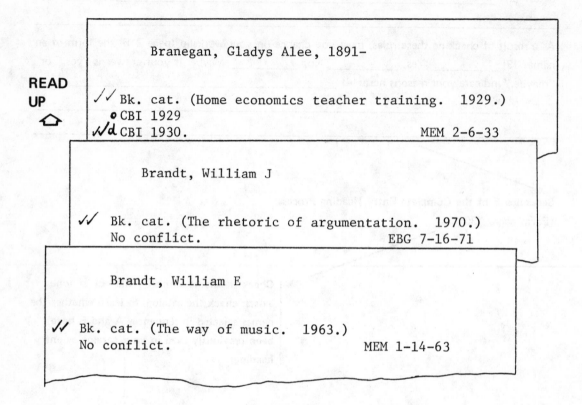

**READ
UP**

* If you wonder why some of these cards follow the "No conflict" method and others do not: Before 1949, every name that was to be established was automatically searched in bibliographies. Thus, name authority cards begun before 1949 almost always include references to bibliographies. After 1949, the "No conflict" principle began to be used, and bibliographies were searched only to resolve actual or potential conflicts. See pages 92-93.

Bronstein, David

READ
UP

✓✓ Bk. cat. (Everyday spiritual reception. 1968.)
No conflict.   HMS 3-6-69

Bronson, Wilfrid Swancourt, 1894-

✓ Bk. cat. (W.M.Reed, The sea for Sam. 1935.): Wilfrid
    S. Bronson.
✓/d CBI 1933-37.   HED 3-9-38

Bronson, Walter Cochrane, 1862-1928.

✓ Bk. cat. (English poems. 1907.): Walter C. Bronson.
✓/d Bk. cat., jacket: b. 1862.
✓/d BIP 1928: d. 1928.   NAS 12-12-30

Reed-Hill, Robert E
    xHill, Robert E   Reed-

READ
UP

✓✓ Bk. cat. (Physical metallurgy principles. [1964]):
    Robert E. Reed-Hill.
✓✓ LC cd.
No conflict.   CEB 10-6-64

Reed, William Maxwell, 1871-

✓✓ Bk. cat. (The sea for Sam. 1935.): W. Maxwell Reed.
✓/d CBI 1933-37.   HED 3-9-38

Reed, Joan

✓✓ Bk. cat. (Pizer, M. Come listen! 1966.)
No conflict.   SET 5-9-67

EXERCISE

After studying the above authority file, please indicate below:

Which of the three names on your workslip (page 215) **cannot** be corrected on the basis of the authority file? (1) _____

Can this name be left in the form in which it is listed on the workslip? Justify your answer.
(2) _____ Yes; _____ No; Reason: _____

_____

Write the other two names in the exact form in which they should be listed as entry headings.
(3) _____

_____

_____

Sequence F of the Complete Entry Heading Process
(From pages 130-131)

Record the names selected in final form on
the workslip, in their proper place.

EXERCISE

This is easy. Correct the workslip (Page 215) on the basis of the preceding answers.

Now you have gone through all of the sequences listed on pages 130-131. It was a long process. But, as mentioned earlier, it takes longer to read about, and study, a process than to do it routinely with the sophistication that comes from experience. Once you have gained experience, you will be able to take many shortcuts, to combine some steps, and to skip others. Your work will go quickly.

PART C:
PERSONAL NAME ENTRY HEADINGS AND THE AACR

CHAPTER EIGHT **AACR CHOICE-OF-ENTRY-HEADINGS RULES FOR PERSONAL NAMES**

HIGHLIGHTS

Table Number One: This chapter is constructed around a table that summarizes the basic AA rules for selecting main or added entry headings. While emphasizing choice of personal names, the table is also a guide to all other AA choice-of-entry-heading rules. The first breakdown of this table is on page 225; the fourth, and most detailed, breakdown on page 227. In general, the table is divided into main and added entry rules dealing with individual authorship; rules dealing with multiple authorship in which the contribution of any one author is *not* distinct; rules in which it *is* distinct; rules for books of unknown or uncertain authorship; and added entry headings rules based on the concept of the user's approaches and convenience, as explained in Chapter 4.

Among the terms listed in Table Number I are the following: *Editor:* Depending on the role an editor had in preparing a text, he may not receive any entry heading, or he may receive an added entry heading as a supporting collaborator, or the main entry heading as the book's creator. *Author-title Added Entries:* These are added entry headings consisting of an author's name and the title of one of his works. They are used to cause, for example, a discussion of a book to be filed next to the main entry for that book. *Analytical Added Entry Heading:* This is an added entry heading for a part of a work, rather than for the whole work. *Anonymous Works:* Works of unknown authorship fall into three categories: (1) Author is not indicated in the book, and reference works give no indication either; (2) Author is not indicated in the book, but reference works give a reasonably definite indication of authorship; (3) Author is not mentioned in the book, but reference works give definite indication of authorship.

The Three Dimensions of AA Rule 33: The preliminary note of this rule permits the cataloger to use his judgment and to look at the book being cataloged (1) from the dimension of the entire book. (List a book under the person(s) responsible for its intellectual content as a whole. Don't list it under people who contributed little, because hardly anyone would look for *this* work under *these* names.) (2) From the dimension of part of a book. (You may make an added entry heading for a person responsible for only part of a work.) (3) From the dimension of the person whose name becomes a heading in a catalog. (If your patrons need to know what you have by any one person, you may make an entry heading for any of his contributions, large or small, regardless of what the other rules say.)

The "Rule of Three": Many entry heading rules, and many descriptive cataloging rules, employ the number 3 as dividing line between one type of action and another. For both, entry headings and descriptive cataloging, the "Rule of Three" can be codified like this; "1, 2, 3 in any one category—use all; 4 or more in any one category—use only the first."

The "Rule of Three" is an arbitrary device, based on two assumptions: (1) The first-mentioned name in any one category (author, editor, assistant, etc.) is typically its principal creator; (2) The involvement of 4 or more authors (or editors, etc.) divides the intellectual responsibility so much that there is little chance a reader will approach the book through any but its principal creators.

When combining the "Rule of Three" for descriptive cataloging, and for entry headings, names are occasionally transcribed descriptively for which no added entry headings are made.

AA CHOICE-OF-ENTRY-HEADING RULES FOR PERSONAL NAMES

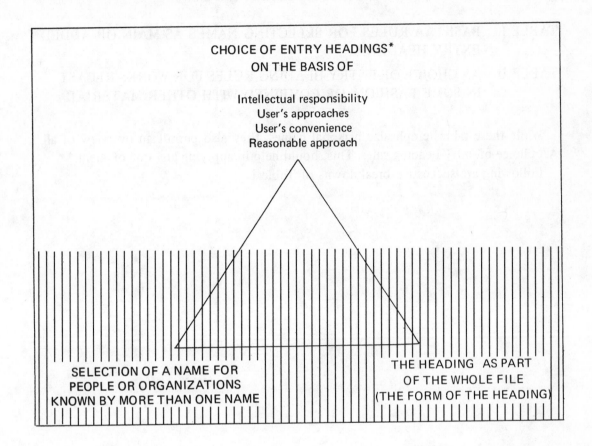

CHOICE OF ENTRY HEADINGS*
ON THE BASIS OF

Intellectual responsibility
User's approaches
User's convenience
Reasonable approach

SELECTION OF A NAME FOR
PEOPLE OR ORGANIZATIONS
KNOWN BY MORE THAN ONE NAME

THE HEADING AS PART
OF THE WHOLE FILE
(THE FORM OF THE HEADING)

We now turn to the individual AA rules on selecting personal names for main and added entry headings. Before proceeding, please review Chapter 2 (pages 48-64) which illustrates typical choice-of-entry-heading situations, and pages 102-105 of Chapter 4, which summarize AA's four basic choice-of-entry-heading concepts.

* From page 110.

All AA choice-of-entry-heading rules* fall into a definite pattern. With respect to personal names, this pattern can be summarized in two tables:

TABLE I.   BASIC AA RULES FOR SELECTING NAMES AS MAIN OR ADDED ENTRY HEADINGS.

TABLE II   AA CHOICE-OF-ENTRY-HEADING RULES FOR WORKS RECAST IN SOME FASHION, OR COMBINED WITH OTHER MATERIAL.

While these tables emphasize personal names, they also permit an overview of **all** AA choice-of-entry-heading rules. This should help in applying any one of them.** Following are successive breakdowns of Table I.

* The various headings—personal name, corporate name, real title, uniform title, form headings—were mentioned on pages 28 to 45.

* See also page 124.

First Breakdown of
TABLE I
BASIC AA RULES FOR SELECTING NAMES
AS MAIN OR ADDED ENTRY HEADINGS

RULES BASED ON THE CONCEPT OF INTELLECTUAL RESPONSIBILITY. (pages 12, 32, 58, 102)	ADDED ENTRY HEADING RULES* BASED ON THE CONCEPT OF THE USER'S APPROACHES AND CONVENIENCE. (pages 58, 59, 102, 104)

Second Breakdown of
TABLE I
BASIC AA RULES FOR SELECTING NAMES
AS MAIN OR ADDED ENTRY HEADINGS

RULES BASED ON THE CONCEPT OF INTELLECTUAL RESPONSIBILITY. (Pages 12, 32, 58, 102) THESE COVER:			ADDED ENTRY HEADING RULES* BASED ON THE CONCEPT OF THE USER'S APPROACHES AND CONVENIENCE. (Pages 58, 59, 102, 114)
Individual authorship: A book created by one author or editor or compiler. (Pages 117-178)	Multiple authorship or editorship or compilership: A book for which several people have approximately equal responsibility.	Books of unknown or uncertain authorship.	

* See pages 32 to 39 for examples of main entry headings selected on the basis of the user's approaches rather than of intellectual responsibility.

Third Breakdown of

T A B L E I

BASIC AA RULES FOR SELECTING NAMES AS MAIN OR ADDED ENTRY HEADINGS

RULES BASED ON THE CONCEPT OF INTELLECTUAL RESPONSIBILITY. (Pages 12, 32, 58, 102.)

Individual authorship: A book created by one author or editor or compiler. (158)

Multiple authorship or editorship or compilership: **equal** responsibility This can be: THESE COVER: A book for which several people have approximately equal responsibility

Situations in which the precise contribution of any one author etc. is **not** distinct, that is, **shared**, or **joint** authorship (159-163) or editorship or compilership, in which the

- principal author, editor, or compiler **is indicated** and there are
  - 1 - 3 authors
  - 4 or more authors
- principal author, editor, or com-piler is **not** indi-cated and there are
  - 1 - 3 authors
  - 4 or more authors

Situations in which the precise contribution of any one author etc. **is** distinct, that is, **multiple** author-ship (164-169) or editorship or compilership, with the book

- **having a collective** title**
  - and its compiler or editor **is clearly** indicated
  - and its compiler or editor **is not** clearly indicated
- **not having** a collective title**
  - **but having** a collective title page***
  - **and not** having a collective title page***

Books of **unknown** or uncertain authorship.

ADDED ENTRY HEADING RULES* BASED ON THE CONCEPT OF THE USER'S APPROACHES AND CONVENIENCE. THESE INCLUDE: Situations in which added entry headings, such as the book's title, or the names of people or organizations can be used as additional approaches to a work, although no authorship or collaboration is involved. (58-59, 104, 171, 173) (tracings.))

---

* See pages 32-39 for examples of main entry headings selected on the basis of the user's approaches, rather than of intellectual responsibility.

** A title that is obviously intended to fit the whole book rather than only a part of a book (In other words, the typical title. Books of multiple authorship have occasionally no such title, but only separate titles for each contribution.)

*** A title page that is obviously intended to fit the whole book rather than only a part of a book. (In other words, the typical title page. Books of multiple authorship have occasionally no common (collective title page, but only separate title pages for each contribution.)

Study the preceding breakdown of Table I carefully and refer to the text pages indicated in it. Then study the following, final breakdown. Note that it lists the pertinent AA rules. The following pages will guide you through these rules by means of exercises and text.

TABLE I:

BASIC AA RULES FOR SELECTING NAMES
AS MAIN OR ADDED ENTRY HEADINGS.

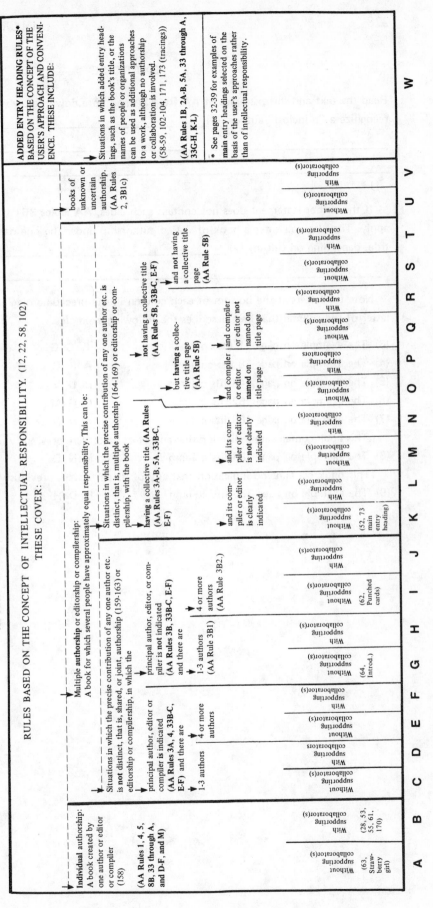

EXERCISE

Read the text and the examples of **AA Rule 3A** and note down below what clues AA uses to recognize a "principal" author. (1) _____

_____

_____

If the author statement does not contain such clues, **AA Rules 3B1 (first paragraph) and 3B2** apply. They let you enter a book of shared authorship under the one named first, or under its title, depending on (fill in) (2) _____

_____

Note the letters at the bottom of each column in the preceding diagram. Circle (below) the letter of the column that best describes the following examples.

(3) The example on page 51 fits column   B   C   G

(4) The example on page 78 fits column   A   B   C

(5) The example on page 148 fits column   B   U   V

(6) The example on page 182 fits column   C   G   M

(7) The example on page 183 fits column   K   M   N

  (This book contains no indication that any of its parts were previously published separately.)

(8) The example on page 184 fits column   M   N   Q

  (This book contains no indication that any of its parts were previously published separately.)

(9) The example on page 189 fits column   B   D   H

Read **AA Rules 4 and 5,** and indicate below which one is intended for material previously published separately, or in other editions, but now combined in a new combination, (1)_____ and which one deals with material newly written for publication at this time (2) _____ .

An editor usually plays one of several roles which are defined on AA page 344. Please read this definition, for it will show that, according to the part an editor had in preparing a text, he may not even be mentioned in the book being cataloged (pages 171 and 196) and would thus typically not receive an added entry heading, or he may be mentioned as a supporting collaborator (pages 53 and 201), in which case he might well receive an added entry heading, or he may actually be the organizer and creator of a work (pages 52, 172 and 174).

EXERCISE

With which of the editor's roles mentioned above does **AA Rule 4A** deal? (3) _____

_____

With which of these roles does **AA Rule 33D** deal? (Ignore, for our purposes, the reference to serial publications; they are outside the scope of this text.) (4)_____

_____

Some Comments on Rules Listed in Table I (Page 227)

(1) AA Rules 3, 4, and 5 tell you to make in certain situations the main entry heading for a work under its title. If you wonder how such a rule can be grouped under the concept of "Intellectual Responsibility," be patient. This will be discussed on pages 240 - 242.

(2) AA Rule 5: The term "author-title added entry" in this rule refers to an added entry heading that consists of an author's name plus the title of one of his works. It is used to cause this particular added entry to be filed in proper alphabetical sequence, for example next to the entry for a book that it may discuss. Here is a typical author-title added entry.

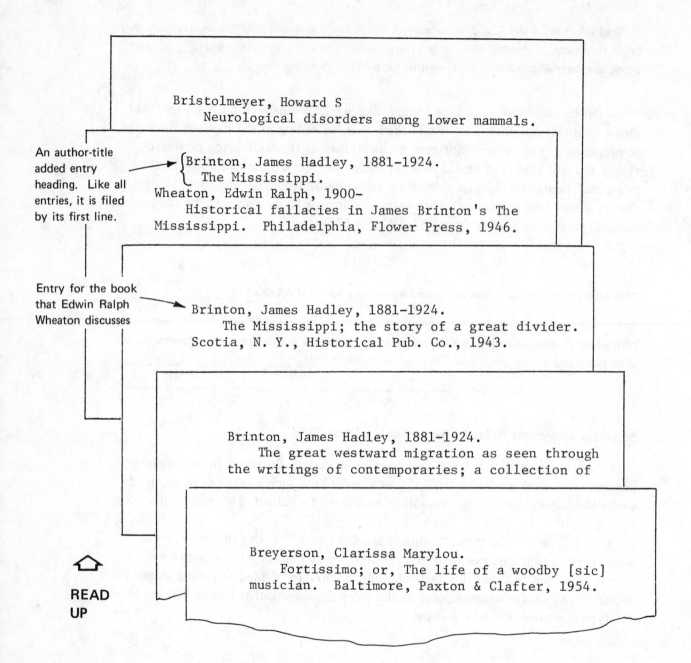

Bristolmeyer, Howard S
    Neurological disorders among lower mammals.

An author-title
added entry
heading. Like all
entries, it is filed
by its first line.

Brinton, James Hadley, 1881-1924.
  The Mississippi.
Wheaton, Edwin Ralph, 1900-
    Historical fallacies in James Brinton's The
Mississippi. Philadelphia, Flower Press, 1946.

Entry for the book
that Edwin Ralph
Wheaton discusses

Brinton, James Hadley, 1881-1924.
    The Mississippi; the story of a great divider.
Scotia, N. Y., Historical Pub. Co., 1943.

Brinton, James Hadley, 1881-1924.
    The great westward migration as seen through
the writings of contemporaries; a collection of

Breyerson, Clarissa Marylou.
    Fortissimo; or, The life of a woodby [sic]
musician. Baltimore, Paxton & Clafter, 1954.

READ
UP

(3) AA Rules 5B (example) and 33 (Preliminary note): The term "Analytical added entry" in this rule is explained on AA page 343, under "Analytical entry." Its distinguishing characteristic is that it describes a part of a larger work, whereas we ordinarily catalog a whole work as a unit. Thus, an "analytical added entry heading" is an added entry heading for a part of a work rather than for the whole. This added entry heading may be a name, the title of a work, or of a part of a work, or it may be an author-title added entry heading.

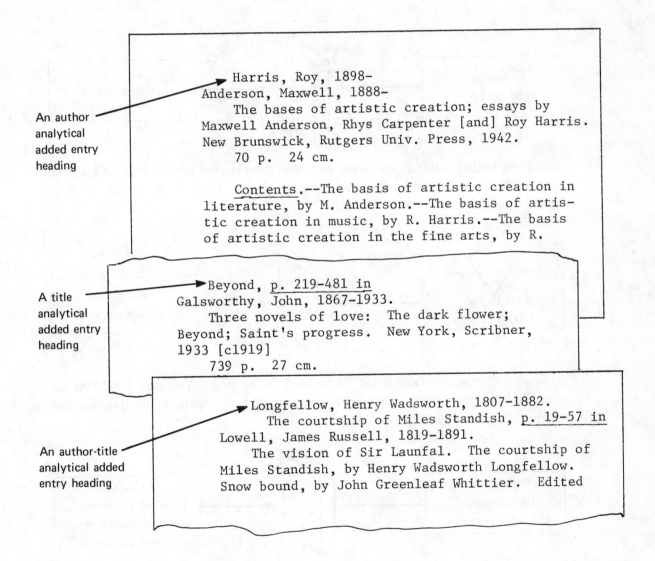

An author analytical added entry heading

Harris, Roy, 1898-
Anderson, Maxwell, 1888-
    The bases of artistic creation; essays by
Maxwell Anderson, Rhys Carpenter [and] Roy Harris.
New Brunswick, Rutgers Univ. Press, 1942.
    70 p.   24 cm.

    Contents.--The basis of artistic creation in
literature, by M. Anderson.--The basis of artistic creation in music, by R. Harris.--The basis
of artistic creation in the fine arts, by R.

A title analytical added entry heading

Beyond, p. 219-481 in
Galsworthy, John, 1867-1933.
    Three novels of love: The dark flower;
Beyond; Saint's progress. New York, Scribner,
1933 [c1919]
    739 p.   27 cm.

An author-title analytical added entry heading

Longfellow, Henry Wadsworth, 1807-1882.
    The courtship of Miles Standish, p. 19-57 in
Lowell, James Russell, 1819-1891.
    The vision of Sir Launfal. The courtship of
Miles Standish, by Henry Wadsworth Longfellow.
Snow bound, by John Greenleaf Whittier. Edited

(4) Three Dimensions of **AA Rule 33**: Be aware of the three dimensions in the **"Preliminary Note" of AA Rule 33**. They give the cataloger authority to use his judgment.

First dimension: The whole book being cataloged is the focus. Like the other rules studied so far, it says in effect: List a work under the person(s) responsible for its intellectual content as a whole.

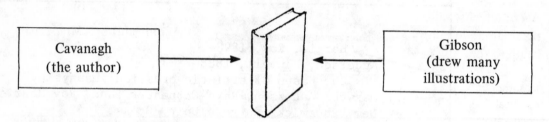

But don't bother listing it under the names of people who contributed only a small part, or who just helped a bit, because hardly anyone would look for this work under these names.

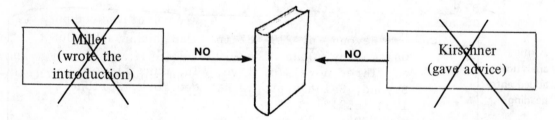

Second dimension: Part of the whole book is the focus. You may also make an entry heading for a person responsible only for part of a work. ("Analytical added entries." See also page 228.)

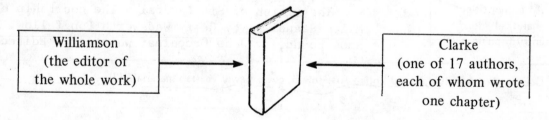

Third dimension: The catalog as a whole, and the person are the focus. If your patrons need to know what you have by any one person, you may make an entry heading for any of his contributions, whether big or small, regardless of what the other rules say.

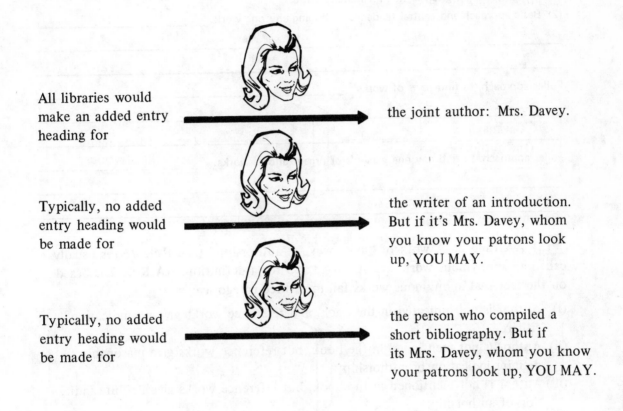

All libraries would make an added entry heading for → the joint author: Mrs. Davey.

Typically, no added entry heading would be made for → the writer of an introduction. But if it's Mrs. Davey, whom you know your patrons look up, YOU MAY.

Typically, no added entry heading would be made for → the person who compiled a short bibliography. But if its Mrs. Davey, whom you know your patrons look up, YOU MAY.

You may make these added entries if your patrons seem to need them. But it would be foolish to carry this too far. See pages 104 and58

EXERCISE

Does **AA Rule 3** cover both "joint" and "multiple" authorship? (1) _____

_____

Does it, like **AA Rule 4,** and unlike **AA Rule 5,** cover newly written material? (2) _____

_____

In what way does **AA Rule 8B** permit the cataloger to use his judgment? (1) _____

_____

_____

Summarize the central tendency of **AA Rule 33 (through A, and D-F, and M)**, noting the three different approaches given in its "Preliminary Note."

(2) Basic approach and central tendency in finding any one work: _____

_____

_____

Fuller approach, to find parts of works: _____

_____

_____

Fuller approach, to find any one person's or organization's works: _____

_____

_____

(5) **AA Rule 2**: A work of "unknown . . . authorship" (**AA Rule 2A**) is usually called an **anonymous work**. See AA page 343 for a definition. **AA Rule 2** is based on the fact that anonymous works fall into three categories:

(i) Author is not indicated in the book, and reference works give no indication, either;

(ii) Author is not mentioned in the book, but reference works give reasonably definite indication of authorship;

(iii) Author is not mentioned in the book, but reference works give definite indication of authorship.

Be sure to distinguish in your own mind between an anonymous work and a pseudonymous author. A definition of the term "Pseudonym" is on AA page 346. See also pages 71-76.

An "author-title reference" (**AA Rule 2B**)* refers from a name-plus-book-title to another-name-plus-book title. While the usual see-reference refers from a name to another name and thus leads to *all books listed under the second name* (page 73-78), the author-title reference refers only from one possible entry for a particular book to the *real entry for that book*. It is used nowadays only for the situation described in **AA Rule 2B** and looks like this:

Smith, Walter James
Memoirs of Buckwheat Country
<u>see</u>
Boucher, John Charles, 1931-
Memoirs of Buckwheat Country.

EXERCISE

Study the AA rules listed below, and jot down the concepts that cause added entry headings to be made for people or organizations that have *no* intellectual responsibility for a work. These rules exist because they furnish additional reasonable approaches to a work. (Page 104.)

AA Rule 1B_____

_____

AA Rules 2A, 2B_____

_____

AA Rule 5A_____

_____

AA Rule 33A _____

_____

_____

AA Rules 33H, 33L_____

_____

_____

* For "author-title added entry" see pages 229-231.

The purpose of the following exercise is to show how the specific rules you have just studied, when viewed together, fall into a pattern.

EXERCISE

Please fill in the blank spaces below with whichever of the following expressions applies. You may use any one of them as often as needed.

THE WORK'S TITLE
AUTHOR
THAT AUTHOR
AUTHOR, EDITOR, OR COMPILER
THE HEADING APPROPRIATE TO THE FIRST WORK LISTED OR BOUND IN THIS WORK
THE PERSON NAMED FIRST ON THE TITLE PAGE

If an author or editor or compiler seems to have principal intellectual responsibility for a work, make the main entry heading under (1) _____

_____

If you know definitely (judging by the book you are cataloging) or probably (judging by reference works) that a certain person is the author of the book, make the main entry heading under (2) ____

_____

_____

If several people are the authors of a work, one of whom seems to have principal responsibility, make the main entry heading under (3) _____

_____

If one, two, or three people are the authors of a work but none seems to have principal responsibility, make the main entry heading under (4) _____

_____

If the author's name is not available, if the author has no name, or if the fact of authorship is uncertain, make the main entry under (5) _____

_____

If the work being cataloged is a collection of different pieces, or of many bits of information gathered by an editor or compiler who, however, seems *not* to assume principal responsibility for the work's intellectual content, make the main entry under (6) _____

_____

If four or more people are the authors of a work, but none of them, nor an editor, seems to have principal responsibility for it, make the main entry under (7) _____

_____

If the work being cataloged is a collection of different pieces without an overall title, make the main entry under (8) _____

_____

For the following review exercise you will need to consider every rule studied in this chapter. Be sure to refer to the AA freely as you go along. Even experienced catalogers do this, for guidance.

EXERCISE

Considering every AA rule studied so far, indicate below what main entry heading is needed for each given situation, and what added entry headings you would make—definitely, possibly, or not at all. Do not indicate the form of each heading, but *do* cite the pertinent rule number.

EXAMPLE	Make MAIN ENTRY under	WOULD make ADDED ENTRY under	MIGHT make ADDED ENTRY under	Would NOT make ADDED ENTRY under
(A single work) By John Doe & James Miller	Doe 3A	Miller 3A, 33B		
The collected works of John Doe. Introduction by James Miller. (1)				
(A single work) By John Doe. With assistance of James Miller. (2)				
(A single work) By John Doe. Illustrated by James Miller. (3)				
(A single work) By John Doe, James Miller and Jane Smith. (4)				
(12 papers by 12 authors, presented at a conference. The authors are listed only in the Table of Contents.) The title page reads: (Title) Edited by John Doe (5)				

	Make MAIN ENTRY under	WOULD make ADDED ENTRY under	MIGHT make ADDED ENTRY under	Would NOT make ADDED ENTRY under
(A single work) By John Doe, James Miller, Jane Smith, & Arthur Roe. (6)				
(12 papers by 12 authors, presented at a conference. Title page contains only title & imprint. Editor has signed the Preface, authors are listed in Table of Contents.) (7)				
(A single work. No author is named in it. Reference books indicate that James Gadsden or Julius Sterling Morton might have written it.) (8)				
(A single work, by the Société des amis des bibliothèques. Title page indicates that it was translated into English by James Miller, & that Jules Gabin drew the illustrations. (9)				

	Make MAIN ENTRY under	WOULD make ADDED ENTRY under	MIGHT make ADDED ENTRY under	Would NOT make ADDED ENTRY under
(Title page reads): Letters to his wife Mary By John Doe. (Preface indicates that the original manuscripts of most of these letters are in the Putztown, Pa., Historical Museum.) (10)				
(Reprints of stories, newspaper articles, etc., written over the past 70 years by many authors. Title page reads): Highlights of Lame Duck, S.D. Edited by J. M. Doe under the guidance of the Lame Duck Historical Society which sponsored this work. (11)				
(A single work) By John Doe. (Preface indicates that the statistical formulae which form an important part of the work were developed with the advice of James Miller.) (12)				

THE "RULE OF THREE."

Many entry heading rules employ the number three as dividing line between one type of action and another. Here is a summary:

AA Rule 2A: When entering a work of unknown or uncertain authorship under its title, make added entries for 1, 2, or 3 persons to whom authorship has been attributed. **Therefore, implied:** If authorship has been attributed to 4 or more persons, make no added entries for them.

AA Rule 3A: If a work of shared authorship is entered under 1 person or organization, make added entires for the other authors only if not more than 3 are involved. **Therefore, implied:** If 4 or more persons or organizations share authorship, make no added entries for them.

AA Rules 3B1, 3B2: If 2 or 3 authors are involved, make main entry under the first one listed and added entries under the others. If 4 or more authors are involved, enter under title and make one added entry for the first author listed.

AA Rules 5A, 5B: Make author-title added entries if not more than 3 works are included in the collection. **Therefore, implied:** If 4 or more works are included, make no author-title added entries for them.

If more than 3 works, but not more than 3 authors are included, make added entries for these authors. **Therefore, implied:** If 4 or more authors' works are included, make no added entries for these authors.

AA Rule 33B: If up to 3 authors are involved, make added entries under the authors not selected for the main entry heading. **Therefore, implied:** If 4 or more authors are involved, make no added entries for them.

If the main entry is under a category other than an author, make added entries for 1, 2, or 3 authors. **Therefore, implied:** If 4 or more authors are involved, make no added entries for them.

In descriptive cataloging the number 3 is also the dividing line. For books by 2 or 3 joint authors, editors, or compilers all names are transcribed in each category in the author statement. In books by 4 or more joint authors, editors, or compilers only the first name on the title page in each category, is listed in the author statement followed by the phrase [and others] if the title is in English and [et al.] if it is in another language. In the case of other contributors—illustrators, translators, etc.—the same convention is observed.

Davis, Allison, 1902-
    Relationships between achievement in high school, college, and occupation: a follow-up study [by] Allison Davis and Robert Hess, with the assistance of Jack Forman [and others] Chicago, University of Chicago, 1963.

Two authors: more than three other contributors.

Fox, Robert S
    Pupil-teacher adjustment and mutual adaptation in creating classroom learning environments, by Robert S. Fox, Ronald O. Lippitt [and] Richard A. Schmuck, with collaboration of David Epperson, Margaret Luszki [and] Elmer Van Egmond. [Ann Arbor] Inter-center Program of Research on Children

Three authors; three other contributors.

For entry headings as well as for descriptive cataloging, this "Rule of Three" can be codified like this: *1, 2, 3 in any one category—use all; 4 or more in any one category—use only the first.* Remember that it applies separately to each category of author, editor, supporting contributor, etc.

The "Rule of Three" is an arbitrary decision based on two assumptions: (1) The first-mentioned name in any one category (author, editor, assistant, etc.) is typically its principal creator;* (2) The involvement of four or more authors (or editors, etc.) divides the intellectual responsibility so much that there is little chance a reader will approach the book through any but its principal creators.

When combining the "Rule of Three" for descriptive cataloging and for entry headings, names are occasionally transcribed descriptively for which no added entry headings are made.

---

* When the first-mentioned name in any one category is obviously not its principal creator, the rules permit flexibility: *cf.* **AA Rule 3A**, third example; also **AA Rule 33**.

* Pages 17 and 46-48 discuss transcription without added entry headings because of the *role* an individual had.

EXERCISE

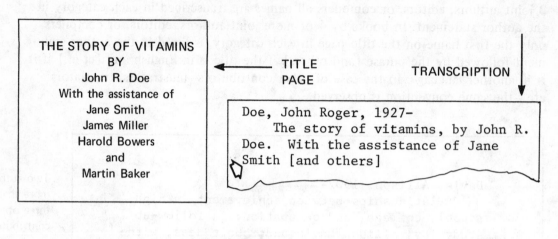

According to **AA Rules 33A and 33H,** should an added entry tracing be made for Smith?

(1) _____ Yes; _____ No.

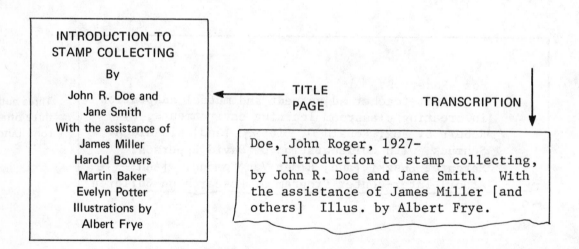

According to the AA Rules, should added entry tracings be made for (2)

Smith _____	Yes; _____	No.	Bowers: ___ Yes; _____	No.
Frye: _____	Yes; _____	No.	Baker: ____ Yes; _____	No.
Miller: _____	Yes; _____	No.	Potter: ____ Yes; _____	No.

REVIEW EXERCISE

On the basis of the information given below, and of the pertinent AA rules, indicate for each book what main and added entry heading(s) you would select, and list the number(s) of the rule(s) used. Do not indicate the form of these headings, but do study **AA Rule 33P**, and indicate for each book whether or not a title added entry should be made.

THREE TALES OF HANS ANDERSEN

WITH TWENTY-TWO ILLUSTRATIONS
BY
LINLEY SAMBOURNE

MACMILLAN AND CO., LIMITED
ST. MARTIN'S STREET, LONDON
1910

CONTENTS

THE DAUNTLESS TIN SOLDIER	1
THUMBELISA	13
THE LITTLE MERMAID	39

ILLUSTRATIONS

	PAGE
Initial	1
"Soldiers! Soldiers!"	2
"The maid-servant and the little boy ran down at once to look for him"	5
"'Look out,' said one, 'there is a tin soldier!'"	6
"So they made a boat"	7
"The soldier . . . sailed away down the gutter"	8
"Phew! how he gnashed his teeth and shouted to the sticks and straws: 'Stop him! Stop him!'"	9

Main entry heading:

_____

Selected on basis of AA Rule(s):

_____

Added entry heading(s), if any:

_____

_____

Selected on basis of AA Rule(s):

_____

A Symposium on

STEROID HORMONES

Edited by
EDGAR S. GORDON

THE UNIVERSITY OF WISCONSIN PRESS
————— 1950 —————

With Contributions By

S. A. Asdell	I. Chester Jones
S. Bird	Charles D. Kochakian
John J. Bittner	Seymour Lieberman
Konrad Bloch	F. W. Lorenz
H. H. Cole	G. F. Marrian
Nicholas E. Collias	Harold L. Mason
Konrad Dobriner	Carl R. Moore
L. V. Domm	Edward C. Reifenstein, Jr.
Louis F. Fieser	Leo T. Samuels
Thomas F. Gallagher	J. J. Schneider
Roy O. Greep	Ulrich V. Solmssen
Hans Hirschmann	Charles W. Turner
Frederick L. Hisaw	Gray H. Twombly
Charles B. Huggins	Eleanor H. Venning
R. R. Humphrey	Albert Wettstein
Robert A. Huseby	Abraham White
Dwight J. Ingle	Alfred L. Wilds

Publisher's Note

ADDITIONAL
SAMPLE PAGES
FROM THIS
BOOK ON
FACING PAGE

For bibliographical reasons, Dr. Edgar S. Gordon, chairman of the committee responsible for this book, has been designated editor. Listing volumes of essays written under separate authorship presents problems to bibliographers which do not easily lend themselves to practical solution. The Press, therefore, feels that scholars will be grateful for a simple entry under which this book may appear in files, catalogues, and bibliographies.

Main entry heading:

_____

Selected on basis of AA Rule(s):

_____

Added entry heading(s), if any:

_____

Selected on basis of AA Rule(s):

_____

ADDITIONAL SAMPLE
PAGES FROM "STEROID
HORMONES."

Preface

Progress in the understanding of the part played by steroid compounds in the regulation of animal function and behavior has ac-

In order to summarize and correlate this mass of information arising from experimental work in scores of laboratories, a symposium was arranged to cover both fundamental and applied aspects of steroid research. The participants are recognized authorities in their respective fields and are representative of the various subdivisions of biological science that have contributed to the expansion and development of this subject.

The present volume is a collection of the major papers presented at this meeting. Unfortunately, it has not been possible to provide a verbatim report of the many informal discussions which took place in the round

The symposium was made possible through the generosity of the Wisconsin Alumni Research Foundation by means of funds administered by the Graduate School of the University of Wisconsin and through a grant from the National Research Council Committee on Growth acting in behalf of the American Cancer Society. Grateful acknowledgment is made to these two sponsors as well as to the committee on arrangements which planned the program.

Edgar S. Gordon

Madison, Wisconsin
September 1, 1949

Contents

VOLUME 1

ADDITIONAL
SAMPLE PAGES
FROM THIS
BOOK ON
FACING PAGE

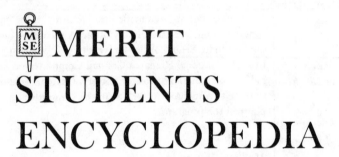

MERIT
STUDENTS
ENCYCLOPEDIA

BERNARD S. CAYNE
EDITOR-IN-CHIEF

WILLIAM D. HALSEY
EDITORIAL DIRECTOR

LOUIS SHORES
SENIOR LIBRARY ADVISOR

CROWELL-COLLIER EDUCATIONAL CORPORATION

Main entry heading: Added entry heading(s), if any:

_____   _____

Selected on basis of AA Rule(s):   Selected on basis of AA Rule(s):

_____   _____

CHAPTER NINE AACR CHOICE-OF-ENTRY-HEADING RULES FOR RECAST AND COMBINED WORKS

HIGHLIGHTS

Table Number Two: This chapter is constructed around a table that summarizes AA rules for works that someone other than the original creator has changed in some fashion, and for works that were combined with other material to form a new work. The table is on page 258. The situations which it describes are illustrated on pages 253-257.

In all cases described, two individuals are involved, either of whom might become the main entry heading. Actually, the degree of change from the original to the changed edition, or the predominance of original material as against the added material, determine the selection of the main entry heading. The central tendency of the AA rules for such works is:

For Changed Works: If the new work is essentially like the original, make the main entry heading under the original author. But if the new work differs considerably from the original, make the main entry heading under the new author.

For Works That Have Been Combined With New Material: Use as main entry heading the name of the author who created the greater part, or who is presented as its chief creator.

For both categories, added entries are made for the person not chosen as main entry heading.

How to Recognize a Table Two Entry Heading Situation: Decision as to the degree of change, or predominance of one element over the other (and thus, the choice of the main entry heading) is made on the basis of the following clues, contained in the book being cataloged: (1) The author's intent and purpose, as expressed in the preface or foreword; (2) Proportion of each type of material; (3) Wording on the title page; (4) Typographical devices on the title page; (5) Sequence of names on the title page. Few books in this category contain all these clues. Whatever clues exist in one book will usually confirm each other. If not, follow the above order of precedence.

The Spectrum of Situations: An overall view of the situations listed in Tables I (page 227) and II (page 258) shows that many contain similar elements, but with different degrees of emphasis. If the situations with similar elements are grouped together as chains, the links in each chain can be arranged by increasing or decreasing degree of emphasis. A partial example of such a chain will illustrate this.

| Text without illustrations | 50 per cent text; 50 per cent illustrations | Illustrations without text |

Viewing cataloging situations (including entry heading situations) as links of a chain permits viewing each situation in the context of similar, but not identical, situations. It permits an overview of these situations and their entry heading rules.

AA CHOICE-OF-ENTRY-HEADING RULES FOR RECAST AND COMBINED WORKS

Table II,* which you will study next, comprises works which someone other than the original creator *changed* in some fashion, and works that were *combined with other material* to form a new work. Examples are the novel which has been condensed and republished, the collection of one person's letters published together with that person's biography by another writer, or the novel that has been recast as a play. (See also pages 56-58.)

Although two different "authors" or "elements" are involved in each such case, the choice of main entry heading is not problematical because of the two traditional basic guidelines: (1) When cataloging a work, look at the *whole* work in hand, not just an isolated section; (2) Whenever possible, make the main entry under the person or organization *chiefly* responsible for the intellectual content of the whole work being cataloged. These guidelines result in the following central tendency for main entry headings:

For changed works: If the complete new work is essentially like the original, make main entry heading under the original author. But if the new work is quite different from the original, make main entry heading under the new author.

For works with two elements: Use as main entry heading the name of the author who created the greater part, or who is presented as its chief creator.

---

* Mentioned on page 224.

If these two diagrams represent subject matter

And if this symbol repre- sents a book

For works republished in a different form

For works consisting of two elements

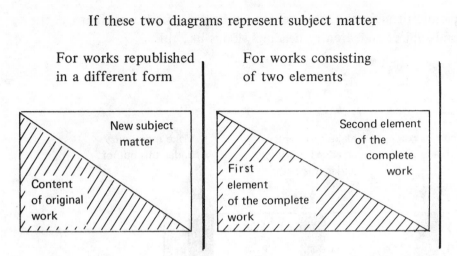

New subject matter

Content of original work

First element of the complete work

Second element of the complete work

the *main entry heading* for such a book is selected as follows:

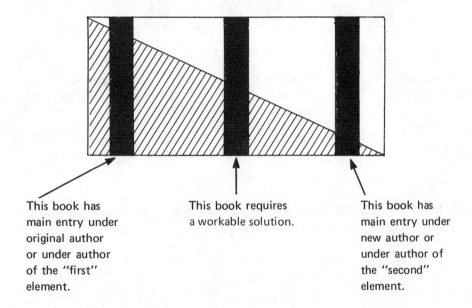

This book has main entry under original author or under author of the "first" element.

This book requires a workable solution.

This book has main entry under new author or under author of the "second" element.

The degree of change, or the predominance of one element over another, is the criterion for selecting the main entry heading. An added entry heading is made for the other author or element.

The combined picture of main and added entry headings for such works, apart from title, series, and subject added entry headings, looks like this:

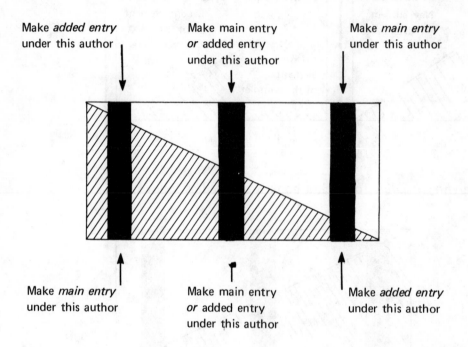

Make *added entry* under this author

Make main entry *or* added entry under this author

Make *main entry* under this author

Make *main entry* under this author

Make main entry *or* added entry under this author

Make *added entry* under this author

Any such book may also have supporting collaborators who may or may not receive added entry headings.* A typical case might be:

Selections
from
Shakespeare's

OTHELLO

Edited and with notes by
John Peters
Illustrations by
James Miller

* See pages 240-242.

EXERCISE

To learn the precise meaning of each term that you will encounter in Table II and be able to visualize the situation it represents, get a good dictionary (desk size dictionary will do, but not pocket dictionary), study the following diagrams, and fill in the dictionary definitions.

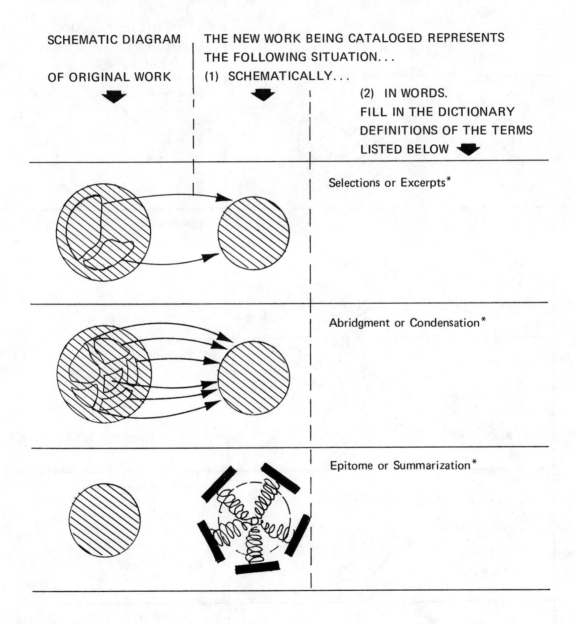

SCHEMATIC DIAGRAM

OF ORIGINAL WORK

THE NEW WORK BEING CATALOGED REPRESENTS THE FOLLOWING SITUATION...

(1) SCHEMATICALLY...

(2) IN WORDS.
FILL IN THE DICTIONARY
DEFINITIONS OF THE TERMS
LISTED BELOW

Selections or Excerpts*

Abridgment or Condensation*

Epitome or Summarization*

* For our purposes, these two terms are synonymous.

SCHEMATIC DIAGRAM

OF ORIGINAL WORK

THE NEW WORK BEING CATALOGED REPRESENTS
THE FOLLOWING SITUATION...

(1) SCHEMATICALLY...

(2) IN WORDS.
FILL IN THE DICTIONARY
DEFINITIONS OF THE TERMS
LISTED BELOW

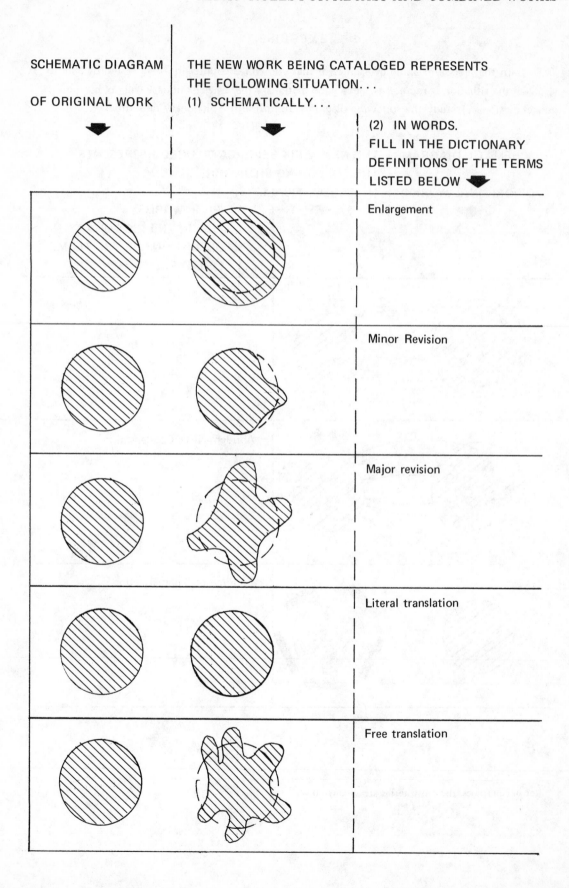

Enlargement

Minor Revision

Major revision

Literal translation

Free translation

SCHEMATIC DIAGRAM OF ORIGINAL WORK ⬇	THE NEW WORK BEING CATALOGED REPRESENTS THE FOLLOWING SITUATION... (1) SCHEMATICALLY... ⬇	(2) IN WORDS. FILL IN THE DICTIONARY DEFINITIONS OF THE TERMS LISTED BELOW ⬇
(circle)	(square)	Dramatization (Your dictionary may use "dramatize.")
(square)	(circle)	Novelization (Your dictionary may use "novelize.")
(circle)	(scalloped circle)	Versification
(circle)	(irregular blob)	Adaptation
(circle)	(dashed circle)	Paraphrase (may be humorous or satirical)

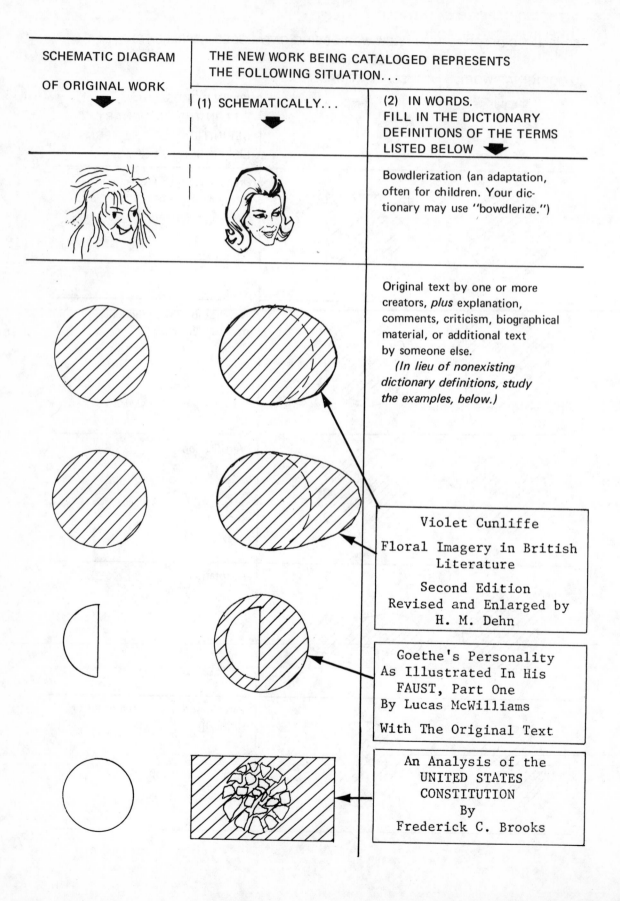

SCHEMATIC DIAGRAM OF ORIGINAL WORK ⬇	THE NEW WORK BEING CATALOGED REPRESENTS THE FOLLOWING SITUATION...	
	(1) SCHEMATICALLY... ⬇	(2) IN WORDS. FILL IN THE DICTIONARY DEFINITIONS OF THE TERMS LISTED BELOW ⬇
		Bowdlerization (an adaptation, often for children. Your dictionary may use "bowdlerize.")
		Original text by one or more creators, *plus* explanation, comments, criticism, biographical material, or additional text by someone else. *(In lieu of nonexisting dictionary definitions, study the examples, below.)*

Violet Cunliffe

Floral Imagery in British Literature

Second Edition
Revised and Enlarged by
H. M. Dehn

Goethe's Personality
As Illustrated In His
FAUST, Part One
By Lucas McWilliams

With The Original Text

An Analysis of the
UNITED STATES
CONSTITUTION
By
Frederick C. Brooks

THE WORK BEING CATALOGED REPRESENTS THE FOLLOWING SITUATION. . .SCHEMATICALLY	. . . AND IN WORDS. . .

Author and artist as collaborators;
Art reproductions plus text by someone else.
(In lieu of nonexisting dictionary definitions, study the examples below.)

<table>
<tr><td>

MIRACLES OF THE DESERT

A Pictorial Essay

Photographs by
Franklyn Bunce
Text by Jessica White

</td><td>

The Paintings of
Karl Blechen

With Notes and a
Biography
of the Artist
By Benton Milam

</td></tr>
</table>

The terms illustrated on the preceding pages represent cataloging situations listed in Table II. This table is arranged in three columns that correspond to the diagrams on pages 251-252. Table II should be read as follows: *Selections (This is the first situation listed in the left-hand column and means): If the book being cataloged is a selection of passages from a book by Mr. "A" with no, or with only minor additions by Messrs. "B" or "C," make main entry under Mr. "A's" name, on the basis of AA Rule 1A.*

TABLE II

AA CHOICE-OF-ENTRY-HEADING RULES FOR WORKS

RECAST IN SOME FASHION, OR COMBINED WITH OTHER MATERIAL*

Material altered in some way by someone other than the original author but still in the same literary form. *Not involving a true re-writing of the original text.* Make main entry under *original author.*	Material combined with other material by someone other than the original author. Main entry decision depends on the *proportion* of each type of material (page count) and/or the *intent and purpose* of the new work as expressed in its title or prefatory matter. If proportion and purpose conflict, *purpose takes precedence.*	Material altered rather extensively by someone other than th the original author, and in a different literary style or form. Involves actual *re-writing* of the text. Make main entry under *"new"* author
Selections excerpts **AA Rule 1A** Abridgment Condensation Enlargement **AA Rule 14A** Minor revision Literal translation **AA** of a work. **Rule 15A** (A collection of translations from different authors is treated as a collection: AA **Rule 15B, Rule 5, Table I.**)	Original text by one author plus explanation, comments, criticism, biographical materials, or additional text by someone else. **AA Rules 9, 11** Author and artist as collaborators **AA Rule 8A** (Artists as supporting collaborators are covered in **Rule 8B, Table I.**) Art reproductions plus text **AA Rule 8D**	Adaptation Bowdlerization Dramatization Epitome Novelization **AA Rule 7A** Paraphrase Summarization (as per footnote on AA page 32) Versification Free translation **AA Rule 15A** Major revision **AA Rule 14B**
without supporting collaborator(s) / with supporting collaborator(s)	without supporting collaborator(s) / with supporting collaborator(s)	without supporting collaborator(s) / with supporting collaborator(s)

* The concept of "Related Works," AA Rule 19, is not part of this table.

Many of the rules listed in Table II are new to you. Take the time now to read through them, and to think about them. You will soon need them for an exercise.

How to Recognize a Table II Entry Heading Situation

The basic, and usually only, source for gathering entry heading information about a book is the book itself.* Typically, the book being cataloged will indicate the degree of change, or the predominance of one element by one or more of the following:

(1) *The author's intent and purpose* as expressed in the preface or foreword

TITLE PAGE:	PREFACE:
The Book of Job	". . . I have endeavored to cast this familiar story in a setting intelligible to today's audience. Purists may be shocked by seeing Job in the guise of a disk jockey, but. . ."

(2) *the proportion of each type of material*

300 pages of one author's work together with 10 pages of someone else's comments about this work	as against	Selected sentences from one author's work, quoted to illustrate certain points in a 300-page treatise by someone else

(3) *the wording on the title page*

. . . adapted for children by (someone other than author)
. . . translated from the French by . . .
. . . based on . . .
. . . Second edition by (someone other than the original author)

* See also page 153ff.

(4) *typographical devices on the title page*

Poinsettia Pointers

By

James Smith and

ROBERT KLEIN

(5) *the sequence of names on the title page*

Sunny Mexico, a Pictorial Travelogue

Photographs by (one person)

Text by (another person)

Very few books contain all five kinds of clues for such entry heading situations. Usually the clues within any one book will confirm each other. If they do not, follow the above order of precedence.

EXERCISE

Considering the AA Rules studied for Table II (but not forgetting those from Table I), indicate below the situation which each work represents, what main entry heading is needed for it, and what added entry headings, including title added entry headings, you would make—definitely, possibly, or not at all. Do not indicate the form of each heading, but *do* cite the pertinent rule number(s).

	THE TITLE PAGE READS:	Situation	Make MAIN ENTRY under	WOULD make ADDED ENTRY under	MIGHT make ADDED ENTRY under	Would NOT make ADDED ENTRY under
E X A M P L E	Selections from A. S. Buckley's EDUCATION FOR LIVING Edited by John Martin Illustrations by James Smith	selections from one work	Buckley 1A		Martin 33D; Smith 8B, 33F; title of original: Education for living. 33P, last para.	title 33P1
	LITTLE WOMEN a play in four acts By Marly Higgins. Based on the novel by Louisa May Alcott (1)					
	GESEGNETE HÄNDE von Adele Comandini (Verso of title page states: Ubersetzt aus dem Englischen. Originaltitel: Dr. Kate, Angel on snowshoes.) (2)					

THE TITLE PAGE READS:	Situation	Make MAIN ENTRY under	WOULD make ADDED ENTRY under	MIGHT make ADDED ENTRY under	Would NOT make ADDED ENTRY under
Goethe's FAUST A selective and edited translation by Jason Smith (Preface states: "... negative and sordid aspects were de-emphasized ... in particular it was found desirable to let Marguerite stay alive in happy motherhood and send Mephistopheles back to Hell in defeat...") (3)					
An analysis of Mark Twain's social consciousness as expressed in his "Innocents Abroad" by James Doofer (Note: This work includes the original text and the somewhat longer analysis.) (4)					

THE TITLE PAGE READS:	Situation	Make MAIN ENTRY under	WOULD make ADDED ENTRY under	MIGHT make ADDED ENTRY under	Would NOT make ADDED ENTRY under
Beloved episodes from THE INNOCENTS ABROAD by Mark Twain. Edited by Charles Martin (Note: The editor contributed 19 pages of comments, the text from "Innocents Abroad" is 193 pages.) (5)					
CINNAMON TOAST by Ellen Teachgood. (Preface states: "This adaptation of Harold Blackburn's 'Bitter Bread' was written to permit its introduction to a wider audience...") (6)					
Familiar letters of Clinton Eastwood and his wife Daphne. With a biography of Daphne Eastwood by Cloe Birch. (Note: The biography is on pages v-xxxii, the letters on pages 1-411.) (7)					

THE SPECTRUM OF SITUATIONS

An overall view of the situations listed in Tables I (page 227) and II (page 258) shows that many contain similar elements, but with different degrees of emphasis. If the situations with similar elements are grouped together as chains, the links in each chain can be arranged by increasing or decreasing degree of emphasis. Here are some examples:

The text-plus illustrations chain

Text without illustrations	Text plus supporting illustrations	Illustrations at least as important as text	Illustrations plus supporting text	Illustrations without text

The one-or-more authors chain

One author	One author plus supporting collaborator(s)	Shared authorship with collective title (Principal author indicated)	Shared authorship with collective title (Principal author not indicated)	Shared authorship without collective title

The less-and-less-like-the-original chain

A work	Literal translation	Minor revision	Major revision	Adaptation; Free translation; Paraphrase; or Recasting into another literary form

EXERCISE

Fill in the missing links.

The largest-to-smallest-version chain

An enlarged version of a work	The work as originally written	(1) _____ _____ _____	Its epitome or summarization

The selections chain

A complete work	(2) _____ _____ _____	Selections from this work with comments by someone else	Sentences quoted from the work in someone else's treatise

The anonymous-author-chain (has three stages)

(3)_____ _____ _____	_____ _____ _____	_____ _____ _____

Viewing entry heading situations as links on a chain permits viewing each situation in context, as part of a spectrum that allows an easier overview of these situations and of the corresponding entry heading rules.

REVIEW EXERCISE

On the basis of the information given below, and of the pertinent AA Rules, indicate for each book what main and added entry heading(s) you would select, and list the number(s) of the rule(s) used. Do not indicate the form of these headings, but do study AA Rule 33P and indicate whether or not a title added entry should be made.

The Complete Library of World Art

ALL THE PAINTINGS OF **GIORGIONE**

Text by LUIGI COLETTI

Translated by PAUL COLACICCHI

CONTENTS

HAWTHORN BOOKS, INC.

Publishers · New York

FOR YOUR INFORMATION:
Pages 7-78 contain a biography, notes, a description of each painting, and similar matter by Luigi Coletti.

Beginning on page 79 are 120 pages of reproductions of Giorgione's paintings.

Main entry heading:

_____

Selected on basis of AA Rule(s)

_____

_____

Added entry heading(s):

_____

Selected on basis of AA Rule(s)

_____

_____

They Wrote on Clay

The Babylonian Tablets Speak Today

By

EDWARD CHIERA

Late Professor of Assyriology
The University of Chicago

Edited by

GEORGE G. CAMERON

Instructor in Oriental Languages
The University of Chicago

The University of Chicago Press · Chicago

ADDITIONAL SAMPLE PAGES
FROM THIS BOOK ARE ON
FACING PAGE

Preface

ONE day Professor Chiera was guiding some visitors through the exhibition halls of the Oriental Institute of the University of Chicago. They stopped first in front of the huge Assyrian bull or "cherub," which he himself had found and brought to this country, then passed through the Assyrian Hall containing the massive stone reliefs from the palace of Sargon of Assyria. As they turned to enter the room containing the ancient clay tablets and records, one of the members of the party chanced to remark, "Now that we've seen the most interesting things, let's rush through here as quickly as possible."

That was so typical of the average attitude toward Babylonian-Assyrian discoveries that Professor Chiera, stopping short, said, "Wait a minute! The real interest starts here," and proceeded to discuss some of the important information that we may secure from these ancient "books of clay." This volume is an enlargement of the talk he gave there.

Fortunately, before his last illness he had written the first draft of a book intended for this purpose. Friends urged its posthumous publication, and at the request of Mrs. Chiera I have prepared this edition. In it I have endeavored to retain as far as possible Professor Chiera's style and method of presentation. We may be sure that the talk he gave that day in the museum halls was well received; let us hope that this edition of the book which he left unfinished will meet with a similar reception.

GEORGE G. CAMERON

CHICAGO, ILLINOIS
January 3, 1938

Table of Contents

ADDITIONAL SAMPLE PAGES
FROM "THEY WROTE ON CLAY."

Main entry heading:

_____

Selected on basis of AA Rule(s)

_____

Added entry heading(s):

_____

_____

Selected on basis of AA Rule(s)

_____

_____

Prologue

FROM A LETTER OF THE AUTHOR TO HIS WIFE

This evening I made my usual pilgrimage to the mound covering the ancient temple tower. It is only a few hundred yards from our camp, and it is pleasant to ascend to the summit of that tower, which dominates the landscape. This I generally do in the evening, after supper, in the bright moonlight. Today I have come with the ambition of jotting down my impressions, for the spectacle moves me deeply.

Seen from below, it does not look so high as might be expected of a Babylonian temple tower. Did not that of Babylon pretend to
Thoug
still fr
boundl
finally
high m
of pest
nearer.
remains

On a
and no
and can

Acknowledgments

TO THE many people who have assisted in the publication of *They Wrote on Clay*, this brief note is dedicated. For their invaluable assistance in editing the manuscript, I am most grateful to Professors A. T. Olmstead and W. F. Geers, to Drs. W. H. Dubberstein, R. M. Engberg, and I. J. Gelb, and to Mrs. Erna S. Hallock, Miss Doris R. Fessler, and my wife, Frances T. Cameron. Especial appreciation is accorded the University of Chicago Press, in particular Professor Gordon J. Laing, Miss Mary D. Alexander, and Mr. Herman J. Bauman.

To the Oriental Institute and its Director, Professor John A. Wilson, I am indebted for permission to use illustrations from the

pages 36, 37, 69, 81, 87 (bottom), 97, 113, 179, 180, 182, 185, 188, and 189: Mrs. Edward Chiera.

GEORGE G. CAMERON

DEATH TAKES A HOLIDAY

A Comedy in Three Acts

BY

WALTER FERRIS

BASED ON A PLAY OF THE SAME TITLE
BY
ALBERTO CASELLA

SAMUEL FRENCH
Thos. R. Edwards   Managing Director
NEW YORK   LOS ANGELES
SAMUEL FRENCH LTD.   LONDON
1930

---

18   DEATH TAKES A HOLIDAY   [ACT I

DUKE
She's quite safe in the garden, Marie.

PRINCESS
Yes, of course. But I'm so . . . shaken, tonight.

STEPHANIE
She has many friends, but she's a lonely child.

DUKE
She seems too gentle and lovely to be real, sometimes.

PRINCESS
I wish she were like other children. I've tried to bring her up to be sensible, but it's so difficult to make an impression.

DUKE (*smiling*)
She just fades, if things aren't pleasant. I've seen her.

PRINCESS
Yes, she simply doesn't hear.

DUKE
It's a very normal and alert little mind.

PRINCESS
But such a dreamy one.

BARON
Marry her off. Nothing like marriage to spoil your dreaming.

CORRADO (*crossing up to steps*)
Thanks Baron. I'm the prospective bridegroom, you know.

Main entry heading:

_____

Selected on basis of AA Rule(s)

_____

_____

Added entry heading(s):

_____

_____

Selected on basis of AA Rule(s)

_____

_____

CHAPTER TEN

BASIC AACR ENTRY HEADING PATTERN FOR PERSONAL NAMES

HIGHLIGHTS

The AA tend to use as entry heading a person's commonly known name, the name which he tends to use himself, for example in the books he writes.

The "Circle of Information": In building entry headings for personal names, it is useful to view the formally spoken name as a circle of information:

Charles William Snyder

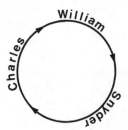

The typical entry heading is constructed by following the circle, starting with the surname:

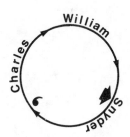

Snyder, Charles William.

If available, or if needed for distinction from other names in our catalog, we add the life date(s). Sometimes the function which the individual exercised is added. This results in the

Basic 4-element Entry Heading Pattern:

3 Elements For The Person (Each of these may consist of one or more parts.) (These elements remain constant in any one catalog.)			1 Element For The Function (Changes with the person's role.)
Surname(s)	Forename(s), Initial(s) or combination	Date(s) or other distinguishing terms	
Snyder,	Charles William,	1867-1959,	<u>ed.</u>

Punctuation and Spacing: In personal name entry headings, the four elements are ordinarily separated by commas, and if the last element (whichever this may be) is complete, the entry heading is closed by a period. However, a birth date without death date is merely followed by a hyphen, and commas are omitted after any incomplete element.

Enough space is left after any incomplete element to permit future completion. By convention, this means: 8 spaces after initials, 6 spaces after the hyphen following the birth date, if the "element for the function" is also used.

BASIC AA ENTRY HEADING PATTERN FOR PERSONAL NAMES

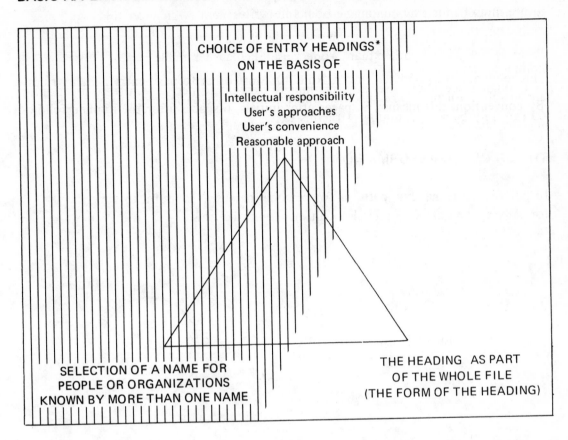

CHOICE OF ENTRY HEADINGS*
ON THE BASIS OF

Intellectual responsibility
User's approaches
User's convenience
Reasonable approach

SELECTION OF A NAME FOR
PEOPLE OR ORGANIZATIONS
KNOWN BY MORE THAN ONE NAME

THE HEADING AS PART
OF THE WHOLE FILE
(THE FORM OF THE HEADING)

We now turn to the most frequently used form-of-entry-heading rules for personal names, that is, the patterns in which different types of personal names can be effectively recorded as entry headings. Before proceeding, please review pages 67-76 which discuss the need for consistency and distinction in entry headings; pages 105-119 which summarize AA's basic form-of-entry-headings concepts; pages 137-138 which provide a guide to AA's form-of-entry heading rules; and pages 142-147 which list the pertinent sequence of steps.

* From page 110.

The **AA** tend to use a person's *commonly known name,* the name which he tends to use himself, for example in the books he writes:

Wodehouse, P. G.

rather than Wodehouse, Pelham Grenville.

This tendency is formulated in **AA Rule 40.** Most other form-of-entry-heading rules are merely refinements, or specific applications, of this basic rule. Study **AA Rule 40** carefully before continuing with this text.

THE CIRCLE OF INFORMATION

In building entry heading patterns for personal names, it is useful to view the formally spoken name as a circle of information, like this:

CHARLES WILLIAM SNYDER

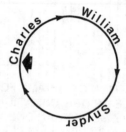

When listing "ordinary" names, that is, names consisting of one or more forenames and a surname, as headings in catalogs, bibliographies, telephone directories, or wherever else people's names are listed alphabetically, select as the first element the surname, followed by a comma, and add the forenames or initials in regular order, like this:

SNYDER, CHARLES WILLIAM

Telephone directories add the address, which helps to distinguish people with identical names; bibliographers and catalogers add the date(s) if conveniently available or needed for distinction.

Snyder, Charles William, 1867-1959.

FOUR ELEMENTS

The basic entry heading pattern for people known by a combination of forenames and surnames consists of four elements:

3 ELEMENTS FOR THE PERSON (Remain constant in anyone catalog. Pages 68-70)			1 ELEMENT FOR THE FUNCTION (Changes with the person's role.)
SURNAME	FORENAME(S) or INITIAL(S) or combination	DATE(S) or other DISTINGUISHING TERMS	FUNCTION PERFORMED IN CREATING A PARTICULAR WORK
Always used in complete form	Always used in the fullest form conveniently available. Should be sufficiently complete to distinguish similar names used as entry headings in the catalog. (Pages 67-68.)	Dates should be used if conveniently available. Dates or (if none are available) distinguishing term *must* be used if forenames do not help to distinguish similar names used as entry headings in the catalog.	Added rarely, on basis of specific AA Rules. Since most entry headings are for authors, *not* used to indicate this obvious role, but only other roles, usually expressed in abbreviated form, such as *comp.* (compiler), *ed.* (editor), *illus.* (illustrator), *tr.* (translator), *joint author, joint comp.,* etc.
SNYDER,	CHARLES WILLIAM,	1867-1959.	
SNYDER,	CHARLES WILLIAM,	1867-1959,	*ed.*
SNYDER,	CHARLES WILLIAM,	1867-1959,	*tr.*

Each "element for the person" may consist of one or more parts:

Rosen, Perry, 1930-
Brown, Hugh Victor
Phillips, Edwin Allen, 1915-
Thoreau, Henry David, 1817-1862.
Brosbøll, Johan Carl Christian, 1816-1900.
Sirijos-Gira, Vytautas, 1911-
Sánchez Azcona, Juan, 1876-1938.
Schmidt-Nielsen, Knut Størtebecker, 1915-

EXERCISE

To get familiar with the basic entry heading pattern, copy the above names into the blank spaces on page 276, including the punctuation.

Examine the entry headings below to determine what information the cataloger did, or did not, have in each case. Each represents a slightly different situation.

Berrey, Lester V   1907-
Bauer, Albert, 1913-
Tibbets, D   Daniel
Czerny, Carl, 1791-1857.
Greenwood, J   E   G   W
Child, Charles Manning, 1869-1954.
Braslavskii, A   P
Moor, Fred Bennett, 1893-
Tannenbaum, Samuel Aaron, 1874?-1948. (Note the ?)
Moody, William T

ONE NAME, ONE ENTRY HEADING FORM IN ONE CATALOG

If a name is used more than once as entry heading, the "three elements for the person" remain constant,* but the "element for the function" changes with the function.

EXERCISE

You have used in your catalog the following added entry heading for a book's translator:

Pendleton, Andrew M   1931-   *tr.*

You now receive another book, of which the same Mr. Pendleton is author. The main entry heading for the new book is

(1) _____

Several years later, you use his name again as entry heading, but this time, you must use for some reason his complete forenames (Pendleton, Andrew Martin, 1931-   ) rather than just his initials. (This happens very seldom.) Should you

(2)(a) _____ Fill in the middle name on the cards already in your catalog?

   (b)_____   Leave the old cards alone and use the full name only on the new cards?

   (c) _____ Make see-also references from the first form to the second, and *vice versa*?

* See also pages 68-70, 95, and 276.

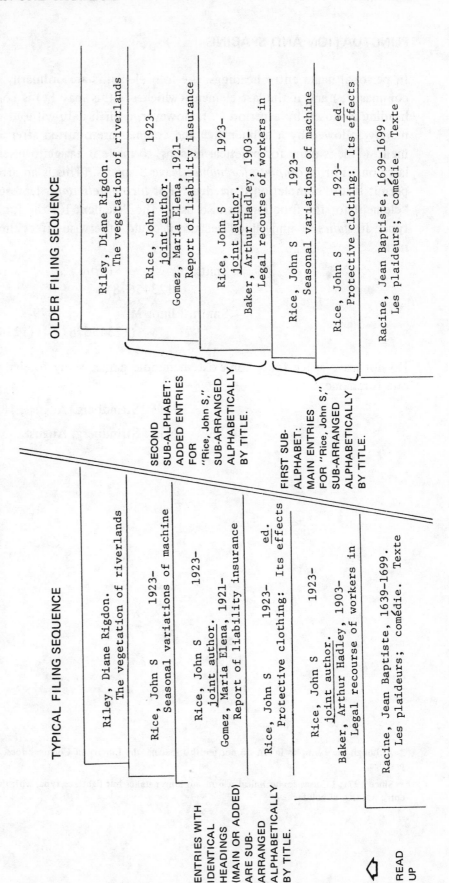

Effect of "Function" Element on the Filing

Typically, the "element for the function" does not affect the filing sequence. Most libraries file by the first line, regardless of whether it shows an author, editor, or joint author. See column at left for the typical situation. Some libraries, however, use an older method through which the "element for the function" does affect the filing sequence. See Column at right for an example.

TYPICAL FILING SEQUENCE

Riley, Diane Rigdon.
    The vegetation of riverlands

Rice, John S   1923–
    Seasonal variations of machine

Rice, John S   1923–
    joint author.
Gomez, Maria Elena, 1921–
    Report of liability insurance

Rice, John S   1923–   ed.
    Protective clothing: Its effects

Rice, John S   1923–
    joint author.
Baker, Arthur Hadley, 1903–
    Legal recourse of workers in

Racine, Jean Baptiste, 1639–1699.
    Les plaideurs; comédie. Texte

ENTRIES WITH IDENTICAL HEADINGS (MAIN OR ADDED) ARE SUB-ARRANGED ALPHABETICALLY BY TITLE.

READ UP

OLDER FILING SEQUENCE

Riley, Diane Rigdon.
    The vegetation of riverlands

Rice, John S   1923–
    joint author.
Gomez, Maria Elena, 1921–
    Report of liability insurance

Rice, John S   1923–
    joint author.
Baker, Arthur Hadley, 1903–
    Legal recourse of workers in

Rice, John S   1923–
    Seasonal variations of machine

Rice, John S   1923–   ed.
    Protective clothing: Its effects

Racine, Jean Baptiste, 1639–1699.
    Les plaideurs; comédie. Texte

SECOND SUB-ALPHABET: ADDED ENTRIES FOR "Rice, John S," SUB-ARRANGED ALPHABETICALLY BY TITLE.

FIRST SUB-ALPHABET: MAIN ENTRIES FOR "Rice, John S," SUB-ARRANGED ALPHABETICALLY BY TITLE.

The older method, shown at right, is not recommended: The use of sub-alphabets makes it easy to overlook any one title.

PUNCTUATION AND SPACING

In personal name entry headings, the four elements are ordinarily separated by commas (,) and if the last element (whichever this may be) is complete, the entry heading is closed by a period (.). However, a birth date without death date is merely followed by a hyphen (-) and commas are omitted after any incomplete element. (This is done for practical reasons, to make it easier to insert information later on.) For *incomplete forenames* leave 8 spaces. (This is an arbitrary figure, to permit future completion if needed.* For *incomplete dates* leave 6 spaces if the "element for the function" is also used. The "element for the function" is typically typed in *italics* or underlined because it could otherwise affect the filing arrangement.**

> Smith, E   Kirby.
>   (12345678)
>
> Smith, Elinor M   1879-   *ed.*
>   (12345678)   (123456)

Do not leave space for a non-existent middle name. Many foreign persons have only one forename.

> Strindberg, August, 1849-1912.
>
> Not: Strindberg, August   1849-1912.

---

* Although the examples in AA do not use this spacing, the Library of Congress does. This text follows "LC" practice.

** Since 1971, LC uses for technical reasons no longer italics but lightface type, with the main part of the main entry heading in boldface.

AA and the Basic Entry-Heading Pattern*

The following sections in the AA deal with the basic pattern although they express it in different words. Please read them, along with the following comments.

1) "Introductory Notes" to the section "Enfry of Name," AA pages 80-81.
    The examples in point (1) of the "Introductory Notes" are exceptions, based on the fact that in some languages, names are *formally spoken in inverted order:*

Smith John   *rather than*   John Smith.

2) AA Rules 46 through 46A.
    Note that this, and other, rules contain the expression "Enter under. . .," which means variously:
    "Use as the first element in the heading. . . " *or*
    "Use as the complete entry heading. . ."
    The context always clarifies the meaning. This text also uses this expression.

3) AA Rules 52-53.

    The typical pattern for dates is:

    > Smith, John, 1924-
    > Smith, John E   1901-1966.

    The alternative pattern is rarely used, and only when the person is obviously no longer living and it is doubtful that his other date can be found:

    > Smith, John, d. 1825.
    > Smith, John, b. 1859.

    The examples in AA Rules 52 and 53 unfortunately omit the final punctuation mark. It should be used for completed headings.

4) "Designation of function in headings," AA pages 10-11.

Study these sections carefully before doing the following exercise.

---

* Differences between the AA and the ALA patterns are discussed in Chapter 18.

EXERCISE

Put the following facts into proper entry heading form.

EXAMPLE

Joseph Nathan Kane
born: 1899   Kane, Joseph Nathan, 1899-
_____

William Joseph Long
born 1867; died 1952   (1) _____

J. Robert Campbell
born 1946; edited this work   (2) _____

C. A. Thomas
Date of birth unknown   (3) _____

Georg Schneider
born 1876; died 1960   (4) _____

You are cataloging another book by C. A. Thomas
and learn now that his first name is Charles and
he was born in 1933   (5) _____

Title page reads:
    PEKING OPERA MAKE-UP;
      AN ALBUM OF CUT-OUTS
         Designed by
         Chang Kuang-yu
         Peking

    Foreign Language Press   (6) _____

An entry heading for Kate Greenaway as
creator of important illustrations in a children's book. She lived from 1846 to 1901.   (7) _____

Clara Louise Avery, who was born in 1891.
You have no one else by this name in your
catalog.   (8) _____

Daniel Defoe, who was probably born in 1661
and died in 1731.   (9) _____

The following headings are already listed in
your catalog:
    Johnson, Walter (for a book published in
Iowa in 1899, on the national bankruptcy act).
    Johnson, Walter, 1867-
(for a book published in 1912 in England, on
British archeology).
    Now you must establish a heading for
Walter Johnson who wrote a book on "The
diseases of young women," published in
London in 1849. He has an "M.B." degree
(Medicinae Baccalaureus.)   (10) _____

CHAPTER ELEVEN

SURNAMES WITH PREFIXES

HIGHLIGHTS

Prefixes are the letters or words which stand before the main part of a surname as it is spoken, but not necessarily as it is listed. Prefixes may consist of words, derivations, articles, or prepositions. They may merge with the main part of the surname, or be written separately. Some are capitalized, others are not, all according to the custom of the language or the individual.

AA Entry Rules for Surnames with Prefixes: For specific rules, the main part of this text refers to the AA. Overall, this group of rules is divided into three parts, as follows:

(A) If the prefix and the main part of the surname are hyphenated or combined, enter under the prefix.

(B) If the prefix is attributive, enter under the prefix—except for Spanish and Portuguese attributive prefixes, which are separated from the main part of the surname.

(C) In all other cases, enter under either the prefix or another part of the surname on the basis of the person's language or personal preference.

Order of Precedence for Discovering a Person's Language or Personal Preference: (1) Clues in the book being cataloged, and the AA, will show the pattern customary in the person's language. Only if you have reason to suspect that a person prefers a different pattern for his own name, turn to (2) Native reference works. If none are available, use (3) Any other reliable reference work. If these do not help, turn to (4) The AA rules for the language of the *name* (rather than for the language of the *person*).

If the typical language pattern and personal preference differ, personal preference takes precedence.

Three Entry Heading Patterns for Surnames with Prefixes: The following three names illustrate that, depending on where one begins the "Circle of information," that is, depending on the person's language (or, sometimes, preference) names with separately written prefixes can fall into one of three patterns:

The three names as formally spoken:

    Max Theodor von Erp.   Antoine Du Verdier.   Jean de la Fontaine.

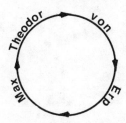 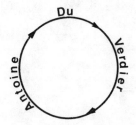 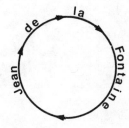

The three names as entered according to different AA rules:

    Erp, Max Theodor von.   Du Verdier, Antoine.   La Fontaine, Jean de.

Individual See-references for Surnames with Prefixes: Since readers will not always know under what form to look for foreign names with prefixes, see-references must be made. Since they refer to one individual they are also called "individual see-references." If a prefix consists of more than one part, more than one see-reference may be made. Deicsion depends on the cataloger's judgment. The technique for making such references with the "Circle of information" is described on page 298.

General See-references for Surnames with Prefixes: An alternative technique is to make see-references that apply equally to all names beginning with a particular prefix. The heading for such a reference consists solely of the prefix, or part of the prefix, and the content consists of an explanation rather than reference to any one name. Since general see-references do not necessarily file in the same place as individual see-references, it is best to make both kinds of references.

SURNAMES WITH PREFIXES

Some surnames consist of more than one word. Which of these words should be the first element in the entry heading?*

      Walter De la Mare

      Herman Smitt Ingebretsen

      Margaret Bourke-White

Listing these people automatically under the last part of their name as formally spoken (Mare, Ingebretsen, White) would often differ from their national custom, sometimes from their own preference, and thus from the way they are referred to in the literature, in reference works and bibliographies. To learn the general AA attitude toward such names,** read the first paragraph of the "Introductory Notes" on AA page 80.

EXERCISE

List below the two guidelines which the "Introductory Notes" on AA page 80 give on entering surnames that consist of more than one word.

_____

_____

_____

_____

  * See also pages 89 and 277.

 ** Differences between the ALA and AA patterns for such names are discussed in Chapter 18.

DEFINITIONS

This chapter deals specifically with **AA** Rules for surnames with prefixes.* Prefixes are the letters or words which stand before the main part of a surname as it is *spoken,* but not necessarily as it is *listed.*

NAME AS FORMALLY SPOKEN	NAME AS LISTED IN ENTRY HEADING:
Herbert von Elmsdorf	Elmsdorf, Herbert von
Francis William Von Elmsdorf**	Von Elmsdorf, Francis William

Prefixes may consist of *words* or *derivations:*
  A', Ap', Fitz, M', Mac, Mc, O', Saint, Sainte, San, Santa
or *articles:*
  el, l', la, le, les, li, lo
or *prepositions:*
  af, am, auf, auf dem, auf der, auf'm, aus'm, d', da, dagli, dai, dal, dalla, dalle, das, de, dei, de la, de las, de los, degli, del, della, delle, des, dos, du, im, in, ten, ter, van, van den, van der, van't, ver, vom, von, von der, zu, zum, zur

(For purposes of this text, an article is the foreign equivalent of the English "the," and a preposition is the foreign equivalent of the English "of" or "of the.")

Prefixes may consist of one or more words; some merge with the main part of the surname, others are written separately; some are capitalized, others are not; all according to the custom of the language or the individual.

---

* One example is on page 177-179.

** In the first example, "von" is written with a small "v" because the name is German; in the second example with a capital "V" because the name is English. Note that AA entry headings for western languages always start with a capital letter.

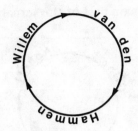

Willem <u>van</u> <u>den</u> Hammen

Thomas <u>A</u>'Beckett

Robert <u>Mc</u>Kibbin

Stanley S. <u>Fitz</u>Gibbon

Menno <u>ter</u> Braak

Joseph Max <u>von</u> Frankenstein

George R. <u>Mac</u> Neal

Howard Winston <u>O</u>'Bennington

Juan <u>Santa</u> Lucia

Walter <u>De La</u> Mare

AA Entry Rules for Names with Prefixes

Within the framework of **AA Rule 40,** and the somewhat narrower framework of the **"Introductory Notes"** on **AA page 80,** the pertinent AA Rules* divide prefixed names into three categories:

(A) If the prefix and the main part of the surname are *hyphenated or combined,* enter under the prefix.

<u>Ter</u>-Tatevosîan, Dzhon Gurgenevich

<u>Saint</u>-Benoît, Claude

<u>Mac</u>Donald, William

<u>Auf</u>demkamm, Theodor

<u>De</u>lacroix, Ferdinand Victor Eugène

* The pertinent rule numbers are cited on the next few pages.

(B) If the prefix is *attributive,* enter under the prefix*—except for Spanish and Portuguese attributive prefixes, which are separated from the main part of the surname.

<u>A'</u>Beckett, Gilbert Abbott

<u>Fitz</u> Gibbon, Abraham Coates

<u>Øvre</u>-Eide, Olaf

<u>San</u> Cristóval, Evaristo

<u>Ben</u> Maÿr, Berl

BUT: Santos, Antonio <u>Dos</u>

* There is no separate AA Rule for attributive prefixes. This cateogry is implied. Attributive prefixes are prefixes that qualify the main part of a surname:

  Ben, Fitz, Mc, Mac = "Son of"
  A', O' = "A descendant of"
  San = "Saint."

Most contracted prefixes are also attributive and (except for Spanish and Portuguese contractions) entered under the contraction. The following prefixes are contractions in French, German, and Italian:

CONTRACTION	ORIGINALLY	MEANING	LANGUAGE	SAMPLE ENTRY HEADING
Am	An dem	At the	German	AmBerg, Wolfgang
Aus'm	Aus dem	From the	German	Aus'm Weerth, Ernst
Des	De les	Of the	French	Des Aulnoyes, François
Del	De il	Of the	Italian	Del Mare, Angela
Della	De la	Of the	Italian	Della Chiesa, Mario
Du	De le	Of the	French	Du Bouchet, André
Im	In dem	In the	German	ImOberdorf, Ronald
Vom	Von dem	From the	German	Vom Ende, Erich
Zum	Zu dem	To the	German	Zum Berg, Hans
Zur	Zu der	To the	German	Zur Linde, Otto

(C) In all other cases enter under either the prefix or another part of the surname, on the basis of the person's *language or personal preference**

> Figuerosa, Francisco <u>de</u> (Page 316)
> <u>De</u> Amicis, Pietro Maria (Page 317)
> <u>La</u> Chasse, Pierre <u>de</u> (Page 318)

This is codified in **AA Rules 46E through 46E1**. Study these rules before continuing with this text.

THREE ENTRY HEADING PATTERNS FOR NAMES WITH PREFIXES

Depending on the person's language (or, sometimes, preference) names with separately written prefixes can fall into one of three patterns. Study these carefully and note the punctuation.

---

* Clues on how to tell a person's language and personal preference, and sources to consult, are on pages 292-293.

(1) ENTER UNDER LAST ELEMENT OF SURNAME

4 ELEMENTS FOR THE PERSON (Remain constant in any one catalog. 68-70)				1 Element for the Function. (Changes)
Main Part of Surname	Forename(s) or Initial(s) or Combination	Complete Prefix	Date(s) or Other Distinguishing Term	Function Performed in Creating a Particular Work
Aa,	Karl	von der,	1876-1937.	
Aa,	Jan Simon	van der,	1895 -	
Aubigné	Théodore Agrippa	d',	1552-1630.	

The above names as formally spoken:

    Karl von der Aa

    Jan Simon van der Aa

    Théodor Agrippa d'Aubigné

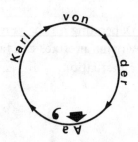

(2) ENTER UNDER PREFIX

3 ELEMENTS FOR THE PERSON (Remain constant in any one catalog. 68-70)			1 Element for the Function. (Changes)
Complete Prefix Plus Main Part of Surname	Forename(s) or Initial(s) or Combination	Date(s) or Other Distinguishing Term	Function performed in creating a particular work
Du Verdier,	Antoine	1544-1600.	
Da Ponte,	Lorenzo	1749-1838.	
De La Mare,	Walter	1873-1956.	

The above names as formally spoken:

    Antoine Du Verdier

    Lorenzo Da Ponte

    Walter De La Mare

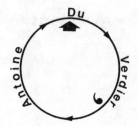

(3) SPLIT THE PREFIX

4 ELEMENTS FOR THE PERSON (Remain constant in any one catalog. 68-70)				1 Element for the Function. (Changes)
Article plus Main Part of Surname	Forename(s) or Initial(s) or Combination	Preposi-tion	Date(s) or Other Distinguish-ing Term	Function performed in creating a particular work
La Fontaine,	Jean	de,	1621-1695.	
L'Hôpital,	Michel	de,	1505?-1573	

The above names as formally spoken:

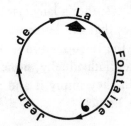

    Jean de La Fontaine

    Michel de L'Hôpital

      Once you know a person's name, language and (if needed) preference, the circle of information technique will lead to the desired AA pattern.

EXERCISE

You may wish to practice with some of the names on the preceding pages.

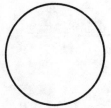
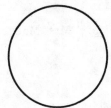
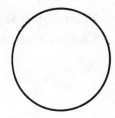

CLUES ON HOW TO TELL A PERSON'S LANGUAGE

(Note that the language of a *person* may differ from the language of that person's *name*. For example, Walter De La Mare carried a typically French name but was a British poet and novelist. His language was English, and his name is entered in English fashion:

De La Mare, Walter

NOT La Mare, Walter de (the French fashion).   )

(1) Often, the book being cataloged is a guide:
Title page: "...by Pieter ten Hoff..."
Verso of title page: "...Translated from the Dutch by..."

Title page: "...by Gertrud von Le Fort..."
Blurb: "...Her contributions to German poetry..."

Title page: "...par Josephine d'Anvers..."
Clues on the author's language: The text is in French; the absence of a translation note implies that the book was originally written in French; the book is published in France; the Introduction is written by someone else with a typically French name. Taken individually, none of these clues proves that the writer's language is French. But they imply it and make it safe to assume that Josephine d'Anvers' language is French.

Such clues can be anywhere in the book being cataloged. See also Chapter 7, pages 153-220.

(2) Sometimes it is necessary to consult reference works to be sure.

Clues on How to Tell Personal Preference

(1) Typically, from the book being cataloged.
Title page: "BY ELIZABETH MACNAUGHTON." (the typical entry heading pattern for such names is "MacNaughton, Elizabeth," with a capital "N." But other parts of the book imply that her personal preference differs):

Spine: Macnaughton.
Caption underneath frontispiece: "Mrs. Macnaughton at her desk."

But beware: Personal names that form part of a sentence are given in regular order: ("...These lucid essays by Veronica Winchell...") In many languages, surnames are *spoken* with the prefix before, but *entered* with the prefix following, the surname.* Therefore, the spelling or sequence of surnames with separately written prefixes in a regular sentence is not necessarily an indication of personal preference.

Preface: "...These poems by de Musset..."
But entry heading: Musset, Alfred de (since his language was French.)

Preface: "...Indeed, del Rio shows that..."
But entry heading: Rio, Antonio del (since his language was Spanish.)

In such cases, the capitalization of the names in the text is sometimes a clue. To discover it, re-read the above examples and the two "Elmsdorf" examples on page 286.

(2) Rarely it is necessary to consult bibliographies or reference works to learn personal preference.

Priority of Sources for Learning a Person's Language or Personal Preference

First-choice source: The language pattern of the person (rather than of the person's name**) as given in the book being cataloged. This is justified because most people follow their standard language pattern. Use other sources only if the first-choice source seems inaccurate—not just incomplete.

Second-choice source: Native reference works.

Third-choice source: Any other reliable reference works.

Fourth-choice source: Assume that the apparent language of the name is also the language of the person, and follow the rules for the language of the name. Often, this makes it necessary to guess from the appearance of the name: Jean Baptiste de Moulin seems to be French; Lin-van-Tran seems to be Vietnamese. But guesswork is only a last resort in any bibliographical activity.

---

* See "Definitions," first paragraph, on page 286.
** Remember that the language of a person may differ from the language of that person's name. See page 292.

EXERCISE

Put the following names into the desired language patterns. Watch the capitalization: Use upper and lower case letters such as "Aa, Karl von der." You may refer freely to this text and **AA Rules 46E and 46F**.

	LANGUAGE		
MAX THEODOR VON HAGEN	German	(1)	_____
JOHANNES VAN DER WAALS	Dutch	(2)	_____
DAISY FITZ GIBBON	English	(3)	_____
GUSTAVE DU TOUR	French	(4)	_____
ARIS VAN BRAAM	Dutch	(5)	_____
WALTER VANDERCAMP	English	(6)	_____
JAMES FRANCIS MACMILLAN	English	(7)	_____
ERICH ZUR LINDE	German	(8)	_____
KLAUS VON BRAUN	German	(9)	_____
	Swedish	(10)	_____
	Afrikaans	(11)	_____
	English	(12)	_____
OTTO SANTA CLARA	English	(13)	_____
	Spanish	(14)	_____
DOMINIC D'ACOSTA	French	(15)	_____
	Italian	(16)	_____
LEOPOLDO DELLA SANTA	Italian	(17)	_____
	English	(18)	_____
CHESTER O'CONNOR	English	(19)	_____
	French	(20)	_____

MARTIN DU GARD English (21) _____

 French (22) _____

 German (23) _____

 Afrikaans (24) _____

CHARLES ALFRED DE MORGAN English (25) _____

 Swedish (26) _____

 Modern Italian (27) _____

 French (28) _____

 Dutch (29) _____

 Spanish (30) _____

ALFRED D'ALBERT French (31) _____

 German (32) _____

 English (33) _____

 Afrikaans (34) _____

EMIL DE LA TOUR English (35) _____

 Swedish (36) _____

 French (37) _____

 Belgian (38) _____

 German (39) _____

 Dtuch (40) _____

 Spanish (41) _____

SEE-REFERENCES FOR PREFIXED SURNAMES

Is your head swimming now? This is understandable. Just remember that AA did not create these different forms for otherwise identical names; the people themselves did, over the course of centuries. As a result, the various Emils de la Tour can be filed in catalogs, bibliographies, and telephone directories under "D," "L," or "T," depending on their language or personal preference.

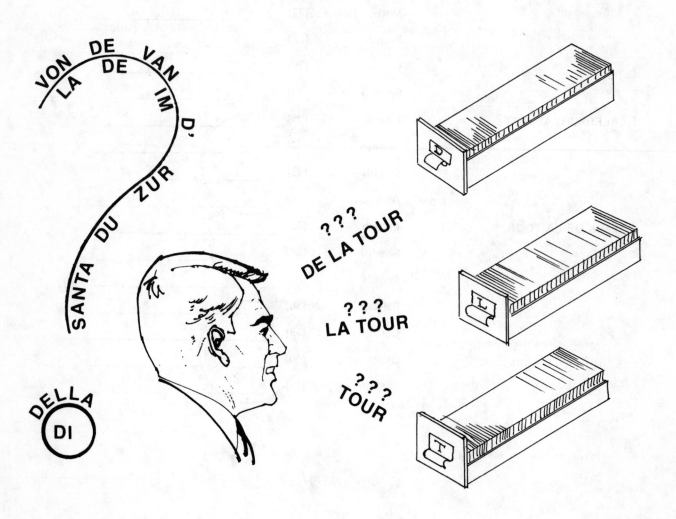

Most readers tend to look automatically under the prefix for English prefixed names (De La Tour; Le Gallienne) but will not always know under what form to look for a foreign prefixed name. See-references are needed for foreign names with prefixes.

Pages 77-79 of this text indicate that see-references refer from a form of a name under which a reader might reasonably look, to the form under which it is listed. Pages 79-82 showed a typical format, pages 99-101 the technique of turning a see-reference tracing into a see-reference. Please review these pages to refresh your memory.

When the rules do not indicate what cross-references to make (as with **AA Rules 46E and F**) the "Circle-of-information" technique* is of help.

Begin by thinking of the name in regular order, as a circle of information

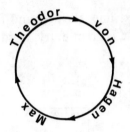

Insert the comma after the surname.

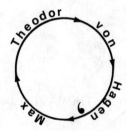

* See pages 274-275.

Begin the see-reference with the word under which you *think* some readers may reasonably look for this name. Capitalize this first word, and go full circle.

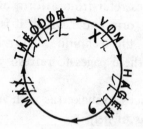

Von Hagen, Max Theodor

Add, in the next line, the <u>see,</u> and for the last line complete the circle once again, starting with the correct entry word. Then add the date.

> Von Hagen, Max Theodor
> <u>see</u>
> Hagen, Max Theodor von, 1831-1906.

EXERCISE

Make a see-reference for THOMAS DU JARDIN, whose language is French. He was born in 1945.

(1) _____

_____

_____

Make two see-references for JEAN DE LA FONTAINE whose language was French. He was born in 1821, died in 1893.

(2) _____   _____

_____   _____

_____   _____

General See-References for Prefixed Surnames

The above references refer to one individual and are thus "Individual see-references." Some catalogs and bibliographies use also, or instead, "general explanatory see-references," that is, see-references that apply equally to all names beginning with a particular prefix.

De la Fontaine, Jean
  see
La Fontaine, Jean de, 1821-1893.

AN INDIVIDUAL
SEE-REFERENCE

De
  Names beginning with the prefix De are entered under the prefix or the part of the name following the prefix, variously in different languages. If the name looked for is not found under the prefix, search should be made under the part of the name following the prefix.

A GENERAL SEE-
REFERENCE AS
USED IN THE
NATIONAL UNION
CATALOG

For an example of a general see-reference to be filed under the prefix "De la," see **AA Rule 121B2.***

A general see-reference should be accurate but brief enough so the patron can both read and retain the message. Here are two possible versions of a general see-reference to be filed under "La."

La

    Names beginning with the prefix <u>La</u> are entered under the prefix, or the part of the name following the prefix, variously in different languages. If the name looked for is not found under the prefix, search should be made under the part of the name following the prefix.

    Names beginning with the prefix <u>De la</u> are entered under the <u>De la</u> or <u>La</u> or the part of the name following the prefix, variously in different languages.

ONE POSSIBLE
BRIEF
VERSION

La

    Most names which begin with this article are entered under it. (Even if written separately, the prefix and the remainder of the name are filed as though they were written as one word.) However, when this prefix, written as a separate word, occurs at the beginning of the surname of a person whose language is Dutch, the surname is entered under the part of the name following the prefix.

    When the article <u>La</u> forms part of the prefix <u>De la,</u> written as separate words at the beginning of the surname of a person whose language is English or Swedish, or whose nationality is South African, the surname is entered under the prefix <u>De la.</u> If the person's language is French or German, the surname is entered under the prefix <u>La.</u> In other cases the surname is entered under the part of the name following the prefix <u>De la.</u>

A LONG AND
PRECISE
VERSION.

IS IT
HELPFUL?

Like entries, see-references are filed by their first line. The following illustration shows that the cataloger's decision on making general or individual see-references, or both, for prefixed names, affects their placement in the catalog.

---

* In this example, the next to the last sentence should be corrected to read: "If the person's language is French or German, the surname is entered under the prefix La." (If the reason for this correction is not clear, re-study the "German" part of **AA Rule 46E1.**)

SEE-REFERENCES FOR PREFIXED NAMES IN
A FILE OF CATALOG CARDS

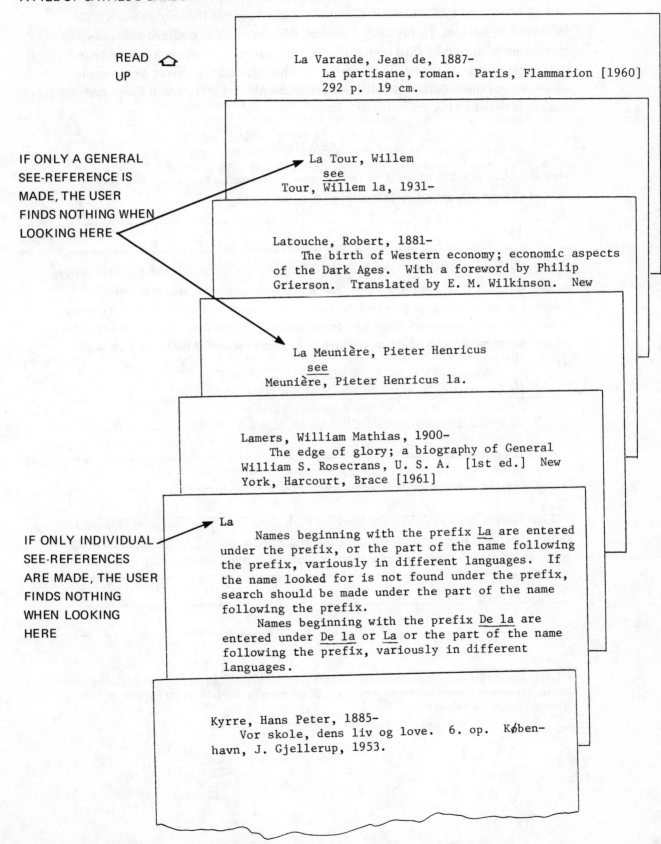

READ UP

La Varande, Jean de, 1887-
    La partisane, roman. Paris, Flammarion [1960]
292 p. 19 cm.

IF ONLY A GENERAL
SEE-REFERENCE IS
MADE, THE USER
FINDS NOTHING WHEN
LOOKING HERE

La Tour, Willem
        see
Tour, Willem 1a, 1931-

Latouche, Robert, 1881-
    The birth of Western economy; economic aspects
of the Dark Ages. With a foreword by Philip
Grierson. Translated by E. M. Wilkinson. New

La Meunière, Pieter Henricus
        see
Meunière, Pieter Henricus 1a.

Lamers, William Mathias, 1900-
    The edge of glory; a biography of General
William S. Rosecrans, U. S. A. [1st ed.] New
York, Harcourt, Brace [1961]

IF ONLY INDIVIDUAL
SEE-REFERENCES
ARE MADE, THE USER
FINDS NOTHING
WHEN LOOKING
HERE

La
    Names beginning with the prefix La are entered
under the prefix, or the part of the name following
the prefix, variously in different languages. If
the name looked for is not found under the prefix,
search should be made under the part of the name
following the prefix.
    Names beginning with the prefix De la are
entered under De la or La or the part of the name
following the prefix, variously in different
languages.

Kyrre, Hans Peter, 1885-
    Vor skole, dens liv og love. 6. op. Køben-
havn, J. Gjellerup, 1953.

Decisions as to whether to make only a general see-reference for prefixed sur-names or individual see-references, or both, depends on the estimated cataloging time and cost, and the apace in the catalog, weighed against the usefulness of such references to the user. In any case, a general see-reference for prefixed surnames must begin with, and be filed under, the element common to all such names, that is the prefix, or part of the prefix. Therefore, even if general see-references are made whenever possible, additional individual see-references are still needed for some names, as shown in the following question.

EXERCISES

Turn to Exercise 299-300. Which of the two individual see-references for La Fontaine could be dropped in favor of a general see-reference?

(1) _____

_____

Make a brief general explanatory see-reference to be filed under the preposition <u>Von</u>. Do not use staccato phrases; use full sentences, but be economical with words. For your information: Surnames of persons whose language is English or whose nationality is South African are entered under "Von"; those who speak German or one of the Scandinavian languages are entered under the part of the name following the prefix, even if the prefix consists of the words "von der."

(2) _____

_____

_____

_____

_____

_____

_____

_____

_____

_____

CHAPTER TWELVE

COMPOUND SURNAMES

HIGHLIGHTS

Compound surnames are family names consisting of two or more proper names.

Forms of Compound Surnames: Compound surnames may or may not be hyphenated; one or both proper names may contain a prefix; or the proper names may be connected by conjunctions, all according to the custom of the language or of the individual.

Priority of Sources for Learning a Person's Language or Personal Preference: (1) Clues in the book being cataloged, and the AA, will show the pattern customary in the person's language. Only if you have reason to suspect that a person prefers a different pattern for his own name, turn to (2) Native reference works. If none are available, use (3) Any other reliable reference work. If these do not help, turn to (4) The AA rules for the language of the *name* (rather than for the language of the *person*). If the typical language pattern and personal preference differ, personal preference takes precedence.

Entry Heading Patterns for Compound Surnames: The standard entry heading for compound surnames is entry under the first surname. This pattern is used for (A) Hyphenated surnames; (B) Surnames that are known to be compound; (C) Surnames that seem to be compound, *unless* the bearer is American or speaks Portuguese or a Scandinavian language.

3 Elements for the Person (These elements remain constant in any one catalog)			1 Element for the function (changes with the person's role)
Surnames	Forename(s), Initial(s) or combination	Date(s) or other distinguishing terms	
Roselli Cecconi,	Mario,	1881-1939,	<u>ed.</u>

Less frequently, entry is under the last element of a compound surname, namely for (D) Portuguese compound surnames; (E) Surnames that seem to be compound, if the bearer is American or speaks Portuguese or a Scandinavian language.

4 Elements for the Person (These elements remain constant in any one catalog)				1 Element for the function (changes with the person's role)
Part of surname used as entry element	Forename(s), Initial(s) or combination	Other parts of surname	Date(s) etc.	
Zayas,	Enrique	Saladrigas y,		tr.

If personal preference differs from the above patterns, personal preference takes precedence.

Combining the Rules for Prefixed and Compound Surnames: When the entry element is a prefixed surname, the rules for prefixed surnames are combined with the rules for compound surnames.

When is a Surname Compound? Most names can be "parsed" easily into forename(s) and surname(s), but the following special situations can make recognition of a compound surname difficult: (a) In all languages, typical forenames are sometimes used as surnames; (b) Conversely, in the United States, surnames are often used as forenames, especially middle names. (c) Very rarely, an apparently compound, hyphenated surname, is actually two surnames of two different individuals. (d) Occasionally, apparently compound surnames are actually surnames consisting of two parts that form a meaningful phrase. Such phrases are never broken.

Individual See-references for Compound Surnames: Since readers and librarians cannot be expected to know always under which of its parts a compound surname is entered, see-references are essential. The technique for making them, with the "Circle of information," is described on page 320.

COMPOUND SURNAMES

Compound surnames* are family names consisting of two or more proper names. Such names are discussed on pages 100-101, 139-141, 176-177, and 277 of this text.

Forms of Compound Surnames

Compound surnames may be hyphenated

Eugenie	Breitbart-Schuchmann
Theodore	Watts-Dunton

or not

Mario	Roselli Cecconi

One or both proper names may contain a prefix

Leander	McCormik-Goodhart
Guy	Du Rousseaud de La Combe
Christian	Knorr von Rosenroth
Theobald	von Beethmann-Hollweg
Henri Joachim	de Bijll Nachenius

or the proper names may be connected by conjunctions

Ovidio	Saraiva de Carvalho e Silva
Federico Carlos	Sainz de Robles
Enrique	Saladrigas y Zayas

* Differences between the ALA and AA patterns for such names are discussed in Chapter 18.

In building entry heading patterns for compound surnames it is useful to view the formally spoken name as a circle of information.*

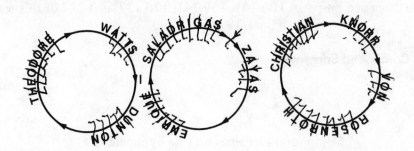

AA Entry Rules for Compound Surnames

Within the framework of **AA Rule 40**, and the somewhat narrower framework of the "Introductory Notes" on AA page 80, any part of the surname can serve as the first element of the entry heading, depending on the person's language or individual preference.

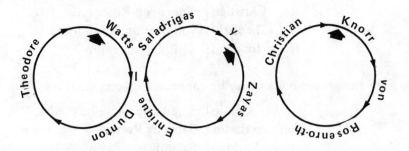

Watts-Dunton, Theodore

Zayas, Enrique Saladrigas y

Knorr von Rosenroth, Christian

If language pattern and personal preference differ, personal preference is followed: As with prefixed surnames, personal preference takes precedence over the standard language pattern.

---

* See pages 274-275.

EXERCISE

If Mr. Zayas, in the preceding example, preferred to be known as Mr. Saladrigas y Zayas, his name would be entered as (1)_____

_____

Why should preference take precedence? (2) _____

_____

STANDARD ENTRY HEADING PATTERN FOR COMPOUND SURNAMES

Entry under the first element of the compound surname is made for:

(A) Hyphenated surnames. This applies also where the second element is a self-selected place name.*

(B) Surnames that are known to be compound.

(C) Surnames that seem to be compound, unless the bearer is American** or speaks Portuguese or a Scandinavian language, in which case enter under the second element.

---

* This is done very rarely, and only by individuals in the same profession, or writers on the same topic, who bear identical common fore- and surnames, to permit distinction.

** The AA Rule actually states, "unless the bearer's language is English." But in general, English names that *seem* to be compound are, while United States names that *seem* to be compound, are not.

These three categories result in the following:

(1) STANDARD PATTERN: ENTRY UNDER THE FIRST ELEMENT; THAT IS, UNDER THE COMPLETE COMPOUND SURNAME (Similar to basic pattern, page 276).

3 ELEMENTS FOR THE PERSON (Remain constant in any one catalog, Pages 68-70)			1 ELEMENT FOR THE FUNCTION (Changes with the person's role).
SURNAMES	FORENAME(S) or INITIAL(S) or COMBINATION	DATE(S) or other DISTIN— GUISHING TERMS	FUNCTION PERFORMED IN CREATING A PARTICULAR WORK
Watts-Dunton,	Theodore,	1832-1914.	
Roselli Cecconi,	Mario,	1881-1939.	
Du Rousseaud de La Combe,	Guy,	d. 1749.	
Knorr von Rosenroth,	Christian,	1636-1689.	
Tessitore Donato,	Giovanna,	1949-	

The above names as formally spoken:

    Theodore Watts-Dunton
    Mario Roselli Cecconi
    Guy Du Rousseaud de La Combe
    Christian Knorr von Rosenroth
    Giovanna Tessitore Donato

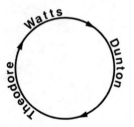

Entry under the last element of a compound surname is made for:

(D) Portuguese compound names.

(E) Surnames that seem to be compound, if the bearer is American* or speaks Portuguese or a Scandinavian language.

These two categories result in the following:

(2) LESS FREQUENT PATTERN: ENTRY UNDER THE LAST ELEMENT OF A COMPOUND SURNAME.

4 ELEMENTS FOR THE PERSON (Remain constant in any one catalog. Pages 68-70)				1 ELEMENT FOR THE FUNCTION (Changes with the person's role).
THE PART OF THE SURNAME THAT IS USED AS ENTRY ELEMENT	FORENAME(S) or INITIAL(S) or COMBINATION	OTHER PARTS OF THE SURNAME IN REGULAR ORDER	DATE(S) or OTHER DIS-TINGUISHING TERMS	FUNCTION PERFORMED IN CREATING A PARTICULAR WORK
NOTE: NO COMMA Zayas,	Enrique	Saladrigas y .		
Hilprecht,	Hermann Volrath**,		1859-1925,	ed.

The above names as formally spoken:

Enrique Saladrigas y Zayas
Hermann Volrath Hilprecht**

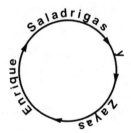

---

* The AA Rule actually states, "unless the bearer's language is English." But in general, English names that *seem* to be compound are, while United States names that *seem* to be compound, are not.

** **Not a compound name,** although it sounds like one. The bearer was American, and "Volrath" was a middle name. See point (E), above.

Enter under the first, last, or any other element of a compound surname:

(F) Persons whose personal preference differs from their typical language pattern (See pages 306-307).

Although worded and arranged differently, the above concepts are based on **AA Rule 40** and the **"Introductory Notes" on AA page 80,** and are expressed specifically in **AA Rules 46B** through **46D.** Study these carefully before continuing with this text.

COMBINING THE PATTERNS FOR COMPOUND AND PREFIXED SURNAMES

When part of the compound surname is prefixed,* the rules for both types of names of that language are combined.

For the French compound surname of Guy | Du Rousseaud | de La Combe | :
>   Du Rousseaud de La Combe, Guy.
> NOT   Rousseaud de La Combe, Guy du.

For the German compound surname of Catharina Elisabeth | von Bolsen | -Lederle | :
>   Bolsen-Lederle, Catharina Elisabeth von.
> NOT   Von Bolsen-Lederle, Catharina Elisabeth.

* See Chapter 11, pages 283-302.

Once a person's name, language and, if needed, preference are known, the "Circle of information"* will lead to the desired AA pattern.

EXERCISE

You may wish to practice with some of the names on the preceding pages.

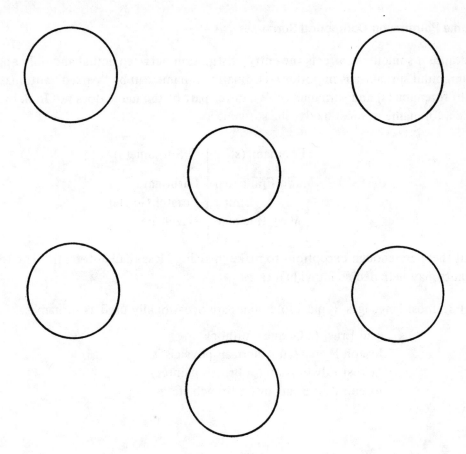

* See pages 274-275.

CLUES ON HOW TO TELL A PERSON'S LANGUAGE AND PERSONAL PREFERENCE*

The same clues apply for compound surnames as for prefixed surnames. (See pages 292-293 and 176-177) The same priorities for consulting sources also apply. (See page 293.)

Some Pointers on Compound Surnames

Because it sometimes affects the entry, distinction between actual and only apparently compound surnames is important. Ordinarily, a name can be "parsed" automatically into forename(s) and surname(s): Whatever part of the name does not look or sound like a forename is, most likely, the surname.

Forename(s)	Surname(s)
Mario Francesco	Carbonara
Emma	Förster Gessler
Mary Imogene	Hazeltine

But there are enough exceptions to make "parsing" less than automatic. The following points may help decide individual cases.

(a) In most languages, typical forenames are occasionally used as surnames.

> Paul <u>Ernst</u> (a German author)
> Joseph <u>Henry </u>(an American physicist)
> August Edwin <u>John</u> (a British painter)
> Joseph <u>Paul</u>-Boncour (a French statesman)

---

* Clues on detecting a compound surname are on pages 303-310.

(b) Conversely, in the United States, surnames are often used as forenames, especially middle names. Thus, to the uninitiated, some ordinary American names may seem to be compound.

> Erle Stanley Gardner : *Surname:* Gardner
> *Entry heading:* Gardner, Erle Stanley.

> Dixon Ryan Fox : *Surname:* Fox
> *Entry heading:* Fox, Dixon Ryan.

An American name that looks compound, almost never is (see **AA Rule 46B4**), but a foreign name that looks compound, often is compound.*

> Spanish: José Rosas Moreno: *Surname:* Rosas Moreno
> *Entry heading:* Rosas Moreno, José.

> German: Anton Sepp von Reinegg: *Surname:* Sepp von Reinegg
> *Entry heading:* Sepp von Reinegg, Anton.

(c) Very rarely, an apparently compound, hyphenated, surname is actually the surnames of different individuals.**

> *Title page:* Maxwell-Honegger

Clues to the authors' different identities are typically in other parts of the book being cataloged.

---

* This was mentioned on page 139.

** For hyphenated surnames consisting of name-place, see text page 307, point (A) and **AA Rule 46C.**

Introduction: "We have tried to. . ."
Preface, written by someone else: "The authors succeeded. . ."
Copyright notice: "Copyright 1965 by James Maxwell and Andreas Honegger."

(d) Occasionally, apparently compound surnames are actually single surnames consisting of two parts, as mentioned in footnote 10, AA page 82.

Vincente Antonio de Espirito Santo
(Espirito Santo = Holy Ghost, in Spanish)

Camilo Castelo Branco
(Castelo Branco = White Castle, in Portuguese)

Irrespective of other rules, such meaningful phrases are never broken in entry headings:

Espirito Santo, Vicente Antonio de.
Castelo Branco, Camilo, 1825-1890.

(e) Spanish and Portuguese names are compound more often than not. For Spanish men and unmarried women,* the sequence of units in a compound surname is typically as follows:

---

* The patterns for married women are described on pages 323-329.

Forename(s)	Father's surname		Mother's surname		Entry heading
Eugenio	Restrepo	y	Soler	:	Restrepo y Soler, Eugenio.
María	Herrera		Pérez	:	Herrera Pérez, María.

Omission of the conjunction is
beginning to be common.

In Portuguese and Brazilian compound names, however, the mother's surname is generally the first part of the compound. This is the reason for **AA Rule 46B3a.** (See also text page 309.)

Forename(s)	Mother's surname		Father's surname		Entry heading
José Francisco	de	Sá	Teles	:	Teles, José Francisco de Sá.

A clue for either sequence is that conjunctions hardly ever stand among the forenames. Typically, they are used to separate the forenames from the surname(s), or to separate different parts of the surname.

Forename(s)	Surname(s) with conjunction(s)
Martinho Augusto	da Fonseca
Manuel	de la Puente y Olea
Carlos	Rosas Morales y Carbo
EXCEPTION: Xiomara de la Caridad	Pelegrino Moscaso

(f) Clues that help to decide whether or not a surname is compound, and which part of the name to use as entry element, are typically in the book being cataloged, such as the hyphen:

> by F. Schuurmans-De Boer (For a book translated from the Dutch)
>
> > Implies: A compound surname. But also see **AA Rules 46B2, 46C,** footnote 10 on AA page 82, and text pages 307 and 313. Note also that in some languages forenames are sometimes hyphenated.)
>
> by Jean-Pierre Chevalier

the conjunction:

> por Luis Cardoza y Aragon (For a book published in Spain)
> > Implies: A compound surname.

the abbreviation:

> by E. de C. Clarke.
>
> (Implies: Not a compound surname. See footnotes 9 and 11 on **AA** pages 81 and 82. The entry heading is: Clarke, Edward de Courcy.

See also Chapter 7, pages 153-220.

But sometimes the information is conflicting or indecisive. See the following:

EXERCISE

Indicate the probable entry heading for the following situations. The books concerned were published in London. If you can think of several probable entry headings, list both.

First situation

INFORMATION ON SPINE	INFORMATION ON TITLE PAGE
BERWICK SAYERS	BY BERWICK SAYERS

Entry heading is probably (1) _____

Second Situation

INFORMATION ON SPINE	INFORMATION ON TITLE PAGE
BERWICK SAYERS	BY W. C. BERWICK SAYERS

Entry heading is probably: (2) _____

The Preface is signed by W. C. B. S. What clue does that provide? (3) _____

_____

The Bibliography at the end of the volume has an entry for "Sayers, W. C. Berwick." What clue does that provide? (4)_____

The Index at the end of the volume has another book on the same subject by "Sayers, W. C. Berwick." What clue does that provide? (5) _____

_____

If the book itself provides no clue, it may become necessary to check in bibliographies or reference works. If neither book nor bibliographies provide an answer, follow **AA Rule 46B4** and text pages 307-309. But remember that, typically, some name information comes to the cataloger with the book from the Order Department. (See pages 128-129.)

EXERCISE

On the basis of the information given below put the following names into entry heading form. You may refer freely to **AA Rules 46 through 46D.**

	GIVEN INFORMATION:	CORRECT ENTRY HEADING FORM:
Example	Theodore Watts-Dunton (British, born 1832, died 1914)	Watts-Dunton, Theodore, 1832-1914.
	Kurt Otto-Wasow (a German)	1.
	Franklin Knowles Young (American; name on spine: Young)	2.
	Pedro Álvares Cabral (Portuguese navigator, born probably 1460, died probably 1526)	3.
	Edmund Kirby-Smith (American; born 1824, died 1893)	4.
	Roger Babington Smith (Nationality unknown, but book is in English, published in New York, has no indication that it is a translation	5.

GIVEN INFORMATION:	CORRECT ENTRY HEADING FORM:
Viktor von Miller zu Aichholz (Book is published in Wien, in German, born 1845, died 1910.)	6.
Walter Savage Landor (English author, born 1775, died 1864. Spine: Landor)	7.
François de La Mothe Le Vayer (French, born 1583, died 1672)	8.
Eduardo Lozano y Ponce de León (Book is in Spanish, was published in Madrid, apparently not translated)	9.
Hans August von Euler-Chelpin (A German-born, Swedish chemist)	10.
Prudente José de Moraes Barros (Brazilian statesman, born 1841, died 1902. Preface: "Moraes Barros defeated Peixoto in 1894. . ." Caption underneath portrait: Moraes Barros)	11.
Frederick Locker-Lampson (English poet, born 1821, died 1895.)	12.

INDIVIDUAL SEE-REFERENCES FOR COMPOUND SURNAMES

As with prefixed surnames,* see-references are needed that refer from the part of the surname that is *not* the entry element to the form that *is* used as heading. Using the "Circle of information" technique** they look as follows:

Name in regular spoken order:
    Eugenie Breitbart-Schuchmann
Cross-reference:

```
      Schuchmann, Eugenie Breitbart-
         see
   Breitbart-Schuchmann, Eugenie.
```

NOTE THE
HYPHEN

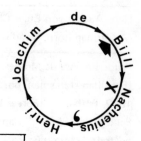

Name in regular spoken order:
    Henri Joachim de Bijll Nachenius
Cross-reference:

```
   Nachenius, Henri Joachim de Bijll
        see
   Bijll Nachenius, Henri Joachim de
```

---

* For see-references for prefixed surnames, see pages 296-302. For basic cross-reference theories and techniques, see pages 77-82 and 99-101.

** See pages 274-275.

EXERCISE

Using the "Circle of information" technique, make see-references for all other names listed on page 205. For your information: Silva's language is Portuguese, Sainz's and Saladrigas's language is Spanish.

CHAPTER THIRTEEN

MARRIED WOMEN'S SURNAMES

HIGHLIGHTS

If a married woman uses a combination consisting of her husband's and her maiden surname, the resulting name looks compound. However, in many languages, such names are not compound but are handled like ordinary surnames, with the maiden name acting as middle name. This is the typical U.S. pattern.

The compound form is used only in those languages and countries in which married women's names are *typically used as compound surnames,* and for those individuals who prefer it.

AA Rule 46B3b, which deals specifically with married women who use both surnames, tells us to make, for most languages, the entry under the husband's surname. Since it is usually not obvious which of the two surnames is the husband's, this text suggests another rule of thumb:

Enter a woman who uses both her husband's and her own maiden surname under the first listed surname, *unless* (1) she prefers another form of entry, (2) she is American, or (3) she speaks Portuguese or a Scandinavian language. In those cases, enter under the second surname listed in regular order.

The, "Circle of information" technique can be used to construct such entry headings.

Note also that a woman's compound surname does not necessarily mean that she is married. If the compound surname is her maiden name, it is entered according to the usual rules for compound surnames. See Chapter 12.

Some married women* write under, or use, their maiden surname. Others write under their married surname, without including their maiden surname.

Forename(s)	Maiden surname	Married surname	
Ruth Suzanne	Senn	(omitted)	SELDOM USED FORM IN U.S.
Ruth Suzanne	(omitted)	Boll	MOST COMMON FORM IN U.S.

EXERCISE

According to **AA Rules 40 and 41,** a married woman using the first form listed above, receives the entry heading (1) _____

If she uses the second form listed above, she receives the entry heading (2) _____

_____

Many a married woman uses, particularly in formal situations, a combination consisting of her maiden and her married surnames. The resulting name always *looks* compound, but in many languages it is not compound and is handled like other surnames with a first and a middle name, with the maiden name acting as middle name.

* Differences between the ALA and AA patterns for such names are discussed in Chapter 18.

Formal name in regular order. Typical for U.S.

Forename(s)	Maiden surname	Married surname
Ruth Suzanne	Senn	Boll

Typical entry heading order for U.S.

    Boll, Ruth Suzanne Senn.*

COMPOUND FORM

The compound form, however, is used as entry heading in those languages or countries in which married women's names are *typically used as compound surnames,* and for those individuals of any language who *prefer to be known* by a compound name.

Husband's surname   Maiden surname

        Kiefer-Haefliger Rosemarie.   (Typical Swiss pattern)

        Molina y Vedia de Bastianini, Delfina   (Spanish pattern)

    Husband's surname   Maiden surname

    Individual preference that counteracts the typical national pattern is often shown in the book being cataloged:

---

* Under the ALA Rules (see pages 103, 106-107, and 114) the maiden surname was enclosed in parentheses; a helpful bibliographic device: Boll, Ruth Suzanne (Senn)

Title page: By Ruth Boll-Senn.
Blurb: Ruth Senn Boll has written an imaginative. . .
Entry heading: Boll-Senn, Ruth. <u>Not</u>: Boll, Ruth Senn.

To recall the general framework within which married women's surnames fall, re-read **AA Rules 40, 41, 43, and 46B1-2** before continuing with this text.

AA Rule 46B3b, which deals specifically with married women who use both surnames, makes the point that, except in some languages, entry is under the husband's surname. Please study this rule now.

The problem is that one can not usually tell which of the two surnames on the title page is the husband's, and which the wife's. The following rule of thumb simplifies the AA and will see you through most such situations:

Enter a woman who uses both the husband's and the wife's surnames under the *first surname listed, unless* (1) she prefers another form of entry, (2) she is American, or (3) she speaks Portuguese or a Scandinavian language.

This includes hyphenated names (**AA Rule 46B2**)

Forename(s)	First listed surname	Second listed surname	Entry heading
Ruth Suzanne	Boll-Senn		Boll-Senn, Ruth Suzanne.

and non-hyphenated names, such as this Italian name:

Forename(s)	First listed surname	Second listed surname	Entry heading
Virginia	Carini	Dainotti	Carini Dainotti, Virginia.

But if she prefers entry under the second surname, is American, or speaks Portuguese or a Scandinavian language, enter her under the second surname as listed in regular order, like this Brazilian name.*

Forename(s)	First listed surname	Second listed surname	Entry heading
Maria Yvonne	Atalécio	de Araújo	Araújo, Maria Yvonne Atalécio de

* For learning purposes, use the "Circle of information" technique, explained on pages 274-275. It makes an apparently involved procedure automatic. — Russian, Arabic, African, Asian, and other names that are difficult for westerners and not too frequently encountered in our libraries, are outside the scope of this introductory text.

But note that a woman's compound surname does not necessarily indicate that she is married. The book being cataloged, or reference works, will help arrive at a suitable entry heading decision.

EXERCISE

On the basis of the given information, and the pertinent AA Rules, construct the following
women's names in entry heading form.

CLUES	ENTRY HEADING
EX-AM-PLE Mary Ellen Smith. (Book published in New York.) Blurb: . . . Miss Smith. . .	Smith, Mary Ellen.
Title page: Elizabeth Foreman Lewis. (Book is published in Philadelphia, is not a translation, is dedicated "To my husband and son.")	(1)
Title page: Mrs. Theodore S. Maxwell. (Book is published in Minneapolis. Preface is signed: Helen W. Maxwell.)	(2)
Title page: Germaine Acremant. (Book is published in Paris, blurb indicates: Mme. Acremant, née Poulain.)	(3)
Title page: Constance Beresford-Howe. (Book is in English, is not a translation, is dedicated "To my father, Russell Beresford-Howe.")	(4)
Complete name: Frau Elisabeth Förster-Nietzsche. (Born 1846, died 1935, sister of the German philosopher Friedrich Nietzsche.)	(5)
Title page: Valfrid Palmgren Munch- Petersen. (Book is published in Stockholm. "Valfrid" is a woman's forename.)	(6)

Complete name: Irma von Starkloff Rombauer. (Book is published in English, in New York, is not a translation. Blurb: 'Mrs. Rombauer's new cook book. . .''	(7)
Title page: Ada Perticucci Bernardini. (Book is published in Italy. The book's cover confuses the issue by giving the name as Ada Bernardini Perticucci.)	(8)
Complete name: Eugenia Serrano y Balaña. (Book is published in Madrid.)	(9)
Complete name: Mercedes García y Sánchez de Serna. (Book is published in Barcelona.)	(10)
Title page: Graça Pina de Morais. (Book is published in Lisbon.)	(11)
Title page: Mary Lavater-Sloman. (Book is published in Zürich, in German, and is dedicated to the author's daughters. Blurb: ''Mary Lavater-Slomans Biographie ist . . .'' and ''Diéses Werk von Mary Lavater ist. . .'')	(12)

CHAPTER FOURTEEN **NOBILITY AND GENTRY**

HIGHLIGHTS

The AA combine only titles of nobility, royalty, and religious personages who are known by given name, or byname, with the name proper.

Ranks of Nobility: The ranks of nobility exist on a sliding scale. The English, French, German, Italian, and Spanish ranks of nobility and titled gentry are shown on page 336.

Standard Entry Heading Pattern for "Four Element" Noble Names: Names of British noblemen, and selected other noblemen, consist typically of four elements:

Forename(s)	Surname(s)	Rank with Title-name
James	Fitzgerald,	*Duke of* Leinster.

Typically, surname differs from title-name. The standard entry heading pattern is developed from the individual's complete name as formally spoken, via the "Circle of information" technique. When surname and title-name differ, entry is under the title-name:

Leinster, James Fitzgerald, *Duke of,* 1722-1773.

If surname or title-name are prefixed or compound, the rules for prefixed or compound names are combined with the standard "Four Element Noble Names" pattern. When necessary to distinguish in one catalog between two otherwise identical British noble names, distinction is made with the individual's sequential numbers.

Entry Heading Pattern for British Nobility Known by Surname: Noblemen who tend to be known by their surname rather than their title-name are entered under surname, via an adaptation of the "Circle of information" technique.

Walpole, Horace, *Earl of Orford,* 1717-1797.

Decision whether to enter a British nobleman under surname or title-name is based on the cataloger's judgment. The AA give guidelines in rules **40, 41, and 43**.

See-references for "Four Element Noble Names": Since British noblemen can be known by either surname or title-name, it is essential to make a see-reference from the pattern that was not selected as entry heading to the pattern that was.

When Surname and Title-name are Identical: The following pattern is used for such names, again via an adaptation of the "Circle of information" technique.

Attlee, Clement Richard, *Earl Attlee,* 1883-

Standard Entry Heading Patterns for "Three Element Noble Names": Non-British nobility, and titled British gentry, have names consisting of only three elements: Forename(s), surname(s), and a title which merely indicates rank;

Ludwig *Baron* von Falkenhausen
Sir Henry Landseer
Sir Walter Scott, *Baronet.*

The several entry heading patterns for such names are again developed from the individual's complete names as formally spoken, via the standard "Circle of information" technique, or via its adaptation.

Falkenhausen, Ludwig, *Baron* von, 1844-1936.
Landseer, *Sir* Edwin Henry, 1802-1873.
Scott, *Sir* Walter, *bart.,* 1771-1832.

NOBILITY AND GENTRY

Some names are integrally combined with personal titles. In the AA, only titles of nobility, royalty, and religious personages known by given name or byname are so combined.* When formally spoken,** the title sometimes precedes the actual name, is sometimes contained within it, and sometimes follows it, depending upon usage.

Nobility or aristocracy
    Arthur Wellesley *Duke of* Wellington
    Gertrud *Freiin* von Le Fort   NAMES
    Sir John Robert Seeley

Royalty   AS
    Peter II, *King of Yugoslavia*
    Carlos *Prince of Asturias*   FORMALLY

Religious personages known by given name or byname
    Pope John XXII   SPOKEN
    Saint Francis of Assisi

In AA entry heading form, the title or rank follow the name. Exception: British titled gentry.

    Le Fort, Gertrud, *Freiin* von, 1876-***   NAMES
    Peter II, *King of Yugoslavia,* 1923-1970.   IN
    John XXIII, *Pope,* 1881-1963.   AA
BUT: Seeley, *Sir* John Robert, 1834-1895.   ENTRY HEADING
                                         FORM

* The ALA Rules also added titles of elected heads of state. For a discussion of the pattern for such names in the ALA Rules, see Chapter 18.

** Such names can also be spoken briefly or informally: Pope John, Frau von Le Fort, Prince Carlos.

*** It is necessary to either underline the rank or, on printed cards, type it in a different typeface, to remind the filer that it is ignored in filing. That is, **Sir Arthur** Conan Doyle is filed between **Alfred** Doyle and **Bertha** Doyle, not between Roger Doyle and Thomas Doyle.

ROYALTY AS AGAINST NOBILITY

Before studying entry heading rules for nobility, it is essential to recognize the difference between nobility and royalty. Royalty is the sovereign and immediate family, generally emperors, empresses, kings, queens, and royal and imperial princes and princesses. Although they have surnames and, typically, many forenames they are known by and entered under only their principal forename(s) and title.

Catherine II. *Empress of Russia.*

Charles, *Prince of Belgium.*

ROYAL NAMES IN AA ENTRY HEADING FORM

Nobility, or aristocracy, (called "peerage" in Great Britain) are other people with inherited rank and title who have, at least in our time, no inherited governing responsibility. Depending on their country and custom, their names fall into two categories.

A) "Three element" noble names in regular, that is, spoken, order:

Forename(s)	Title indicating rank	Surname
Friedrich	*Freiherr*	von Hügel

B) "Four element" noble names in regular, that is, spoken, order:

Forename(s)	Surname	Rank with	title-name
John William	Strutt	*Baron*	Rayleigh

Among British nobility, surname and title-name typically differ but are sometimes identical.

Forename(s)	Surname	Rank with	Title-name
Thomas Babington	Macaulay	*Baron*	Macaulay

Typically, noblemen in Category (A) are known by and entered under their surname, those in Category (B) under their title-name. But there are exceptions, depending on usage.

EXERCISE

Please check off the correct answer.

Royalty are known by, and entered under, their (1)____ Forenames and title; ____ Surname or title-name.

Noblemen are known by, and entered under, their (2)____ Forenames and title; ____ Surname or title-name.

On the basis of the examples on pages 333-334, titles of nobility (but not of royalty) are given (3)____ in English; ____ in the vernacular.

RANKS OF NOBILITY

The ranks of nobility exist on a sliding scale. On the next page are listed the English ranks with their French, German, Italian, and Spanish equivalents. Study this table carefully before proceeding with the text.

TABLE OF RANKS OF NOBILITY

(Female ranks given in parentheses)

	English	French	German	Italian	Spanish**
N	Duke of **	duc de ††	Grossherzog von ††	duca di ††	duque de
	(Duchess)	(duchesse)	(Grossherzogin)	(duchessa)	(duquesa)
O			Herzog von ††		
			(Herzogin)		
B					
			Fürst von ††		
I			(Fürstin)		
	Prince ***	prince de ***	Prinz von ***	principe di ***	príncipe de ***
L	(Princess)	(princesse)	(Prinzessin)	(principessa)	(principesa)
I			Pfalzgraf von		
			(Pfalzgräfin)		
T	Marquess of	marquis de	Markgraf von	marchese di	marqués de
	Marquis of	(marquise)	(Markgräfin)	(marchesa)	(marquesa)
Y	(Marchioness)		Landgraf von		
			(Landgräfin)		
	Earl	comte de	Graf von	conte di	conde de
	(Countess)	(comtesse)	(Gräfin)	(contessa)	(condesa)
	Viscount	vicomte de		visconte di	visconde de
	(Viscountess)	(vicomtesse)		(viscontessa)	(viscondesa)
			Baron von		
			(Baronin)		
	Baron	baron de	Freiherr von	barone di	barón de
	(Baroness)	(baronne)	(Freifrau)	(baronessa)	(baronesa)
			Freier von		
			(Freifrau)		
T *		seigneur de	Edler von		
		(de)	(von)		
I	Sir ... Baronet	sieur de	Ritter von		
T	(Lady)	(de)	(von)		
L		chevalier de			
E		(de)			
D					
G	Sir †	... de ...	... von ... ★		
E	(Lady)	(de)	(von)		
N					
T					
R					
Y					

* Gentry are members of the upper class but, strictly speaking, not nobility. But the pattern and rules of entry are the same.

** Depending on the language and the family's custom, the rank is usually, but not always, followed by a preposition such as: of, de, von, zu, di.

*** Distinction must be made between royal princes (who are entered under their forenames according to the rules for royalty) and the sons of the highest noble families who sometimes carry the title "Prince" and are entered according to the rules of nobility.

† The rank of knight, which carries the title "Sir," is personal, not inherited.

†† Some of these families (and even some of lower rank) were formerly sovereign, that is, ruling families. However, they are now known, and thus entered, like other noblemen under their family names or titles. You will learn the specifics on the next few pages.

★ This title is generally inheritable. Occasionally, however, it was granted only as a personal title.

** A few families, the grandees of Spain, carry these ranks "con grandezza" which gave them special privileges. This does not affect the rules of entry, however.

"FOUR ELEMENT" NOBLE NAMES

Names of British, and selected other, noblemen* consist typically of four elements: Forenames(s), Surname(s), Rank with title-name. Typically, the surname differs from the title-name.

In newspaper accounts and conversation most of these elements are ignored and British peers are often referred to by brief generic title, such as "Lord Northcliffe," "Lord Edward Russell," or "The Duke of Leinster." Since titles are inherited such abbreviations could cause confusion if used as entry headings in a permanent bibliographical record. Therefore, the standard AA entry heading pattern is developed from the individual's complete name in regular order, as formally spoken.

"Four Element" Noble Names in Regular Order

Forename(s)	Surname(s)	Rank with	title-name
James	Fitzgerald	*Duke of*	Leinster
Alfred Charles William	Harmsworth	*Viscount*	Northcliffe

Depending on the individual situation, either the surname or the title-name could serve as entry element.

---

* The pattern for British titled gentry will be discussed later on.

(A) *Entry Under Title-name: The Standard Pattern When Surname and Title-name Differ*

When surname and title-name differ the AA typically enters "Four element" noble names under the title-name. The "Circle of information" technique* leads automatically to the AA entry heading.

TITLE-NAME	FORENAME(S) or INITIAL(S) or combination	SURNAME	RANK	DATE(S)	Changes with the person's role
Leinster,	James	Fitzgerald,	*Duke of,*	1722-1773.	
Northcliffe	Alfred Charles William	Harmsworth,	*Viscount,*	1865-1922.	

FOUR ELEMENTS FOR THE PERSON (Remain constant in any one catalog. Pages 68-70) — ONE ELEMENT FOR THE FUNCTION

This concept is codified in Point 3 on AA page 81 and in **AA Rule 47A**. Please study these now.

Prefixed or Compound Noble Names

If the surname, or the title-name, are prefixed or compound, the rules for prefixed or compound names (**AA Rules 46B - E**) are combined with the AA rules for noble names.

* See pages 274-275.

The formally spoken names

Forename(s)	Surname(s)	Rank with	title-name
Edward Burtenshaw	Sugden	*Baron*	St. Leonard's
Edward John Barrington	Douglas-Scott-Montagu	*Baron*	Montagu

result in these AA entry headings:

St. Leonard's, Edward Burtenshaw Sugden, *Baron,* 1781-1875.

Montagu, Edward John Barrington Douglas-Scott-Montagu, *Baron,* 1926-

Sequential Numbers

When necessary to distinguish *in one catalog* between British noblemen with otherwise identical names, the individual's sequential numbers are added. See **AA Rule 47C.**

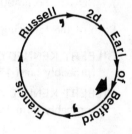

In formally spoken order:
    Francis Russell, second Earl of Bedford
    Francis Russell, fourth Earl of Bedford

In entry heading order:
    Bedford, Francis Russell, *2d Earl of,* 1527?-1585.
    Bedford, Francis Russell, *4th Earl of,* 1593-1641.

Although the individuals' dates help distinguish among them (see page 281 and **AA Rule 52**), adding the sequential number permits filing the names easily in a definite order. For this reason, the A.L.A. Rules *always* included sequential numbers for British noblemen above the rank of Baron.

READ	Norfolk, Thomas Howard, *4th Duke of,* 1536-1572.
UP	Norfolk, Thomas Howard, *3d Duke of,* 1473-1554.
⌂	Norfolk, Thomas Howard, *2d Duke of,* 1443-1524.

EXERCISE

On the basis of **AA Rules 40, 41, 47A, and 47C,** translate the given information into entry heading form. All these individuals are known by their title-name. Instead of using italics, underline.

FRANK PAKENHAM, EARL OF LONGFORD
    [BORN 1905]   (1) _____

QUINTIN MCGRAIL HOGG, VISCOUNT
    HAILSHAM [Family name:
    HOGG; born 1907]   (2) _____

Both of the following names are represented in your catalog:

GILBERT KENNEDY, THIRD EARL OF CASSILLIS   (3) _____
    [probably born 1517, died 1558]

GILBERT KENNEDY, FOURTH EARL OF CASSILLIS
    [probably born 1541, died 1576]   (4) _____

(B) *Entry Under Surname: The Less Frequent Pattern When Surname and Title-name Differ.***

Noblemen who acquired their titles late in life, or who write under their surname, tend to be known by surname rather than title-name. Accordingly, in line with the basic **AA Rules 40 and 41**, entry is under surname. Their rank-with-title-name is appended for identification. For this concept, see **AA Rule 46G1**.

Note that the "Circle of information" technique can still be used partly: Enter forename(s) and surname(s) according to the basic technique (pages 274-275); then add rank with title-name and dates.

Name in regular order:

Horace Walpole, Fourth Earl of Orford.
[English author, born 1717, died 1797, wrote under the name "Walpole," is listed in various reference works and bibliographies under his surname.]

Name in entry heading order:

Walpole, Horace, *Earl of Orford,* 1717-1797.

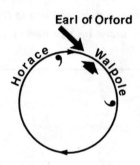

---

* For entry under title-name, the standard pattern, see page 338ff.

EXERCISE

Construct the entry headings that would result if the following individuals were to be entered under surname. Instead of using italics, underline.

James Fitzgerald Duke of Leinster, 1722-1773 (page 337-338)

(1) _____

Edward John Barrington Douglas-Scott-Montagu Baron Montagu, 1926-   (page 339)

(2) _____

Entry Under Surname or Title-Name?

The decision to enter "four element" noble names under the surname (page 341) or the title-name (page 338) is based on the cataloger's judgment. **AA Rules 40, 41, and 43** give guidelines.

EXERCISE

On the basis of **AA Rules 40, 41, and 43,** and the information given below, construct the following name as entry heading. Instead of using italics, underline.

Robert Anthony Eden, Earl of Avon. (British statesman, born 1897, achieved fame under the name "Sir Anthony Eden," never uses his first name, was created late in life Earl of Avon, is now listed in reference works and bibliographies usually under his title-name.)

(3) _____

Surname and Title-name Identical

Although typically surname and title-name differ in a "four element" noble name (page 363ff), they are sometimes identical.

Forename(s)	Surname(s)	Rank with	title-name	
Clement Richard	Attlee		Earl Attlee	IN
Bertrand Arthur William	Russell		third Earl Russell	REGULAR ORDER

If so, enter under surname, using the same formula as for other noblemen entered under surname. See text page 341 and study **AA Rule 47B** which deals with this concept.

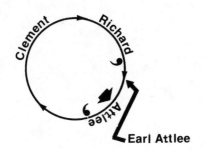

Attlee, Clement Richard, *Earl Attlee,* 1883-
Russell, Bertrand Arthur William, *3d Earl Russell,* 1872-
or Russell, Bertrand Arthur William, *Earl Russell,* 1872-
or, since he does not use his middle names,
Russell, Bertrand, *Earl Russell,* 1872-

IN
ENTRY
HEADING
ORDER

EXERCISE

Construct below the entry headings for the following names, given in regular order. Instead of using italics, underline.

Noel Edward Noel-Buxton, Baron Noel-Buxton, [Family name: Noel-Buxton. Born, 1864, died 1948]

(1) _____

John Arbuthnot Fisher, Baron Fisher. [Family name: Fisher: Born 1841, died 1920.]

(2) _____

See-References for "Four Element" Noble Names

Since, typically, in "Four element" noble names surnames and title-names differ, and since noblemen can be referred to by either name,* a see-reference must be made from the name that was *not* chosen as entry heading. Once both entry heading patterns for "four element" noble names are known, constructing the proper see-reference becomes easy: Select one pattern as entry heading and make a see-reference from the other. The two patterns are described on page 338 (entry under title-name) and 341 (entry under surname).   **AA Rule 120** covers the basic theory of see-references, and **AA Rule 121A3** covers specific application to noble names. names.

---

* The practice of entering British nobility under title-name is not universal. The British Museum, for example, always enters British nobility under their surnames. This has the advantage of listing titled and untitled members of one family together under one surname. But since often different families inherited the same title over the centuries, bearers of one title often are not listed together.

Since British nobility are generally referred to, and known by, title-name, AA's principle of using the "best known" name causes, typically, entry under title-name. The A.L.A. Rules also, typically, entered under title-name.

For a similar problem, see **AA** page 82, footnote 12.

If this pattern is selected for the entry heading. . .

. . .then this pattern is used for the first line of the see-reference*

For: James Fitzgerald, Duke of Leinster

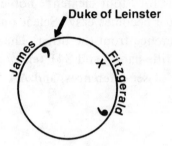

Leinster, James Fitzgerald,
   Duke of, 1722-1773.

Fitzgerald, James, *Duke of Leinster*

Fitzgerald, James, *Duke of Leinster*
       see
Leinster, James Fitzgerald, *Duke of,* 1722-1773.

For: Rodrigo de Sousa Coutinho, conde de Linhares

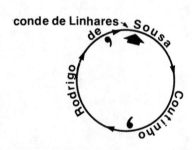

Sousa Coutinho, Rodrigo de,
   conde de Linhares, 1745-1812.

Linhares, Rodrigo de Sousa Coutinho,
   conde de

* For basic cross-reference theory and techniques see pages 77-80 and 99-101. For see-references for prefixed names, see pages 296-302.

Linhares, Rodrigo de Sousa Coutinho, *conde de*
see
Sousa Coutinho, Rodrigo de, *conde de Linhares,* 1745-1812.

EXERCISE

The following names are given in entry heading order. Construct for each one see-reference. Instead of using italics, underline.

Goring, George, Earl of Norwich.

(1)_____

_____

_____

Hailsham, Quintin McGrail Hogg, Viscount, 1907-

(2)_____

_____

_____

Cassillis, Gilbert Kennedy, 3rd Earl of, 1517?-1558.

(3)_____

_____

_____

Is a see-reference needed for the following type of name? Why?

Russell, Bertrand, Earl Russell, 1872-

(4)_____ Yes _____ No.   Reason: _____

_____

STANDARD ENTRY HEADING PATTERNS FOR "THREE ELEMENT" NOBLE NAMES

Unlike British nobility (pages 337-347) most non-British nobility and gentry, and all titled British gentry, lack a title-name. Their names consist of only three elements: Forename(s), Surname(s), and a title which indicates rank (Page 334).

Like the names of British peers, these names often get shortened in conversation or written text: "Sir John," "Freiherr von Lingert," or "Baron Karl" (to distinguish him from his relative, "Baron Ludwig"). But, to avoid confusion, the **AA** entry heading pattern is developed from the individual's name as formally spoken.

Non-British Nobility and Gentry*

For non-British nobility and gentry, these names are typically formally spoken in this sequence:

	Forename(s)	Title indicating rank	Surname(s)
IN	Ludwig	*Baron*	von Falkenhausen [German]
SPOKEN	Carl	**	von Linné [Swedish]
ORDER	Lajos	*báró*	Hatvany [Hungarian]
	Carl Gustaf	*grefve*	Tessin [Swedish]

Since only one surname is involved, entry is automatically under it. The "Circle of information" technique (pages 274-275) leads to the AA entry heading.

---

* For titled British gentry, see pages 336 and 352, for British nobility pages 337-347, and for ranks of nobility, page 336.

** Although "von," "de," and some other prepositions usually denote rank, they play a double role and are considered part of the family name. For this reason they are not italicized or underlined. (For the concept of prepositions see page 286 and the footnote on page 288. For the concept of italics as against underlining see the footnote on page 80.)

	Falkenhausen, Ludwig, *Baron* von, 1844-1936.
IN	
ENTRY	Linné, Carl von, 1707-1778.
HEADING	Hatvany, Lajos, *báró*.
ORDER	Tessin, Carl Gustaf, *grefve*, 1695-1770.

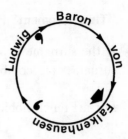

Within the guidelines of **AA Rules 40 and 41** these names are covered by **AA Rule 46G1**. Unfortunately, its examples omit the typical situations.

EXERCISE

Put the following names into entry heading form. (For ranks see page 336). Instead of using italics, underline.

Richard von Volkmann [German, born 1830, died 1889]

(1)_____

Christoph Willibald Ritter von Gluck [German, born 1714, died 1787]

(2) _____

Alfred Guillaume Gabriel comte d'Orsay [French, born 1801, died 1852]

(3) _____

"Three Element" Prefixed or Compound Noble Names*

If the surname is prefixed or compound, the rules for prefixed** and compound***
surnames are combined with the rules for "three element" noble names.

For a French nobleman:

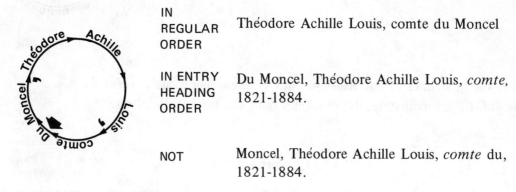

	IN REGULAR ORDER	Théodore Achille Louis, comte du Moncel
	IN ENTRY HEADING ORDER	Du Moncel, Théodore Achille Louis, *comte*, 1821-1884.
	NOT	Moncel, Théodore Achille Louis, *comte* du, 1821-1884.

For a German nobleman:

	IN REGULAR ORDER	Philipp, Prinz von Wied-Neuwied
	IN ENTRY HEADING ORDER	Wied-Neuwied, Philipp, *Prinz* von.
	NOT	Neuwied, Philipp, *Prinz* von Wied-.
	NOT	Von Wied-Neuwied, Philipp, *Prinz*.

---

   * For "Four element" prefixed or compound noble names, see pages 338-339.

  ** Pages 285-302 of this text, and **AA Rule 46E.**

*** Pages 305-322 of this text, and **AA Rules 46B-D.**

EXERCISE

Put the following name into entry heading form. Instead of using italics, underline.

Jean Baptiste François Auguste marquis de La Chataigneraye. [French, born 1785]

(1) _____

Put the following names into entry heading form, and make an individual see-reference for each.

Claude Henri comte de Saint-Simon. [French, born 1760, died 1825]

(2)_____

_____

_____

_____

Novello conte Papaïava dei Carraresi. [Italian, born 1899, surname: Papaïava dei Carraresi]

(3)_____

_____

_____

_____

Titled British Gentry*

Like nobility, these people are sometimes written about, or addressed, by a short form of their name: Sir Arthur, Sir Thomas Beecham. But, for reasons of identification, the AA entry heading pattern is developed from the individual's name as formally spoken.

Regular order, for a knight:

Title of honor	Forename(s)	Surname(s)	Rank
Sir	Arthur Conan	Doyle	

Regular order for a baronet:

Title of honor	Forename(s)	Surname(s)	Rank
Sir	Thomas	Beecham	Baronet

Entry is, of course, under surname. For knights, the basic "Circle of information" technique (pages 274-275) leads to the proper entry heading sequence.

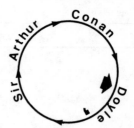

Doyle, Sir Arthur Conan, 1859-1930.**

---

* For ranks of nobility, see page 336. For British nobility page 337-347, for non-British nobility and gentry pages 348-349.

** If you are wondering at this stage why the "Sir" is underlined, please re-read the footnote on page 333.

For baronets, the "Circle of information technique as used for noblemen entered under surname
(page 341) is used. Note that the rank of Baronet
is added in abbreviated form and, for some
reason, with a small "b."

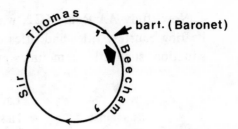

Beecham, <u>Sir</u> Thomas, <u>bart.</u>, 1879-1961.

EXERCISE

Put the following names into entry heading form. Underline instead of using italics.

Sir Philip Montefiore Magnus, Baronet. [Surname: Magnus, born 1906]

(1)_____

Sir Arthur Stanley Eddington. [Surname: Eddington]

(2) _____

Sir Henry Lancelot Aubrey-Fletcher, Baronet. [Born 1887]

(3) _____

Sir Adolf Alexander Fitzgerald. [Born 1890, editor of this work]

(4) _____

Now study **AA Rule 46G2,** which deals with British gentry and with individuals bearing courtesy titles and titles of honor. Note that, depending on the individual's situation, such titles sometimes precede, and sometimes succeed, the forename(s):

Lady Hester Stanhope

as against   Hester, Lady Stanhope *

The book being cataloged, or British reference works, will indicate which form fits a name:

By Lady Hester Stanhope
By Lady Stanhope

and the "Circle of information" technique leads to the proper heading.

EXERCISE

The following names are in regular order. Put them into entry heading order. Use underlining instead of italics.

Sir James Matthew Barrie, Baronet. [born 1860, died 1937]

(1) _____

Friedrich von Flotow. [German, born 1812, died 1883]

(2) _____

Richard Alexander Freiherr von Frankenberg. [German, born 1922]

(3) _____

Thomas Cecil Farrer, Baron Farrer. [British, born 1859, died 1940]

(4) _____

---

* If "Lady" precedes the forename(s), the title was acquired by birth; if it precedes the surname, it was acquired by marriage.

Bruno Baron von Freytag-Löringshoff. [German, born 1912]

(5) _____

Johan August friherre Gripenstedt. [Swedish, born 1813, died 1874]

(6) _____

Sir James Ferguson. [Born 1904]

(7) _____

Sylvia Lady Foot

(8) _____

Archibald Philip Primrose, Earl of Roseberry.

(9) _____

Sholto Douglas, Baron Douglas of Kirtleside. [Forename: Sholto, born 1893]

(10) _____

CHAPTER FIFTEEN **ROYALTY**

HIGHLIGHTS

Royalty is the sovereign, that is, the hereditary rules of a country, and immediate family. Although they have surnames they are known by, and entered under, their principal forename(s) and title.

The entry heading pattern for royalty consists of the individual's official name and numeral, followed by his principal title and life dates. Name and title are given in English if thus commonly used in English-speaking countries.

Henry IV, *King of France,* 1553-1610.

The titles of sovereigns vary with the country and the dynasty. These differences are reflected in the entry heading.

ROYALTY

Royal names are far easier to construct as headings than noble names. As explained on page 334, royalty is the ruler, that is the sovereign, of a country and immediate family. Generally this includes kings, queens, emperors, empresses, and royal and imperial princes and princesses,* but some sovereigns have lesser rank such as Duke or Count.

Like noble names, royal names often get shortened in conversation or written text: King Gustaf, Prince Stephan or, for loyal American admirers of British royalty, the Queen. Conversely, most royalty have several forenames and subsidiary titles. (For example, Queen Elizabeth II of Great Britain is really Elizabeth Alexandra Mary; her consort, Prince Philip, is also Duke of Edinburgh, Earl of Merioneth, and Baron Greenwich.) But for AA entry headings,** only the official forename(s) and the principal title are used since the others are hardly known and thus not apt to be looked for as access points. Is this in line with AA Rule 40?

In line with the same basic rule, the English, rather than the native form of the forename is used in the heading ("Charles" rather than "Karl" for a German emperor) and the English, rather than the native, title ("King of Prussia" rather than "König von Preussen"), provided American readers are apt to know, and thus use, them.

---

* Non-royal princes and princesses, you will recall, are entered under their surname. See page 336.

** Differences between the ALA and AACR patterns for such names are discussed in Chapter 18.

REGULAR ORDER SAME AS ENTRY HEADING ORDER

The name-and-title in regular order become the entry heading, with the forename as entry element.

Official forename(s)	Numeral for reigning Monarch	Principal title	Life dates
Catherine	II,	Empress of Russia,	1729-1796.
Alfonso	III,	King of Asturias and León,	848?-910?
Albrecht,		Archduke* of Austria,	1559-1621.

This concept is covered by **AA Rules 44A3-4,** ** **and 49B.** Whether the English form of a royal name has become "firmly established through common usage," as required by **AA Rule 44A3a,** is generally shown by reference works and bibliographies: If they use the English form, it is usually safe to use it in the AA entry heading.

* Title reserved for royal and imperial Austrian princes and princesses. German: Erzherzog, Erzherzogin.

** The examples in **AA Rule 44A3b** are unusual. For historical reasons, the various King Jans of Poland are known by forename plus surname. This is a-typical. The immediate point of these examples is that only King *Jan* III Sobieski is known to American readers as *John* Sobieski.

A word of caution: Though name and title can be translated, they must be translated literally. Titles of sovereigns vary with the country and the dynasty.

Henry IV, *King of France,* 1553-1610.

Albert I, *King of the Belgians,* 1875-1934.

Francis Joseph I, *Emperor of Austria,* 1830-1916.

Napoleon III, *Emperor of the French,* 1808-1873.

William II, *German Emperor,* 1859-1941.

Elizabeth I, *Queen of England,* 1533-1603.

James I, *King of Great Britain,* 1566-1625.*

These distinctions are often ignored in popular usage but are obeyed in entry headings. Reference works will usually indicate the correct title.

EXERCISE

Make the see-references indicated under "Charles V" in **AA Rule 44A3a.** Instead of using italics, underline. And, if you are wondering why this is necessary, re-read the footnote on page 333.
(1) _____

_____

_____

_____

_____

_____

* Outside the scope of this introductory text is another type of heading which the AA provide for certain official documents issued by sovereigns and other chiefs of state, a form heading such as "Gt. Brit. Sovereign, 1603-1625 (James I)" See **AA Rules 17C1, 80A, and 121B1.**

Explain briefly why these references are helpful to the catalog user.

(2) _____

_____

Turn to **AA Rule 49B1** and give a reason why no see-reference seems necessary for "Clovis, *King of the Franks.*" (3) _____

_____

_____

The next question requires turning to three different places in the AA. (i) Turn to the "Introductory notes" on AA page 173 to refresh your memory about the general purpose of see-references. (ii) Turn to **AA Rule 44B1e** to note the reference indicated for "Catherine II." (iii) Turn to **AA Rule 49B** and note that no equivalent reference is indicated for "Frederick II, *King of Prussia,*" whose native name was "Friedrich."

Question: If you felt that your readers might well look under "Friedrich II, *King of Prussia,*" would you feel free to make a see-reference? (4)_____Yes _____No Reason: _____

_____

In any case, how would this see-reference look?

_____

_____

_____

On the basis of the facts given below, and the pertinent AA Rules, construct entry headings for the following individuals. The names and titles listed are the correct, official, forenames and principal titles. Do not indicate cross-references.

Umberto the First was King of Italy from 1878 to 1900 and lived from 1844 to 1900.

(5) _____

Maria Theresa was Empress of Austria from 1745 to 1780 and lived from 1717 to 1780.

(6) _____

The Empress Marie Louise was consort of Napoleon the First, who was Emperor of the French from 1804 to 1814. She lived from 1791 to 1847.

(7) _____

Edward the Third was King of England from 1327 ro 1377. He lived from 1312 to 1377.

(8) _____

Queen Kaahumanu was consort of Kamehameha the First, who was King of the Hawaiian Islands. She lived from 1772 to 1832.

(9) _____

Amalie was a princess of Saxony and lived from 1794 to 1870.

(10) _____

CHAPTER SIXTEEN

NAMES IN RELIGION

HIGHLIGHTS

For AA entry headings, religious titles are not always added to personal names, but when added, always follow the name.

Christian saints are entered under their names, followed by the title *Saint,* except that a Christian saint who was also a king, emperor or pope, is entered as such

> More, <u>Sir</u> Thomas, <u>Saint</u>, 1438-1535.

> BUT   Gregory II, <u>Pope</u>, d. 731.

Other persons in religion who are known by given name or byname are listed with their religious title.

> Eleanore, <u>Sister</u>, O. P.

> John of Salisbury, <u>Bp. of Chartres</u>, d. 1180.

But persons in religion (other than Christian saints—see above) who are known by surname or title of nobility are entered without their religious titles.

> A cardinal: Suenens, Léon Joseph, 1904-

> An archbishop: Plunkett, William Conyngham, <u>Baron</u>, 1828-1897.

NAMES IN RELIGION

In regular order, religious titles may precede or succeed a person's name, or surround it, or bisect it, depending on his rank.

	<u>Saint </u>Francis of Assisi
IN	<u>Pope</u> John the twenty-third
REGULAR	Léon Joseph <u>Cardinal</u> Suenens
ORDER	Isaac, <u>Bishop of Ninevah</u>
	Robert Grosseteste, <u>Bishop of Lincoln</u>
	Sister Eleanore, <u>O. P.</u>

For AA entry headings, religious titles are not always added to personal names, but when added, always follow the name.

IN AA	
ENTRY HEADING	John XXIII, <u>Pope</u>, 1881-1963.
ORDER	Isaac, <u>Bishop of Ninevah</u>.

THREE TYPES OF NAMES IN RELIGION

Three types of names can be combined with religious titles:

(i)   Ordinary forename-surname combinations. The basic rules for these names were discussed in Chapter 10. The surnames can, of course, be prefixed, compound, or noble. (See Chapters 11-12 and 14.)

(ii) Individuals known by given name only.

(iii) Individuals known by a byname.* The basic AA approach to these two categories is expressed in **AA Rule 49A.** Please read it before proceeding with this text.

RELIGIOUS TITLES NOT ADDED

When Entry is Under Surname or Title of Nobility

Except for Christian saints, who will be discussed later on, persons in religion who are known by surname or title of nobility are entered without their religious titles.

A cardinal:	Suenens, Léon Joseph, 1904-
A bishop:	Grosseteste, Robert, 1175?-1253.
An archbishop:	Plunket, William Conyngham, <u>Baron,</u> 1828-1897.

This is indicated to some extent in **AA Rules 46G4 and 53A.**

---

* Byname: A secondary name or nickname: Saint Anthony *of Padua.*

EXERCISE

Construct entry headings for the following names. Underline instead of using italics. Note that knowledge of chapters 11, 12, and 14 is necessary for this exercise.

Lancelot Andrewes. [Was Bishop of Winchester, lived from 1555 to 1626. "Andrewes" is his surname.] (1) _____

Francis Joseph Spellman. [Cardinal and Archbishop of New York, born 1889.]
(2) _____

Jacques Davy Du Perron. [A Cardinal and a Frenchman, lived from probably 1556 to 1618. "Davy" is his middle name.] (3) _____

_____

Père François d'Aix de La Chaise. ["Père" means "Father," "d'Aix" is his middle name. He was born in 1624 and died in 1709.] (4) _____

_____

Cosmo Gordon Lang. [Was Baron Lang and Archbishop of Canterbury. "Gordon" is his middle name. Lived from 1864 to 1945.] (5) _____

_____

Nicholás Rodríguez Fermosino. [A Spanish Bishop, lived from 1605 to 1669.]
(6) _____

For Saints Who Were Sovereigns Or Popes

Christian saints who also attained the highest worldly ranks*—emperor, king, or pope—are entered only with their wordly titles.

A saint who was also
an emperor: Henry II, Emperor of Germany, 973-1024.

A saint who was also
a pope: Gregory II, Pope, d. 731.

As against a saint who was
neither sovereign nor pope: Francis of Assisi, Saint, 1182-1226.

This is indicated by **AA Rule 49C1**.

EXERCISE

Construct entry headings for the following names. Underline instead of using italics. Knowledge of Chapter 15 is necessary for this exercise. Saint Ferdinand who, as Ferdinand the Third, was King of Castile and Léon. His native name was Fernando and he lived from probably 1199 to 1252.

(1) _____

Saint Pius, who was Pope Pius the Fifth and lived from 1504 to 1572.

(2) _____

---

* For other saints see the next section.

RELIGIOUS TITLES ADDED TO NAMES

For Saints Who Did Not Attain the Highest Worldly Ranks

Conversely, saints **other** than sovereigns or popes* have the title "Saint" added to their name. No other religious title is added unless needed for distinction.
See **AA Rule 49C**

IN AA	A saint who was also	
ENTRY	an archbishop:	Patrick, <u>Saint</u>, 389?-461.
HEADING	A saint who was also	
ORDER	a priest:	Francis of Assisi, <u>Saint</u>, 1182-1226.

For these people, the title "Saint" is added regardless of whether the saint is known by given name, byname, or surname.

IN AA	Anthony, <u>Saint</u>, 251?-350?
ENTRY	Anthony of Padua, <u>Saint</u>, 1195-1231.
HEADING	La Salle, Jean Baptiste de, <u>Saint</u>, 1651-1719.
ORDER	More, Sir Thomas, Saint, 1438-1535.

Note how the rules for other names are combined with those for names in religion. But use only titles by which the saint is commonly known. See **AA Rule 49C3.**

* For saints who were also sovereigns or popes, see the preceding section.

EXERCISE

Construct entry headings for the following names. Underline instead of using italics.
Saint Anselm was Archbishop of Canterbury and lived from probably 1034 to 1109.

(1) _____

Saint Frances Cabrini, lived from 1850 to 1917 and is generally referred to by her surname.

(2) _____

Saint Bernard of Menthon, lived from 923 to probably 1008. "Menthon" is the place generally associated with his name. (3) _____

_____

Saint Gregory: Not one of the popes, but Bishop of Nyssa. His dates are unknown, but he flourished from 379-394. (4) _____

_____

For Other Persons In Religion Known By Given Name Or Byname

The names of persons in religion other than saints, who are known by given name or byname, are listed together with their religious titles. For this concept, please study **AA Rules 49D-F** before proceeding with this text.

IN AA	John XIII, Pope, 1881-1963.
ENTRY	Isaac, Bp. of Ninevah.
HEADING	John of Salisbury, Bp. of Chartres, d. 1180.
ORDER	Eleanore, Sister, O.P.

But remember that persons in religion other than saints, who are known by **surname or title of nobility** are entered **without** their religious titles.* See page 365.

A bishop: Grosseteste, Robert, 1175?-1253.

EXERCISE

Construct entry headings for the following names. Underline instead of using italics.

Pope Pius the Fourth who lived from 1499 to 1565.

(1) _____

Hernando de Talavera was archbishop of Granada, was born in probably 1428 and died in 1507. "Talavera" is a placename, not a surname.

(2) _____

Francis Asbury was an American bishop and lived from 1745 to 1816.

(3) _____

* This chapter is not an attempt to justify the AA rules. It is only intended to help you find your way through them.

CHAPTER SEVENTEEN INDIVIDUALS KNOWN BY MORE THAN ONE NAME

HIGHLIGHTS

Certain individuals are known by, or carry at different times of their lives, more than one name. Among these are British noblemen, kings, popes, and people who change their name legally, write under a pseudonym, enter a religious order, or acquire a title of nobility.

The Type of Name Determines Its Form: These persons are entered under the name by which they are commonly identified. (For example, a monk can be entered under his former secular name.) Whichever name of an individual is selected as entry heading is put into the form appropriate to that type of name.

See-references for Persons Known by More Than One Name: To help the reader who does not look under the better known name, see-references should be made from the "other" form of entry, from the name not chosen as heading. This technique is used when all of a person's works are entered under one form.

See-also References for Persons Known by More Than One Name: In some cases, particularly if both names represent quite different functions, and particularly if both of these functions are represented in the catalog, it might be best to enter each function under the name with which it is associated, connecting the two by see-also references.

Catalogers Need Judgment: The AA permit either of the above techniques. It is up to the cataloger to judge which technique is best for the author, library, and the particular range of patrons served.

INDIVIDUALS KNOWN BY MORE THAN ONE NAME

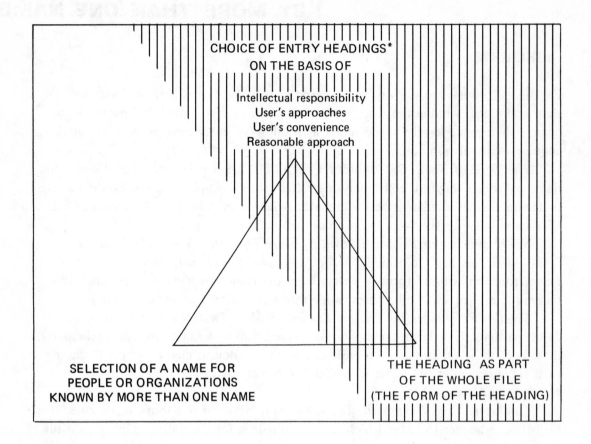

This chapter touches briefly on many form-of-entry heading concepts you have met earlier, and can help in reviewing them.

Many people are known by more than one name, had at one time another name, or use only part of their name.* Yet, only one of these names should be selected as entry heading.** Here are some examples.

---

*   Differences between the ALA and AA pattern for such names are discussed in Chapter 18.

** See pages 67-76 and 105-108.

Which Name to Use as Entry Heading?

surname

or

title-name of a British nobleman?

Jermyn, Henry, <u>Earl of St. Albans</u>

or

St. Albans, Henry Jermyn, <u>Earl of</u>   ?

English form

or

native form of a king's name?

Philip II, <u>K</u>ing of Spain

or

Felipe II, <u>King of Spain</u>   ?

English form of official name

or

official Latin form

or

former secular name of a Pope?

John XXIII, <u>Pope</u>

or

Joannes XXIII, <u>Pope</u>

or

Roncalli, Angelo Giuseppe   ?

name at birth

or

legally adopted name under which an actor became famous?

Brodribb, John Henry

or

Irving, <u>Sir</u> Henry   ?

writer's pseudonym

or

legal name?

Mansfield, Katherine

or

Murry, Kathleen Beauchamp   ?

former secular name

or

later religious name?

Brosnahan, Katharine Mary

or

Eleanore, <u>Sister</u>   ?

full name   De La Mare, Walter John, 1873-1956.

or   or

normally used name of a
British poet and novelist?   De La Mare, Walter, 1873-1956   ?

EXERCISE

Without bothering to refer to individual rules, indicate below in general terms on which basis one or the other of a person's names is selected as entry heading.

_____

_____

_____

The general AA approach to the choice of one among a person's several names is answered by **AA Rules 40-44A, and 45A,** * and on pages 67-76 and 105-118 of this text. Please review these rules before proceeding with the text.

* **AA Rule 44B,** which also treats this matter, is outside the scope of this introductory text.

THE TYPE OF NAME DETERMINES ITS FORM

Whichever of an individual's names is selected as entry heading is put into the form appropriate to that type of name. For example:

(i) The American writer Robert St. Clair wrote under the pseudonyms J. Vincent Barrett, and Vincent Struthers. Both pseudonyms look like "ordinary" names (Chapter 10) and, if used as entry headings, are entered as such.

> Barrett, J Vincent, 1898-
> Struthers, Vincent, 1898-

The real name is prefixed and, if used as entry heading, will be entered as such (Chapter 11).

> St. Clair, Robert, 1898-

(ii) If the English form of his official name is selected as entry heading for Pope John XXIII, it is selected on the basis of **AA Rule 49D** as

> John XXIII, Pope, 1881-1963.

If his secular name were selected (which you, of course, know it should not be) it would be built like any other "ordinary" name:

> Roncalli, Angelo Giuseppe, 1881-1963.

EXERCISE

The purpose of this exercise is not to select the correct name from among several, but to build the name in the various forms called for. Feel free to refer to earlier chapters of this text, and to the AA.

Anthony Charles Robert Armstrong-Jones is the First Earl of Snowdon and was born in 1930. He hardly ever uses the names "Charles Robert" but is known by, and uses, his title. If he is entered under his title-name the heading is:

(1) _____

If he is entered under his surname according to the rules for British nobility known by surname, the heading is:

(2) _____

Edmund Fisk Green legally changed his name to John Fiske and became famous under it as an American historian and philosopher. He lived from 1842 to 1901. If he is entered under his original name, the heading is:

(3) _____

If he is entered under his legally adopted name, the heading is

(4) _____

Miguel Primo de Rivera was Marqués de Estella and lived from 1870 to 1930. "Primo" is one of the surnames of this Spanish nobleman. He is generally known by surname, the title being largely unknown. If he is entered under his title-name, the heading is

(5) _____

If he is entered under his most commonly known name, the heading is:

(6) _____

Clare Booth, born in 1903, gained fame as an American dramatist under her maiden name. She then married Henry Robinson Luce and is now always referred to as Clare Booth Luce. "Robinson" is the middle name. If her maiden name is selected as entry, the heading is

(7) _____

If her married name is selected as entry, the heading is

(8) _____

William Huntington Wright was an American writer, lived from 1888 to 1939, and used the pseudonym S. S. Van Dine extensively. "Huntington" was his middle name, "S. S." did not stand for any particular forenames. If he is entered under his real name, the heading is

(9) _____

If he is entered under his pseudonym, the heading is

(10) _____

Although not as many clues are available as there would be on the job, go back now to your answers 1-10 and indicate which form of name AA would tend to prefer as heading in each given instance.

(11) Anthony Charles Robert Armstrong-Jones: Correct heading: 1_____, 2_____.

(12) Edmund Fisk Green: Correct heading: 3____, 4____ .

(13) Miguel Primo de Rivera: Correct heading: 5____, 6____ .

(14) Clare Booth: Correct heading: 7____ , 8____ .

(15) William Huntington Wright: Correct heading: 9____, 10____ .

SEE-REFERENCES OR ENTRY UNDER BOTH FORMS OF A NAME?

To help the reader who does not look under the better known name, see-references should be made—often but not always—from the "other" form of entry, from the name not chosen as heading.* This is explained in the "Introductory notes" on **AA page 173**, and in **AA Rules 120-121.****

The decision on whether or not to make a see-reference from one form of a name to the other requires judgment on the cataloger's part. The rules permit several approaches, and not all cases are clear-cut.

When the person's role does not change drastically with the name, it seems best to enter all his works under the better known name and make a see-reference from the less well-known form, or from the earlier name.

Armstrong-Jones, Anthony, Earl of Snowdon
see
Snowdon, Anthony Armstrong-Jones, Earl of, 1930-

---

  * For the theory and technique of making see-references, see pages 76-82, 84-86, and 88.

** Most examples in **AA Rule 121A1a** contain, typically, no dates in the first line of the see-reference (See text pages 80-81 for this methodology). Only the references for the two "Father Louis" contain dates in the first line. Since the reader can only see one of these cards at a time, this is a necessary distinguishing device for a library that has works by both men. An alternative is to put both see-references on one card.

Louis, Father
see
Biersack, Louis, 1894-
Merton, Thomas, 1915-1968.

But if both names represent totally different functions, and especially if both these functions are represented in the catalog, it might be best to enter each function under the name with which it is associated, connecting the two by see-also references. One example is Ray Stannard Baker who wrote historical research under his own name, and recreational literature under the pseudonym David Grayson (See pages 71-75).

```
    Baker, Ray Stannard, 1870-1946.            Grayson, David.

       [Heading used for his                 [Heading used for his
        historical works]                      fictional works]

     Baker, Ray Stannard, 1870-1946            Grayson, David.
       see also his pseudonym:                   see also his real name:
   Grayson, David.                          Baker, Ray Stannard, 1870-1946.
```

    The number of entries a library has under a name at the time the "new" name is introduced, and the new name's future use, also affect the decision, since changing existing headings to a new form takes time and is only useful if most readers are really apt to use the new name. For example, a library with a dozen books by and about Sir Anthony Eden would perhaps keep this heading after he had ceased being politically active in his late years, and had been created Earl of Avon. See the Exercise on page 342.

The library's role, and the patrons' assumed approaches to these names, also affect the cataloger's decision. For example, an author who wrote detective stories under many names is best listed under his real name in a scholarly library, so that the user has an easy overview of all his locally available works. But in a public library, where many patrons tend to be loyal to a particular name, it is probably best to list each of his works under the name he used for it, connecting the names by see-also references. A case in point is John Creasey. See pages 75-76.

Or, in a library school library with a collection of children's books but next to no works on mathematics, it is probably best to list Lewis Carroll's famous book for children of all ages under that pseudonym since it is best known for that work. But the main library of a university, which would also have his mathematical treatises written under his own name, might well list all his works under his real name to permit an easy overview. Or, if it wished to keep both parts of his production separate because they appeal to different audiences, it could list each type under the name he used for it.

The two alternative approaches are suggested by **AA Rule 42B and footnote 5 on AA page 74**. Please study these before proceeding with the text.

The rules present the cataloger with the techniques for alternative solutions. The cataloger must then judge which technique works best for the author, library, and the particular range of patrons concerned.

EXERCISE

Go over this section again and fill in below points that the cataloger should consider when deciding whether to enter all of a person's works under one or two forms of his name.

_____

_____

_____

_____

_____

_____

Often, several of the above-listed considerations will interact or conflict. For example, although the person's role may change drastically with the name, it may still be best in a particular library to enter all his works under one name. This is a matter of judgment. In case of doubt, and particularly in general scholarly libraries, it is best to list all of an author's works under the best known name, with a see-reference from the other. Whichever name or names are chosen must use the same degree of fullness in all entries (see pages 68-70) to achieve the necessary consistency and distinction among entry headings. (See page 67.)

BLENDING THE OLD AND THE NEW:
AA ENTRIES IN AN ALA CATALOG

This text tries to show how to select and shape personal names as entry headings for books, according to our present code, the AA. But cataloging is more than just creating a number of entries for one book at a time.

AN ENTRY AS PART OF THE WHOLE CATALOG

An effective catalog demands that each entry, and each group of entries for one book, be designed with the user in mind* and, therefore, as part of a cohesive structure, the catalog.** Cohesiveness can be obtained by cross-references,*** by design-

---

* For the concepts of the user's approaches and convenience, see pages 102-103; for the concept of the reasonable approach, page 104; for the concept of the best known name, pages 105-106 and 376; for reasons for maintaining one degree of fullness for one name in one catalog, pages 68-70. Many studies exist on "the" user's approaches to the catalog. More, and more precise, studies are needed. For an excellent summary and evaluation of these "catalog use studies" see James Krikelas, "Catalog Use Studies and Their Implications," *Advances in Librarianship*, v. 3, p. 195-220 (New York: Seminar Press, 1972).

** The concept of the heading as part of the whole file was summarized on page 108. – The user, and cohesiveness, are also important considerations for bibliographies, but in the typical card catalog they are paramount: It is open-ended, unlike the printed page it permits viewing only one entry at a time, and its size—the largest card catalogs are larger than any printed bibliography—magnifies each error, inconvenience, or inconsistency immensely.

*** For examples and general concepts of cross-references, see pages 73-79 and 84-87; for the technique of making them, page 80-82.

ing headings, especially corporate, uniform title, and form headings,† so that they group together material by one organization and its parts, or material of the same nature; and by maintaining the necessary consistency and distinction, especially among personal name entry headings.††

ALA — AA DIFFERENCES IN CHOICE OF ENTRY HEADINGS

Consistency and distinction are not always easy to achieve since the entries created according to our current AA must be typically interfiled in a catalog created according to our former code, the ALA Rules.††† Sometimes, for example, the two codes differ in their choice of main-entry-heading for the same work, as shown by the following selected examples.*

† Examples of such entries, and the benefit of structuring them, are on pages 29-31 and 39 for corporate entries; 34-38 for Uniform title entries; 37-39 for Form headings.

†† For the concept of Consistency and distinction for entry headings, see page 67, and **AA Rules 52-53**; for Reasons for maintaining one degree of fullness for one name, pages 68-70.

††† *A.L.A. Cataloging Rules for Author and Title Entries.* 2d ed., edited by Clara Beetle. (Chicago: American Library Association, 1949).

* Most of the following examples are selected from the *A.L.A. Cataloging Rules for Author and Title Entries*, and from the *Anglo-American Cataloging Rules*.

(1) **AA Rule 2A:** *Works of Unknown or Uncertain Authorship, or By Unnamed Groups*

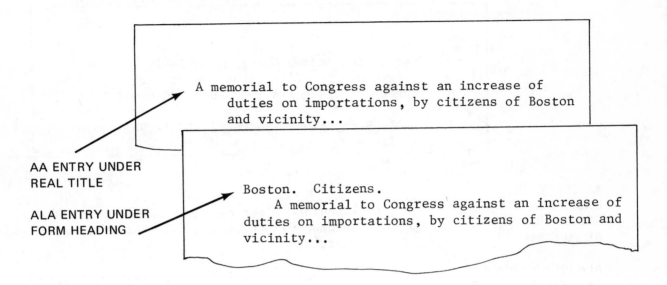

A memorial to Congress against an increase of
    duties on importations, by citizens of Boston
    and vicinity...

**AA ENTRY UNDER
REAL TITLE**

**ALA ENTRY UNDER
FORM HEADING**

Boston. Citizens.
    A memorial to Congress against an increase of
duties on importations, by citizens of Boston and
vicinity...

(2) **AA Rule 3B1b:** *Shared Authorship. Authors' Names in Different Order On Title Page of Later Edition.*

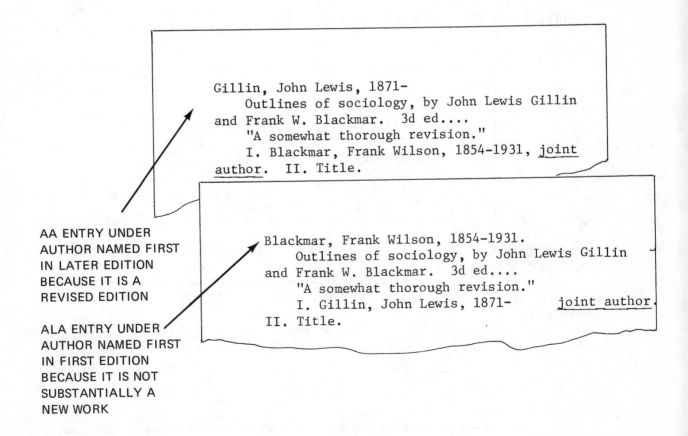

Gillin, John Lewis, 1871-
    Outlines of sociology, by John Lewis Gillin
and Frank W. Blackmar. 3d ed....
    "A somewhat thorough revision."
    I. Blackmar, Frank Wilson, 1854-1931, <u>joint</u>
<u>author</u>. II. Title.

**AA ENTRY UNDER
AUTHOR NAMED FIRST
IN LATER EDITION
BECAUSE IT IS A
REVISED EDITION**

**ALA ENTRY UNDER
AUTHOR NAMED FIRST
IN FIRST EDITION
BECAUSE IT IS NOT
SUBSTANTIALLY A
NEW WORK**

Blackmar, Frank Wilson, 1854-1931.
    Outlines of sociology, by John Lewis Gillin
and Frank W. Blackmar. 3d ed....
    "A somewhat thorough revision."
    I. Gillin, John Lewis, 1871-   <u>joint author</u>.
II. Title.

(3) **AA Rule 4A**: *Works Produced Under Editorial Direction.*

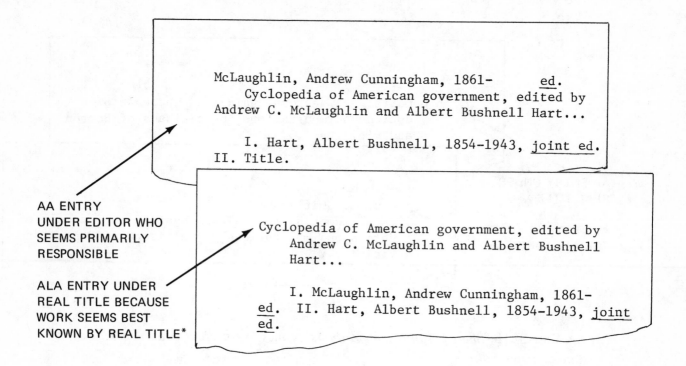

AA ENTRY
UNDER EDITOR WHO
SEEMS PRIMARILY
RESPONSIBLE

ALA ENTRY UNDER
REAL TITLE BECAUSE
WORK SEEMS BEST
KNOWN BY REAL TITLE*

(4) **AA Rule 5A**: *Collection With Collective Title*

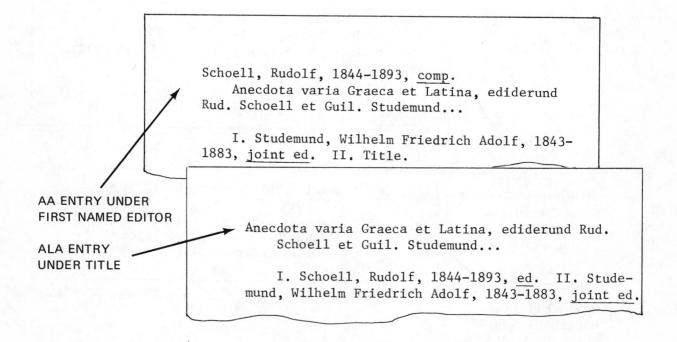

AA ENTRY UNDER
FIRST NAMED EDITOR

ALA ENTRY
UNDER TITLE

* Examples 3 and 4 are not intended to imply that ALA entered every cyclopedia and every collection under
title. They are intended to show a tendency. For a different AA situation, see pages 246-247.

(5) **AA Rule 7A:** *An Adapted Work.*

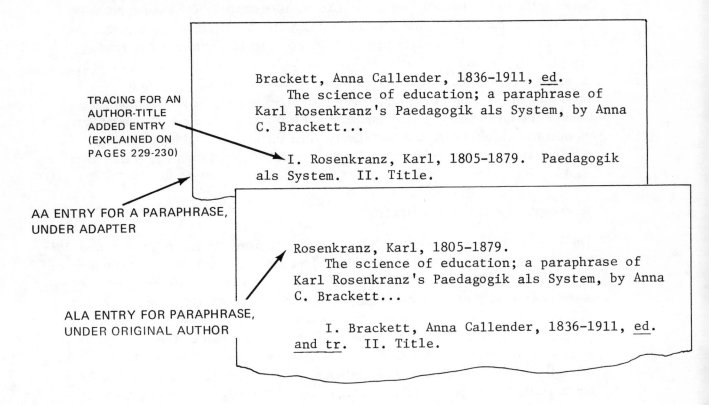

TRACING FOR AN
AUTHOR-TITLE
ADDED ENTRY
(EXPLAINED ON
PAGES 229-230)

Brackett, Anna Callender, 1836–1911, <u>ed</u>.
    The science of education; a paraphrase of
Karl Rosenkranz's Paedagogik als System, by Anna
C. Brackett...

    I. Rosenkranz, Karl, 1805–1879. Paedagogik
als System. II. Title.

AA ENTRY FOR A PARAPHRASE,
UNDER ADAPTER

Rosenkranz, Karl, 1805–1879.
    The science of education; a paraphrase of
Karl Rosenkranz's Paedagogik als System, by Anna
C. Brackett...

    I. Brackett, Anna Callender, 1836–1911, <u>ed</u>.
<u>and tr</u>. II. Title.

ALA ENTRY FOR PARAPHRASE,
UNDER ORIGINAL AUTHOR

EXERCISE

Each of the above examples gets a different main entry heading under the two codes. Indicate below for which examples the total group of main and added entries provides the same approaches under both codes.

ALA & AA PROVIDE SAME COMBINATION OF ENTRIES:

Example 1: ____ Yes ____ No   (If no tracings are shown, none exist)

Example 2: ____ Yes ____ No   (For our purposes, disregard the designation of function.)

Example 3: ____ Yes ____ No

Example 4: ____ Yes ____ No

Example 5: ____ Yes ____ No

Would any of the above examples have one entry filed under the same heading?
(6) _____

Which example would have no entry filed under the same heading? (7) _____

The above examples were selected to show differences rather than similarities between the two codes, yet four out of five furnish essentially the same approaches to a work. Typically (not illustrated above) ALA and AA select the same person as main entry heading. Differences between the two codes in choice of entry heading are relatively rare and are mostly the result of AA's using as main entry heading a person or title that ALA would have used as added entry heading. These differences are not much of a bar to interfiling AA entries in an ALA catalog: since most libraries file their entries by first line, an entry is found in the same place regardless of whether it is main or added. But libraries that file main and added entries in different sequences (see page 279) will find it more difficult to put AA entries in an ALA catalog.

Superimposition: Choice of Headings

The Library of Congress, which sells catalog cards to many American libraries, also helps to cushion the shock because it "has adopted a policy known as 'Superimposition' in applying the new rules.* This means that the [AA] rules for choice of entry [are] applied only to works that are new to the Library [of Congress]. . . . New editions, etc., of works previously cataloged [are] entered [by the Library of Congress under the ALA Rules], in the same way as the earlier editions (except for revised editions in which change of authorship is indicated).** Thus, a number of current Library of Congress catalog cards, and all cards printed prior to 1967,*** contain entry headings selected according to the ALA Rules. As indicated above, this should not cause too many obstacles.

ALA — AA DIFFERENCES IN FORM OF ENTRY HEADINGS

While ALA—AA differences in **choice** of entry headings cause relatively few difficulties when interfiling new entries in an existing catalog, their differences in the **form** of entry headings can be substantial. Please re-read page 108 which gives an overview of this situation.

---

 * This concept was first mentioned on page 109.

 ** U.S. Library of Congress. Processing Department. *Cataloging Service Bulletin 79.* Washington, D.C.: 1967, p. 1.

*** When the AA were adopted

Superimposition: Form of Headings

As with choice, the Library of Congress has adopted the policy of "Superimposition" with respect to the form of the headings. This means that the AA form-rules are "applied only to persons. . . that are being established for the first time. . . New works by previously established authors. . . appear [in the Library of Congress catalogs] under the same headings that were used before. Exceptions to the policy of superimposition [are] largely confined to instances where very few entries are involved and where it is judged that some decided improvement in entry or heading may be obtained by revising existing entries in accordance with the new [AA] rules."*

Therefore, even if an author is new to a library that buys catalog cards from the Library of Congress, or that subscribes to its computer services, the library will typically get entries with headings in the old ALA style for most authors who wrote before 1967,** and for new editions of works that were first published before, 1967, since the Library of Congress is apt to have had such works since before 1967.

An individual library can practice its own "Superimposition" only with authors and works for which it does original cataloging. When it buys cards from the Library of Congress, it virtually must accept L.C.'s decision (ALA choice and form, or AA choice and form), since it would be uneconomical to buy cards and then change them extensively. While in most instances the form of an entry heading is identical under both codes, selected substantial form differences do exist that do affect the place of an entry in a file. The following sections will summarize the most frequent differences and their effect on filing.

---

* U.S. Library of Congress. Processing Dept. *Cataloging Service Bulletin 79.* Washington, D.C.: 1967, p. 1-2.

** When the AA were adopted.

Distinguishing Terms. (Pages 281-282)

AA Rule 53 differs in two respects from ALA:

(1) If dates are not available to distinguish in one catalog different individuals with identical names, both ALA and AA permit adding a term of address, title, initials denoting an academic degree or membership in an organization, etc. But only ALA permitted adding the person's occupation, specialty, or location.

ALA & AA PERMIT THESE	Müller, Heinrich, *Dr. jur.* Müller, Heinrich, *D. I. N.*
ONLY ALA PERMITS THESE	Müller, Heinrich, *of Giessen.* Müller, Heinrich, *of Madrid?* Müller, Heinrich, *pharmacist.* Müller, Heinrich, *writer on copyright.*

(2) Since AA has fewer terms with which to distinguish identical names, it permits listing identical names under the same heading if no suitable terms exist. See **AA Rule 53B** for examples. ALA, however, always insisted on some kind of distinction between identical names for different people.

Effect on filing: Under ALA, different people with the same name were always separated in the file because each had his own distinguishing term. Under AA, they are apt to be amalgamated since the file of identical headings is subarranged by title, not by distinguishing term.

Surnames With Prefixes. (Pages 285-302)

AA Rules 46E-F agree with many ALA headings. The chief differences are as follows:

Afrikaans: ALA entered Afrikaans names on the basis of their origin. AA follows local custom by entering always under the prefix.

ALA	AA
Villiers, Anna Johanna Dorothea de	De Villiers, Anna Johanna Dorothea
Wielligh, Gideon Retief von	Von Wielligh, Gideon Retief
But: Du Toit, Stephanus Johannes	Du Toit, Stephanus Johannes

German: ALA entered these always under the part of the surname following the prefix. AA follows the German custom of entering under prefix if it consists of an article or a contraction. (For a list of contractions, see page 288).

ALA	AA
Thym, August am	Am Thym, August
Ende, Erich vom	Vom Ende, Erich
Berg, Hans zum	Zum Berg, Hans
But: Hagen, Maximilian von	Hagen, Maximilian von
Mühll, Peter von der	Mühll, Peter von der

Italian: ALA entered all Italian names whose prefix consisted of a preposition under the part of the surname following the prefix. AA follows Italian custom, entering only modern names almost always under the prefix.

ALA	AA
Arienzo, Nicola d'	D'Arienzo, Nicola
Amicis, Pietro Maria de	De Amicis, Pietro Maria
Mare, Angela del	Del Mare, Angela
But: Da Ponte, Lorenzo	Da Ponte, Lorenzo

Spanish: ALA entered Spanish names almost always under the part following the prefix. So does AA, unless the prefix consists of an article.

ALA	AA
Ripa, Domingo la	La Ripa, Domingo
But: Rio, Antonio del	Rio, Antonio del

Effect on interfiling: In many cases, notably French and English prefixed names, the entry form is identical. In others, the same name is filed quite differently under the two codes. Libraries receiving new editions, or works, of such authors already represented in their catalog, will probably follow the Library of Congress lead and typically keep the old form. But even if individual names are changed to the new form, typically the same **type** of name will file differently, depending on whether an author started writing before or after 1967, when the AA were adopted. Few libraries have the funds to go systematically through their files and change all existing prefixed headings to the AA form.

At least general see-also references seem called for. (See pages 327-331.) Individual see-references are even better. (See pages 297-298 and **AA Rules 120-121 A.**)

EXERCISE

Suppose that you have decided to leave existing entry headings in ALA form if at all possible, but to enter authors new to your catalog under the AA form, if possible.

Looking at different section of your catalog, you find the following headings:

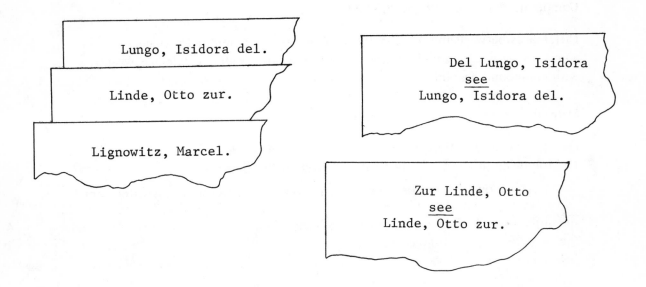

A new book arrives, by the same Otto zue Linde who is already listed in your catalog. Record below the exact main entry heading you will use for this book.

(1) _____

Would you make a see-reference for this name?
(2) _____ Yes _____ No.

You now receive your first book by the twentieth century Italian, Pia Maria Del Mangano. Record below the exact main entry heading and the cross-reference you will use for this name.

(3) Main entry heading: _____

Cross-reference: _____

_____

_____

Compound Surnames. (Pages 305-322)

Differences between the AA and the ALA Rules for compound surnames are rare. In almost every case, it should be easy to interfile into existing catalogs new entries with compound headings.

Married Women's Surnames. (Pages 323-329)

For this category, differences between the AA and the ALA Rules are not frequent. The following differences may result in different headings:

(1) ALA typically enclosed the maiden surname in parentheses, AA does not.*

---

* This was first mentioned on page 325.

ALA	AA
Browning, Elizabeth (Barrett)	Browning, Elizabeth Barrett.
Rose-Troup, Frances (James)	Rose-Troup, Frances James.
Rombauer, Irma (von Starkloff)	Rombauer, Irma von Starkloff.

But, when custom or personal preference clearly indicate it:

Suárez del Otero, Concha.	Suárez del Otero, Concha.
Förster-Nietzsche, Elisabeth.	Förster-Nietzsche, Elisabeth.
Effect on interfiling: None.	

(2) Unless the situation was absolutely clear-cut, ALA tended to translate more foreign married women's names into the standard form than does AA.

ALA	AA
Haavio, Elsa (Enäjärvi)	Enäjärvi-Haavio, Elsa.

Effect on interfiling: In the few cases where this happens, the effect is major and demands individual see-references (See pages 297-298, and **AA Rules 121-121A**). As, for example, with prefixed names, it means that the same type of name can file differently (See pages 392-393).

Nobility and Gentry. (Pages 335-357)

Although their wording differs quite a bit, the effect of both codes on names of nobility and gentry is much the same. Most such names are entered identically under both codes. In a few cases, stylistic differences result which still permit interfiling the old and the new. But a few AA Rules are different enough to require decision. The chief differences are as follows:

(1) ALA used small letters for most, but not all, titles. AA capitalizes according to the rules of the language concerned,* except that it uses small letters for "bart." (Baronet).

<u>ALA</u>	<u>AA</u>
Bacon, Francis, *viscount St. Albans,* 1561-1626.	Bacon, Francis, *Viscount St. Albans,* 1561-1626.
Reventlow, Franziska, *gräfin* zu, 1871-1918.	Reventlow, Franziska, *Gräfin* zu, 1871-1918.

– –

But: Campbell, *Dame* Janet Mary.	Campbell, *Dame* Janet Mary.
Scott, *Sir* Walter, *bart.,* 1771-1832.	Scott, *Sir* Walter, *bart.,* 1771-1832.

Effect on interfiling: None.

(2) ALA always used the numeral for British nobility above the rank of Baron and, if necessary, even for them. AA uses the numeral only if necessary to distinguish two otherwise identical names in one catalog.**

---

* Basic capitalization rules, generally followed in cataloging, with examples, are on AA pages 348-357, and in Appendix II, volume I, of this series.

** This was first mentioned on pages 339-340.

ALA	AA
Wellington, Arthur Wellesley, *1st duke of,* 1769-1852.	Wellington, Arthur Wellesley, *Duke of,* 1769-1852.

Effect on filing: None because of ALA-AA differences. But, internally, the AA Rules can cause problems: If *no one else* with identical name is already in the catalog, no number is needed for the new name. If someone else with identical name *is already in the catalog,* he will have a number if done according to ALA, and AA could automatically also use a number. But if the identical name that is already in the catalog was done since 1967, under AA Rules, it will most likely *not have a number.* In that case, the respective numbers will have to be added to both headings.

(3) ALA used the "four element" entry heading pattern (see pages 337-347) even if the surname and title-name are identical.*

| IN REGULAR ORDER | Thomas Babington Macaulay, Baron Macaulay

Bertrand Russell, third Earl Russell |
|---|---|

ALA	AA
Macaulay, Thomas Babington Macaulay, *baron,* 1800-1859.

Russell, Bertrand Russell, *3d earl, 1872-* | Macaulay, Thomas Babington, *Baron Macaulay,* 1800-1859.

Russell, Bertrand, *Earl Russell,* 1872- |

* For **AA** treatment of this situation, see pages 343-344.

Effect on interfiling: Since the first few words are identical with either code, both forms would probably file together. But the reader must be awake to realize that both forms refer to one individual. Superimposition is advised.

EXERCISE

Suppose that you have decided to leave existing entry headings in ALA form if at all possible, but to enter authors new to your catalog under the AA form, if possible. The following headings are in your catalog, each represented by from two to four entries.

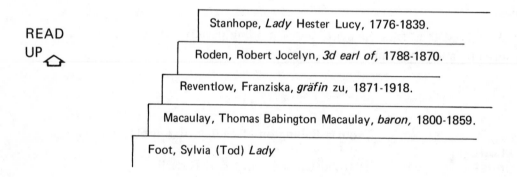

READ
UP

Stanhope, *Lady* Hester Lucy, 1776-1839.

Roden, Robert Jocelyn, *3d earl of,* 1788-1870.

Reventlow, Franziska, *gräfin* zu, 1871-1918.

Macaulay, Thomas Babington Macaulay, *baron,* 1800-1859.

Foot, Sylvia (Tod) *Lady*

You now receive additional books with names as recorded below. Record the form in which you will enter these names in your catalog.

Names as recorded in newly received books:	Entry heading form used for newly received books:
Franziska Gräfin zu Reventlow	(1) _____
Sylvia, Lady Foot. [Blurb: Lady Foot, the former Sylvia Tod]	(2) _____

Bernard Law Montgomery, first
  Viscount Montgomery. [Family
  name: Montgomery. Born 1887]   (3) _____

Robert Jocelyn, Earl of Roden.
  [Upon checking you find that
  he is the first Earl, born 1731,
  died 1797]   (4) _____

Lady Hester Stanhope [born 1776,
  died 1839]   (5) _____

Royalty. (Pages 357-363)

Most royal names are constructed identically under both codes and can, in spite of some stylistic differences, be interfiled easily into existing catalogs. But in a few cases, major differences demand the policy of superimposition. Differences are as follows:

(1) The Catalog Rules of 1908 (see pages 115-116), which preceded the ALA Rules, used small letters for royal titles. Both ALA and AA use capital initial letters for English language titles, except for the word "consort."

<u>1908 Rules</u>	<u>ALA & AA</u>

Gustaf III, *king of Sweden,*
  1746-1792.
	Gustaf III, *King of Sweden,*
	  1746-1792.

Effect on interfiling: None.

(2) For consorts (male and female) of rulers, ALA merely attached the standard title "consort of. . ." to the official forename. AA inserts the consort's own rank.

<u>ALA</u>	<u>AA</u>
Mary, *consort of George V,* *King of Great Britain,* 1867-1953	Mary, *Queen, consort of George V,* *King of Great Britain,* 1867-1953.
Albert, *consort of Victoria,* *Queen of Great Britain,* 1819-1861.	Albert, *Prince Consort of Victoria,* *Queen of Great Britain*, 1819-1861. [His rank and title was "Prince Consort," thus the capital "C."]

Effect on interfiling: Considerable, if the library follows the ALA standard* and sub-arranges identical forenames by designation: "Charles, Duke of. . ." before "Charles, Emperor of. . ." These entries are further sub-arranged by country: "Charles, King of France" before "Charles, King of Sweden," and within any one country the sub-arrangement is by numeral: "Charles I, King of France," followed by "Charles II, King of France."

READ
UP ⌂

Charles, *King of Sweden*

Charles II, *King of France*

Charles I, *King of France*

Charles V, *Emperor of Germany*

Charles, *Duke of Lorraine*

---

* For specifics, see *A.L.A. Rules for Filing Catalog Cards.* Prepared by the ALA Editorial Committee's Subcommittee on the ALA Rules for Filing Catalog Cards. Pauline A. Seely, chairman and editor. 2d ed. Chicago: American Library Association, 1968: Rule 25.

This system separates two entries for one queen, listed according to ALA and AA:

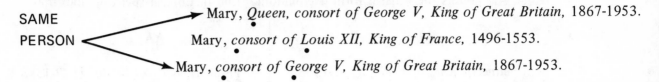

SAME → Mary, *Queen, consort of George V, King of Great Britain,* 1867-1953.

PERSON ← Mary, *consort of Louis XII, King of France,* 1496-1553.

→ Mary, *consort of George V, King of Great Britain,* 1867-1953.

But if the library uses an alternative, older method, both entries can be interfiled easily.* This method sub-arranges identical forenames by rank (sovereigns before noblemen), sub-arranges by country, within country by designation, and within designation by numeral.

READ

UP △

      Charles, *Duke of Lorraine*

       Charles, *King of Sweden*

    Charles V, *Emperor of Germany.*

  Charles II, *King of France.*

  Charles I, *King of France.*

Since, with this method, the major sub-arrangement of royalty is by country, it does not matter if the title differs slightly.

SAME → Mary, *Queen, consort of George V, King of Great Britain,* 1867-1953.

PERSON → Mary, *consort of George V, King of Great Britain,* 1867-1953.

Mary, *consort of Louis XII, King of France,* 1496-1553.

* See *A.L.A. Rules for Filing Catalog Cards.* Prepared by a Special Committee, Sophie K. Hiss, chairman, Chicago: American Library Association, 1942: Rule 17b.

(3) ALA tended to enter rulers under their native forename, that is, their real name. AA prefers the English form if commonly used in English speaking countries.

ALA	AA
Felipe II, *King of Spain,* 1527-1598.	Philip II, *King of Spain,* 1527-1598.
Henri IV, *King of France, 1553-1610.*	Henry IV, *King of France,* 1553-1610.
Napoléon III, *Emperor of the French,* 1808-1873.	Napoleon III, *Emperor of the French,* 1808-1873.
- - - - - - - - - - - - - - - -	- - - - - - - - - - - - - - - -
But: Umberto I, *King of Italy,* 1844-1900.	Umberto I, *King of Italy,* 1844-1900.

Effect on interfiling: Sometimes none (Napoléon is filed as Napoleon) but often considerable (even Henri IV, *King of France* could be separated by several dozen entries from Henry IV, *King of France.* Superimposition is usually needed).

(4) ALA included epithets in the heading, usually in the native language. AA omits them but, like ALA, makes see-references from them.

ALA	AA
Charles, *le Téméraire, Duke of Burgundy,* 1433-1477. [xCharles, *le Téméraire*]* [xCharles the Bold]	Charles, *Duke of Burgundy,* 1433-1477. [xCharles the Bold]

* For an explanation of this, apparently strange, see-reference, read the following paragraph, "Effect on inter-filing."

Friedrich II, *der Grosse, King of Prussia,* 1712-1786. [xFriedrich, *der Grosse*]* [xFrederick the Great]	Frederick II, *King of Prussia,* 1712-1786. [xFrederick the Great]

Effect on interfiling: None, because epithets are disregarded in filing entry headings, (but not in filing cross-references): The heading, "Charles, *le Téméraire, Duke of Burgundy,*" is filed as "Charles, *Duke of Burgundy.*"

"Other" Names Combined With Titles

The ALA Rules were more liberal than the AA in combining names with titles: ALA added titles to more types of names, and sometimes combined several titles in one heading.

(1) ALA added religious titles to all names of persons in religion. AA adds them only to persons known by a given name or a byname, and the title "Saint" to Christian saints who were neither sovereigns nor popes (See pages 363-370).

ALA	AA
Suenens, Léon Joseph, *Cardinal,* 1904-	Suenens, Léon Joseph, 1904-
But: John of Salisbury, *Bp. of Chartres,* d. 1180.	John of Salisbury, *Bp. of Chartres,* d. 1180.

Effect on interfiling: In most cases, none. But the reader must read carefully to be sure that both forms belong to one person.

---

* For an explanation of this, apparently strange, see-reference, read the following text paragraph, "Effect on filing."

EXERCISE

The following names are given in AA form. Fill in the ALA form.

ALA	AA
(1) _____	[The French cardinal] Du Perron, Jacques Davy, 1556?-1618.
(2) _____	[The Bishop of Winchester] Andrewes, Lancelot, 1555-1626.

(2) ALA combined many kinds of titles: The title "Saint" with the titles for sovereigns and high church officials; the titles for heads of state with titles of nobility; titles of nobility with religious titles, etc.*

ALA	AA
Louis IX, *Saint, King of France,* 1215-1270.	Louis IX, *King of France,* 1215-1270.
Pius V, *Saint, Pope,* 1504-1572.	Pius V, *Pope,* 1504-1572.
Fisher, John, *Saint, Bp. of* *Rochester,* 1469?-1535.	Fisher, John, *Saint,* 1469?-1535.
Calleja, Félix María, *conde de* *Calderón, Viceroy of Mexico,* b. 1750.	Calleja, Félix María, *conde de* *Calderón,* b. 1750.
Richelieu, Armand Jean du Plessis, *duc* de, *Cardinal,* 1585-1642.	Richelieu, Armand Jean du Plessis, *duc* de, 1585-1642.

But: [For a former Baron]:

Constantin, *Brother,* 1781-1859.   Constantin, *Brother,* 1781-1859.

---

* An exception are those persons in religion who became ordinary priests, monks, or nuns and thus gave up their worldly titles. These were and are entered usually under their religious name, such as, Sebastian, *Father.*

EXERCISE

The following names are given in ALA form. Fill in the AA form.

ALA	AA
Olav II, *Saint, King of Norway,* 995-1030.	(1) _____
Augustine, *Saint, Abp. of Canterbury,* d. 604.	(2) _____

Effect on interfiling: In most cases, none. But the reader will have to read carefully to be sure that both forms belong to one person.

(3) ALA added the titles of office to the names or elected or appointed heads of state, but not heads of government,* AA adds these and other titles only if necessary to distinguish in one catalog otherwise identical names. (See **AA Rules 46G4 and 53A.**)

ALA	AA
Hayes, Rutherford Birchard, *Pres. U.S.,* 1822-1893.	Hayes, Rutherford Birchard, 1822-1893.
Heuss, Theodor, *Pres. German Federal Republic,* 1884-1963.	Heuss, Theodor, 1884-1963.
But: [For the governor of a state]: Lehman, Herbert Henry, 1878-1963.	Lehman, Herbert Henry, 1878-1963.

* For example, ALA added titles of office to names of presidents and viceroys but not governors or prime ministers.

EXERCISE

The following names are given in ALA form. Fill in the AA form.

<u>ALA</u>   <u>AA</u>

Masaryk, Thomas Garrigue, *Pres.*   (1) _____
  Czechoslovak Republic, 1850-1937.

Gil Fortoul, José, *Pres. Vene-*   (2) _____
  zuela, 1862-1943.

Effect on interfiling: None, but the reader must read carefully to recognize that both forms belong to one person.

Real Name As Against Best Known Name. (Pages 105-109.)

ALA tended to use a person's real, full name, AA the name by which he is commonly identified, whether it is real, shortened, or pseudonymous. Both codes make exceptions. The following examples illustrate only a basic attitude.

	<u>ALA</u>	<u>AA</u>
FULL NAME:	Hughes, Dorothy Belle (Flanagan)	Hughes, Dorothy Belle
MARRIED WOMEN	Stowe, Harriet Elizabeth (Beecher)	Stowe, Harriet Beecher.
	Landseer, *Sir* Edwin Henry, 1802-1873.	Landseer, *Sir* Edwin, 1802-1873.
FULL NAME: NOBILITY & GENTRY	Buckingham and Chandos, Richard Temple Nugent Bridges Chandos Grenville, *1st duke of,* 1776-1839.	Buckingham and Chandos, Richard Grenville, *Duke of,* 1776-1839.
	Duff-Gorden, Lucie (Austin) *Lady,* 1821-1869.	Duff-Gorden, Lucie, *Lady,* 1821-1869.
PSEUDO-NYM	White, William Anthony Parker. [Real name of Anthony Boucher]	Boucher, Anthony.

Effect on interfiling: For pseudonymous names, considerable and requires superimposition. For other names, typically none, but the reader must be careful to realize that both forms belong to one person.

ALA - AACR OVERALL DIFFERENCES:

When the various differences in prefixed names, noble names, title treatment and real, full name as against best known name, are combined, the differences between the old and the new form can be considerable.

ALA	AA
Ende, Thomas vom, *Bp. of Münster,* 1816-1891.	Vom Ende, Thomas, 1816-1891.
Gregorius I, *the Great, Saint, Pope,* 540 (ca.)-604.	Gregory I, *Pope,* ca. 540-604.
Lot, Myrrha (Borodine) 1882-1957.	Lot-Borodine, Myrrha, 1882-1957.
Beaconsfield, Benjamin Disraeli, *1st earl of,* 1804-1881.	Disraeli, Benjamin, *Earl of Beaconsfield,* 1804-1881.
Fernando V, *El Católico, King of Spain,* 1452-1516.	Ferdinand V, *King of Spain,* 1452-1516.
Joannes XXIII, *Pope,* 1881-1963.	John XXIII, *Pope,* 1881-1963.

However, more often than not, a name selected and constructed under the AA can be interfiled automatically in a catalog with ALA entry headings. When this is not possible, the library can most economically bridge the difference with a judiciously applied policy of "superimposition."

THE NEXT CODE

Whatever reaction we may have to the AA and their differences with ALA-based catalogs, a new entry heading code will certainly appear within one generation, probably much sooner. In the past, major new English-language entry heading codes were adopted in 1841, 1876, 1908, and 1949, and 1967, that is, at intervals ranging from 18 to 41 years.* Each new code reflected some changes in approach and some refinements, but also maintained many of its predecessors' approaches. Between the 1949 and the 1967 codes, many new information retrieval techniques were developed, information retrieval technology made rapid progress, international bibliographic standardization became a pervading concern, and the computer began to be a realistic information retrieval device that will probably change bibliographic access techniques over the next few decades. The 1967 AA ignored most of these developments,** probably wisely, since computer technology is still in a state of rapid development—yesterday's impossibility becomes tomorrow's standard practice—and since the progress in information retrieval theories and techniques concerns primarily subject, rather than author or title, approaches. But the whole area of bibliographical access and bibliographical control is in a state of flux. The ongoing development of area-wide library networks and of nation-wide subject-oriented bibliographic networks, and the foreseeable stabilization of the computer's role in bibliographic control make it safe to assume that, within a generation or less, the 1967 AA will join its predecessors in honorable retirement. It will be replaced by a code designed to meet the needs of its day, or perhaps by two codes: one for school and smaller public libraries, another for research-oriented libraries or library departments. Whatever our professional label—librarian or information retrievalist—our professional purpose is to serve our public by providing bridges between recorded material and its potential users. As long as we remember this, we will change our codes from time to time to conform to our current public demands, professional theories and technologies, and personal insight.

---

* See pages 115-116.

** For example, its entry heading rules were written without regard to the computer's ability to sort and file the resulting headings.

APPENDIX I

DESCRIPTIVE CATALOGING: FORMAT, TERMINOLOGY, STANDARD SEQUENCE.

STANDARD FORMAT AND SEQUENCE OF UNITS FOR
ENTRIES ENTERED UNDER PERSONAL AUTHOR, CORPORATE
AUTHOR, OR UNIFORM TITLE.

AA
STYLE
(For sample entry
see page 6.)

```
Call
Num-    Main entry heading.
ber         Title, subtitle [by] Author statement.  Illus-
        trator, Translator, or Other contributors state-
        ment.  Edition statement.  Imprint:  Place of
        publication, Publisher, Date(s).
            Collation:  Pagination, illustration state-
        ment, height.  (Series statement)
            Notes.
            1. Subject tracings:  Major subject.  Other
        subjects treated in depth.  I. Added entry trac-
        ings:  Names in the order of listing in the
        entry.  Title.  Series.
```

PROPOSED
INTERNATIONAL
STANDARD
BIBLIOGRAPHIC
DESCRIPTION
(ISBD)
(Uses standardized
punctuation)

```
Call
Num-    Main entry heading.
ber         Title: subtitle/ author statement.  Illustra-
        tor, Translator, or Other contributors statement.
        -- Edition statement. -- Imprint: Place of publi-
        cation: Publisher, Date(s).
            Collation: pagination: illustration statement;
        height. -- (Series statement)
            Notes.
            International-Standard-Book-Number Binding:
        Price.
            Tracings as in AA style.
```

STANDARD FORMAT AND SEQUENCE OF UNITS FOR
ENTRIES ENTERED UNDER THEIR REAL TITLE.
("HANGING INDENTION")

**AA
STYLE**
(For sample entries
see page 33.)

> Call
> Num-   Title, subtitle [by] Author statement. Illus-
> ber   trator, Translator, or Other contributors
>   statement. Edition statement. Imprint:
>   Place of publication, Publisher, Date(s).
>   Collation: Pagination, illustration state-
>   ment, height. (Series statement)
>
>   Notes.
>
>   1. Subject tracings: Major subjects. Other
>   subjects treated in depth. I. Added entry trac-
>   ings: Names in the order of listing in the
>   entry. Series.

**PROPOSED
STANDARD
BIBLIOGRAPHIC
DESCRIPTION**
(ISBD)
(Uses standerdized
punctuation)

> Call
> Num-   Title: subtitle/ author statement. Illustrator,
> ber   Translator, or Other contributors statement.
>   -- Edition statement. -- Imprint: Place of
>   publication: Publisher, Date(s).
>   Collation: pagination: illustration statement;
>   height. -- (Series statement)
>   Notes.
>   International-Standard-Book-Number Binding;
>   Price.
>   Tracings as in AA style.

APPENDIX II

WORKSLIPS

Definition

A temporary record of bibliographical information. Most frequently, a record on which the cataloger constructs an entry, along with supplemental information, from which the typist prepares, according to a standard formula (see Appendix I), a stencil master for duplication. It may range from an ordinary P-slip to a preprinted, highly organized 5″ x 8″ sheet of thin cardboard.

Workslips are referred to on pages

SAMPLE OF A HIGHLY ORGANIZED WORKSLIP
SUITABLE FOR A LARGE DEPARTMENT.
(TYPICAL SIZE: Anywhere from 5″ x 6″ to 5″ x 8″.)

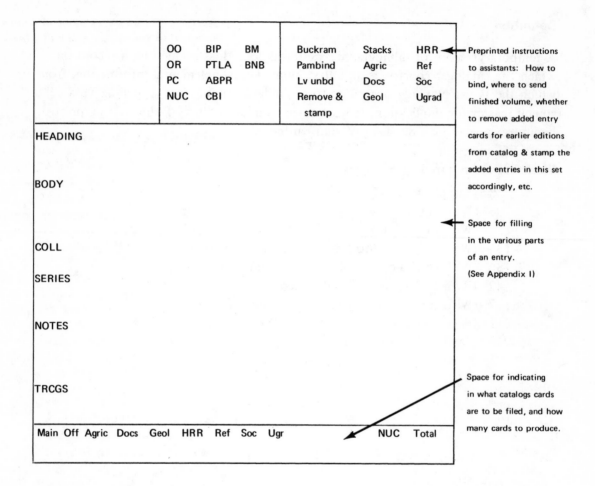

	OO BIP BM	Buckram Stacks HRR	Preprinted instructions
	OR PTLA BNB	Pambind Agric Ref	to assistants: How to
	PC ABPR	Lv unbd Docs Soc	bind, where to send
	NUC CBI	Remove & Geol Ugrad	finished volume, whether
		stamp	to remove added entry

HEADING — cards for earlier editions from catalog & stamp the added entries in this set accordingly, etc.

BODY

COLL — Space for filling in the various parts of an entry. (See Appendix I)

SERIES

NOTES

TRCGS — Space for indicating in what catalogs cards are to be filed, and how many cards to produce.

Main Off Agric Docs Geol HRR Ref Soc Ugr   NUC Total

ON THE BACK OF THE WORKSLIP can be space, for example, (1) for the cataloger's temporary notes to himself, for example when establishing a name; (2) to record itinials of the people handling this volume, with date of receipt; (3) to handle overflow for items from the front of the workslip.

THE VARIOUS AREAS in this workslip can, of course, be re arranged and/or changed in shape. For example, the binding instructions (top right) can be shifted to the back of the workslip. Depending on the library's needs, different units can be added, others can be taken out or shortened, or fewer preprinted labels can be used, to permit greater flexibility.

TO DESIGN A WORKSLIP EFFECTIVELY, one must understand the cataloging process in the library concerned, that is, the movement of book, workslip, and catalog cards from one stage to the next, and the type of information which each stage needs and creates.

SUPPLEMENTARY GLOSSARY OF TERMS USED IN THIS TEXT

This Glossary is intended only as a supplement to the Glossary in the AA Rules. (AA Appendix I, AA page 343ff.)

AA (AACR). *Anglo-American Cataloging Rules, North American Text.* Prepared by the American Library Association, the Library of Congress, the Library Association, and the Canadian Library Association. Chicago, American Library Association, 1967. The official American cataloging code covering both description and entry headings for books, serials, incunabula, manuscripts, and audio-visual materials.

Accession list. A list of all, or selected, titles newly received and cataloged. Many libraries issue such lists periodically to inform their patrons, or as a public relations gesture.

Accession number. A unique number which many (but not all) libraries assign to each book in the order of receipt, or in the order of cataloging. Typically, it has no connection with the call number.

Adaptation. "1. **A rewritten form of a literary work modified for a purpose or use other than that for** which the original work was intended. 2. A new version based upon one or more versions of a given work or story. . . ."*

Added entry, *see* **Entry.**

Added entry heading, *see* **Entry.**

A.L.A. or A.L.A. Rules. *A.L.A. Cataloging Rules for Author and Title Entries.* Prepared by the Division of Cataloging and Classification of the American Library Association. 2d ed., edited by Clara Beetle. Chicago, American Library Association, 1949. (A.L.A. is also the abbreviation for the American Library Association but is not used in this text with this meaning.)

Authority card, *see* **Authority file or list.**

Authority file or list. A record of the exact form of each heading (other than title main or added entries) and the references leading to it, in a particular catalog. If on cards, it is called an Authority File, each heading being listed on a separate Authority card; if on sheets, it is called an Authority list. Typically, a separate file is kept for names (Name authority file), and a separate file or list for subject headings (Subject authority file or list.)

Backbone of a book, *see* **Spine of a book.**

Backstrip of a book, *see* **Spine of a book.**

Bastard title, *see* **Half-title.**

Bibliographical access. Learning of the existence of, or locating, a book, periodical article, film, or other library item through the use of a bibliographical record such as a catalog or a bibliography.

Bibliography. A list of books, pamphlets, filmstrips, maps, or similar items that exist and that may be located anywhere. Like the catalog, it is a list of entries but, unlike the catalog, it is not a list of items owned by any one library. (The term has additional meanings which are outside the scope of this text.)

Blurb, *see* **Jacket of a book.**

Boards, *see* **Cover of a book.**

Book. Also called a "Monograph." A nonperiodical publication containing forty-nine or more pages, not counting the covers. If bound in regular book binding, it consists primarily of leaves sewn together at one edge in groups, or "signatures," and then glued. If bound in "perfect binding" its leaves are simply glued at one edge. In either case the leaves are enclosed by a cover and spine. *See also* **Monograph.**

Book catalog, *see* **Catalog.**

Book cover, *see* **Cover of a book.**

Book jacket, *see* **Jacket of a book.**

Call number. A number, or group of numbers, used to assign a book to its proper location on the shelves. In the United States, the call number consists typically of a subject number (class number) followed by an author number. If the class number is done according to the Library of Congress classification system it is generally called the "L.C. number"; if it is done according to the Dewey Decimal Classification system, it is generally called the "D.D.C. number." *See also* **Accession number; Classification.**

Caption title, *see* **Running title.**

Card catalog, *see* **Catalog.**

Catalog. A compilation of entries which records, describes, and indexes most of the resources of a library. *See also* **Shelflist.**

This glossary is intended only as a supplement to the glossary in the AA.

413

Book catalog. Not necessarily a catalog that lists books. (Most catalogs do list books, but they can also list other things like filmstrips.) Rather, a catalog in the form of a book.

Card catalog. A catalog consisting of cards. On most cards, an entry for a bibliographic item is placed. Typically also contains some cross-reference cards that are used to direct the reader to another entry, and explanatory cards that are used to explain the catalog's structure or other matters.

Classed or classified catalog. A catalog in which author, title, and series entries are in alphabetical order in one file, while subject entries are in another file, arranged numerically by class number (that is, in logical order) rather than alphabetically by subject heading.

Computer catalog. A computer-produced catalog, generally in book form (a book catalog), but can also be produced on cards, or stored on computer tapes, etc.

Divided catalog.

> **Vertically divided catalog**. A catalog divided by type of entry. Typically, one alphabet for subject entries, one for all other entries.

> **Horizontally divided catalog**: A catalog divided by date. One alphabet for all items published or received before a certain date, another alphabet of items published or received after that date.

Official catalog. Typically, a file of main entries that duplicate those in the Public catalog. It is for staff use, typically also contains authority cards, and tends to be used only by large libraries, and only when the distance between public catalog and catalog department is uneconomically great.

Public catalog. A catalog, typically on cards, with main entries, added entries, cross-references, and explanatory cards, and intended for public use, as against the Official catalog. (To the public, it is generally "The" catalog.)

Union catalog. A catalog that lists the cataloged books and/or other materials of more than one library. Typically, it contains only main entries. It can be a card catalog, a book catalog, or a computer catalog.

Catalog card. A card on which an entry is placed in order to be listed in a card catalog.

Classed or classified catalog, *see* **Catalog**.

Classification. The assigning of numbers, letters, or letter-number combinations to library items such as books. These symbols represent either a sub-

ject of the book or its form. Used in the United States primarily as a device for systematic arrangement of books, in some other countries for systematic arrangement of the entries. *See also* **Call number**.

Classified or classed catalog, *see* **Catalog**.

Collective title. A title that is obviously intended to describe the whole book rather than only a part. In other words, the typical title as defined in the AA Glossary. Books of multiple, but not of joint, authorship have occasionally no such title, but only separate titles for each contribution.

Collective title page. A title page that is obviously intended to fit the whole book rather than only a part of a book. In other words, the typical title page. Books of multiple authorship have occasionally no common (collective) title page, but only separate title pages for each contribution. *See also* **Title page**.

Colophon. An inscription found at the end of a book, showing the printer's name, the type used, the date and place of printing, or other typographical details. Sometimes combined in an emblem or printer's device similar to a coat-of-arms.

Computer catalog, *see* **Catalog**.

Copyright notice. A statement, usually on the verso of the title page, indicating who has the exclusive right to reproduce and sell that work. Includes the date this right was registered.

Cover of a book. The front and back halves of the outer shall of a book. For regularly bound books, covers are made of stiff cardboard or paper "boards" that are covered on the outside with plain or plastic-coated cloth, buckram, leather, or paper, and on the inside with plain or decorated paper, the "end paper" which connects the cover to the glued and/or sewn pages. When the boards are covered on the outside with paper only, a book is said to be "bound in boards." When encased in heavy paper without boards, a book of more than forty-nine pages is said to be "paperbound" or a "paperback." If less than forty-nine pages, paper-covered, and stitched down the center back fold, it is called a "pamphlet," and this is known as "pamphlet binding." *See also* **Jacket of a book**.

Cumulative Book Index. A bibliography of new trade books published in the English language. Published monthly, with longer cumulations.

DDC class number, *see* **Call number**.

Dedication. An inscription to honor or compliment a patron, relative or friend, customarily on the first leaf following the title page.

This glossary is intended only as a supplement to the glossary in the AA.

Descriptive cataloging. The description of a book or other bibliographical object in a standardized sequence and format. Sometimes also considered as including entry heading work.

Dewey decimal class number, *see* **Call number.**

Divided catalog, *see* **Catalog.**

End paper, *see* **Cover of a book.**

Entry. The complete unit of description about any item listed in a catalog or bibliography. (The terms "Entry," "Main entry," or "Added entry" as customarily defined are ambiguous because each refers to two different things. The AA Glossary gives these standard definitions. To avoid this confusion, this text distinguishes between an entry (main or added) as the complete record of a bibliographical entity in a catalog or bibliography, and the entry heading (main or added) as the word or words under which an entry is listed.)

Entry heading. The name or words under which an entry is listed. *See also* **Entry.**

Exchange list. A list of titles (usually of duplicate copies) which a library is willing to exchange with another library in return for titles it needs.

Foreword. Fulfills most of the functions of the preface but is typically written by someone other than the author. *See also* **Preface; Introduction.**

Front matter of a book. The pages preceding the text, and made up of some or all of the following items, arranged usually in the order listed: Half-title, frontispiece, title page, verso of the title page, dedication, preface or foreword, table of contents, list of illustrations, introduction. Often it has no page numbers, but if it does, these numbers are apt to be a separate sequence in roman numerals while the main text is numbered in arabic numerals. Because the front matter typically introduces, summarizes, qualifies, or otherwise supports the body of the text, catalogers usually turn to it first to determine the classification number and subject headings which will fit the main matter. But front matter is also essential for entry heading work. See Chapter 7.

Frontispiece. An illustration facing the title page of a book.

Half-title. The brief title of a book or series or collection, printed on a separate page which may (rarely) also carry the author's name. If printed on the recto page preceding the full title page it is also called the "bastard title" or "fly title." If it follows the full title page but precedes the text proper, it should not be confused with the

"caption title" (defined in this Glossary under "Running title.") It has cataloging significance only when it differs from the title as given on the more complete title page or when there is no title page.

Incunabula. Books printed before 1501. (Singular: Incunabulum.)

Index of a book. An alphabetical list of names, places, and topics giving reference to the page in the text on which they are treated or mentioned. While usually in the back of the book, it can appear at the front as it does in the *World Almanac. See also* **Table of Contents.**

Introduction. A separate section in the front matter, or the first part of the text proper, which defines the scope and level of the text, outlines its manner of organization or content, or in some other way provides the reader with perspective on it. It often leads directly into the text proper. For contrast, *see* **Preface.**

Jacket of a book. The printed or unprinted paper cover placed around a bound book. In addition to the author's name and the title, it often contains information about the author, his other works, favorable comments about the book (what has come to be known as the publisher's "blurb"), an indication of the contents, or advertising notices for selected other books put out by the same publisher. *See also* **Cover of a book.**

Library of Congress class number, or L.C. class number, *see* **Call number.**

List of illustrations. A list of the page location of plates, figures, tables, and other illustrative matter in the sequence in which they appear in the book.

Main entry, *see* **Entry**

Main entry heading, *see* **Entry.**

Monograph. A work that is complete in itself. It may consist of more than one physical volume but, typically, does not. In other words, a monograph is what the layman calls a "book." Librarians and bibliographers distinguish monographs from periodicals and other serials which are issued continuously, in successive parts. *See also* **Book.**

Name authority file, *see* **Authority file or list.**

National Union Catalog. A union catalog of books and other items recently cataloged by the Library of Congress and about 1000 other U.S. and Canadian libraries. It is published monthly in book form and cumulates for periods of up to 20 years. (the Pre-1956-Imprints edition covers an even longer period.)

Official catalog, *see* **Catalog**.

Order card. A working card for recording bibliographical and price information used in ordering a book. From it, the actual book order is prepared that is mailed to the vendor, the Order list. The order card is quite separate from the cataloger's Workslip. *See also* **Workslip; Order list**.

Order list. A list of titles which the library wishes to order from the book dealer. These orders are typically copied from individual Order cards. The order list can also be sent out in the form of individual slips.

Overtyping. The process of typing above an entry, that has been multiplied in identical units on a set of unit cards, an added entry heading that determines the added entry's position in the catalog.

Pamphlet, *see* **Cover of a book**.

Perfect binding, *see* **Book**.

Preface. An explanatory note written by the author, and preceding the text, giving the purpose of the book, its sources, the author's qualifications or his reasons for writing the book, or his acknowledgments to persons who have helped him in the work. *See also* **Foreword; Introduction**.

Public catalog, *see* **Catalog**.

Running title. The brief title of a book, appearing at the head of all or half the pages of the main matter of a book. If only half, it generally appears on the verso (left page) and alternatively with a "caption title" on the recto (right page). The latter is the brief title of a section of a book and appears (1) at the head of individual pages and often also (2) at the beginning of each section. The running title has cataloging significance only when it differs significantly from the title page title or when there is no title page. The caption title has cataloging significance only if the cataloger desires to analyze the particular section and has no better source for doing so. These titles are also called "running heads."

Shelflist. A file of cards (or a printed list) arranged in the order in which the books are shelved, that is, by call number. *See also* **Call number; Catalog**.

Signature. Distinguishing letter(s) and/or number(s) printed at the bottom of the first page of each gathering of leaves that form a physical section of the book, to guide the binder in assembling the section correctly. By extension, the sections themselves. *See also* **Book**.

Spine of a book. The part of the outer shell or case of the book which joins the two covers together and holds them over the edge where the pages are sewn or glued together. Sometimes, though rarely, the spine is called the "backbone." Only publications with regular book binding or "perfect" binding have spines. Pamphlets and spiral bound publications do not. *See also* **Cover of a book**.

Subject authority list, *see* **Authority file or list**.

Subject added entry heading, *see* **Subject heading**.

Subject heading. One or more words, usually taken from an Authority file or list, that describe a book's major subject matter(s). In card catalogs, they are typically recorded as tracings at the bottom of a unit card, and overtyped as subject added entry headings to produce subject added entry cards.

Table of contents. A list of the chapters or other divisions of a book, arranged in the sequence in which they appear in the book and listing the pages on which they begin. *See also* **Index**.

Title page. A page or a double page spread at the beginning of a book, giving its title, author or authors (if acknowledged), usually its publisher, and often its place and date of publication. Typically, it includes also other items of information: the edition number, the names of other contributors to the work such as illustrators, translators, or editors, and sometimes even an apt quotation. But, except for title, author and publisher, any of these items may be listed instead on the verso of the title page or even in the preface or foreword. A substitute for the title page is any other part of the book that gives its title and, perhaps, also author and publisher when there is no title page. The most common substitute, especially among papercovered pamphlets of less than 50 pages, is the cover. *See also* **Verso of the title page; Collective title page; Cover of a book**.

Tracings. Librarians' shorthand needed to locate (or "trace") other, related cards, filed in the catalog. Two types of tracings exist:

On authority cards: On an authority card, a tracing is a record of a word or name from which a cross-reference is made to the heading under which the authority card is filed.

On unit cards: On a unit card, a tracing is a record of an added entry heading under which another, overtyped, copy of the unit card is filed. In printed unit cards, tracings appear on the front. This is the preferred location with typed cards as well. However, when space limitations make this impossible, the tracings are put on the back or on a second, extension, card.

Union catalog, *see* **Catalog.**

Verso of the title page. The back of the title page, which usually lists the date and holders of the copyright. It may also carry the dates and numbers of earlier editions and previous impressions and the names address of the printer along with other information concerning the production of the book. *See also* **Title page.**

Workslip. A temporary record of bibliographical information. Most frequently, a record on which the cataloger constructs an entry, along with supplemental information, from which the typist prepares a stencil master for duplication, according to a standard formula. (*See* Appendix I.) Workslips range from ordinary P-slips to pre-printed, highly organized, 5″ x 8″ sheets of thin cardboard. (*See* Appendix II.)

This glossary is intended only as a supplement to the glossary in the AA.

INDEX